D0765165

From Assets to Profits

From Assets to Profits

Competing for IP Value & Return

EDITED BY
BRUCE BERMAN

John Wiley & Sons, Inc.

This book is printed on acid-free paper. 

Published by John Wiley & Sons, Inc., Hoboken, New Jersey.
Published simultaneously in Canada.

Library of Congress Cataloging-in-Publication Data:

From assets to profits : competing for IP value & return / edited by Bruce Berman.
p. cm.
Includes index.
ISBN 978-0-470-22538-7 (cloth)
1. Intellectual capital—Valuation. 2. Intellectual property. 3. Technological innovations—Economic aspects. 4. Patent licenses. I. Berman, Bruce M.
HD53.F75 2009
658.4'038—dc22

2008036348

Printed in the United States of America

10 9 8 7 6 5 4 3 2 1

Also by Bruce Berman

Hidden Value
Profiting from the Intellectual Property Economy
From Ideas to Assets
Investing Wisely in Intellectual Property
Making Innovation Pay
People Who Turn IP into Shareholder Value

For innovation, wherever and however it may appear.

Profits are the lifeblood of enterprise. Don't let anyone tell you different.

—Andy Grove, former CEO and Chairman, Intel

Acknowledgments

A number of dedicated colleagues and friends played a part in *From Assets to Profits*. They include Angelina Lachhman, Alexandra Angel, and Narriman Subrati, who were instrumental with research and the preparation of the manuscript and exhibits. Others who helped with planning, thought development, or feedback were Fred Bratman, James Haggerty, Professor Paul Janicke of the University of Houston, Ron Laurie, Dan McCurdy, Brenda Pomerance, and Professor Alexander Wurzer. Paul DiGiammarino spent many hours with me discussing and analyzing intellectual asset management approaches, as did members of Anaqua's user community, notably Amy Achter of Kimberly Clark, Stephen Harpster of Qualcomm, and Marshall Phelps of Microsoft.

My appreciation to Steve Lozan of CitiGroup Smith Barney who showed me that IP-centric investing is something equity investors can and do participate in; David Wanetick of Incremental Advantage; and Bo Heiden and Ulf Petrusson of the Center for Intellectual Property Studies in Gothenburg, Sweden for providing me a platform for thought and discussion. Kudos, too, to Senior Editor Susan McDermott and her crack team of production people, typographers, and designers at John Wiley & Sons. This is our third collaboration, and her attention to detail made a difference on every page. Also instrumental was Joff Wild, editor of *Intellectual Asset Management* (IAM) magazine, who for the past five years has encouraged my ideas and irreverence in "IP Investor."

The encouragement of readers of my previous books and IAM columns, and those who have attended my presentations, has meant a great deal, as has the support of my wife Sharon and daughter Jenn. My final and greatest debt of gratitude is to the contributors of *From Assets to Profits* and their affiliations for their generous time and commitment.

Contents

About the Editor

Bruce Berman is CEO of Brody Berman Associates in New York, a communications and management consulting firm that focuses on innovative businesses and intellectual assets. Mr. Berman works closely with IP-based businesses and their advisors, to enhance patent and brand values, win disputes, and facilitate transactions. In addition to this book, Mr. Berman is responsible for *Making Innovation Pay—People Who Turn IP into Shareholder Value* (John Wiley & Sons, Inc., 2005). He also edited and contributed to *From Ideas to Assets—Investing Wisely in Intellectual Property* (John Wiley & Sons, Inc., 2002), a widely acclaimed book about the business of IP. His articles, reviews, and book chapters have appeared in many publications, including *Nature Biotechnology, The National Law Journal,* and *The Book of Investing Rules* (*Financial Times*, Prentice Hall, 2003), which The Motley Fool called one of the all-time best investment books.

Mr. Berman has guest-lectured at Columbia University School of Business, and chaired panels and organized IP business conferences for Incremental Advantage, *The Wall Street Transcript,* the Intellectual Property Owners' Association, and, in 2005 and 2007, the Center for Intellectual Property Studies (CIP Forum) in Gothenburg, Sweden. He has donated his time and expertise in support of the International Intellectual Property Institute (IIPI), the Brookings Institution, and other leading foundations. Mr. Berman's column, "IP Investor," appears regularly in *Intellectual Asset Management (IAM)* magazine, and he serves on the editorial advisory boards of *IAM* and *Patent, Strategy & Management.* He is an honors graduate of The City College of New York (CCNY) and holds a master's degree from Columbia University.

Introduction

Innovation profoundly affects every business and investor. While most executives believe that new ideas are the currency of choice, few agree on the best ways to profit from them. *From Ideas to Profits* is a search for how invention rights become business assets and the ways they can be converted into return.

Along the way, contributors to this book confront questions facing managers and businesses who rely on innovation. These questions include:

- When do IP rights like patents become business assets?
- What are the best business models for an IP holder to achieve return or advantage?
- Who in fact, are IP investors and how do they affect innovation?

IP value typically escapes the balance sheet. Revenues from patent licenses are attractive to some because they are easily understood. But royalty generation is one of many ways intellectual assets can be monetized. It is not the definitive way. Many companies under pressure to perform get sucked into the competition to build patent stockpiles and generate fees. Some have called licensing income an "addiction"; a mythological siren song that seduces otherwise intelligent CEOs and financial analysts.

Return on intellectual assets means different things to different IP holders. The dynamics of deploying invention rights have changed dramatically over the past twenty years and there is a burden on patent owners today to extract meaningful returns on high cost of R&D. This is especially true of operating companies that are engaged in selling products as opposed to licensing them. It is difficult to pinpoint the role

IP rights play in protecting products' market share or maintaining their profit margins. It is even more difficult to capture their impact on overall business performance. A company may know that some of its patents vaguely support objectives, but seldom can it measure their impact on profitability, the lifeblood of a company.

Useful Consequences

Wikipedia defines profit as "the making of gain in business activity for the benefit of the owners of the business." The word comes from Latin meaning "to make progress" and is defined in two different ways, one for economics and one for accounting. "A key difficulty in measuring either definition of profit," notes Wikipedia, "is in defining costs." I would add that another challenge is identifying "advantage." Another definition of profit from BrainyQuote also is worth considering:

> Accession of good; valuable results; useful consequences; benefit; avail; gain; as, an office of profit.

Unfortunately, there currently is no line on a 10-K report called "useful consequences." Goodwill does even less to explain things. IP value is a relative term that depends on context for meaning. Defining it in terms of royalties generated or damages awards won is too narrow for most IP holders. The patent revenue model is currently a very nasty business, often accompanied by disputes, distraction from day-to-day business and costly litigation. The economics of licensing may work for some IP holders, but not for the majority. For most companies, IP supports the business; for a few, it is the business.

Royalties are typically high margin cash flows that both C-level executives and credit ratings agencies respond to. Strategic patent advantage is vague and abstract. The formidable challenge faced by CEOs and their advisors is how to capture and articulate the meaning of strategic advantage and translate it into the language of income statements and balance sheets. Without a fiscal handle on intellectual assets otherwise ethical fiduciaries run the risk of mismanaging valuable assets, undermining return and facing regulatory scrutiny and shareholder suits. Settling a case for $50 million, as RIM could have in 2002, is with hindsight a better management decision than having to pay $612 million three years later.

Non-practicing entities (NPEs) hold patents but do not engage in product sales. They include small businesses, universities and independent inventors. Some companies dismiss them blanketly as patent speculators or "trolls." These independent holders have for the past twenty years or so challenged conventional thinking about how IP rights are best deployed. By identifying successful products that infringe patents they have been granted or have acquired, some NPEs can extract lucrative settlements and licensing fees from fearful operating companies. Many believe NPEs have an unfair advantage because they do not sell products and cannot be counter-sued. But not all NPEs are harmful to innovation.

Large portfolio owners employ patents (primarily) for freedom to sell their products. However, about 15% of U.S. patents granted are to independent inventors. Another 15–20%, or so, are awarded to small companies and universities. That means about one third of patents are held by small under-capitalized entities, most without products, seeking a return on their ideas. How a business chooses to use its patents is often determined by its industry, size and willingness to do battle for what is theirs.

Uncertainty about patent validity and value, and the lack of pricing transparency, inhibit IP transactions. They in turn create market inefficiencies that are good for buyers, bad for sellers, and hard on valuations. A surge in patent brokerage activity and public auctions is beginning to create a more efficient market for IP-related deals, including mergers and acquisitions.

Jungle Logic

Some readers will view *From Assets to Profits* as a cautionary tale, an ode to strategic IP representing a move back to basics when patent rights were viewed as defensive shields. Others will see it as a call to manage innovation more imaginatively and globally. Still others will conclude that it is a rationale for speculators. The truth is that all are correct. The chapters of *FATP* are divided between those that advocate strategic use of IP rights and those that regard IP as instruments for direct revenue generation.

In my previous book, *Making Innovation Pay*, a dozen prominent IP practitioners regarded the importance of patent licensing for maximum return. But a singular focus on direct revenue generation, while lucrative to some, is not appropriate for the majority of patent holders. In *From*

Ideas to Assets we considered how IP rights are business resources. In *From Assets to Profits* the focus is on understanding the appropriate monetization strategies for a particular business and group of rights.

It is becoming apparent that innovation exists less within a jungle of competing rights, but in an eco-system that relies on symbiosis as much as natural selection. Some of those operating in this environment like trolls may appear to be less savory characters than others. But like the "good" bacteria that inhabit one's digestive tract, some hosts serve a necessary purpose. Survival in the IP world is complex and requires competition to assure quality and success. Identifying, nurturing, acquiring, measuring, conveying, and profiting from intellectual assets are in their infancy. As IP management matures it is becoming clearer there are many ways to generate a return, but that some are more difficult to discern than others. The contributors to *From Assets to Profits* believe this book will help make it less so.

Bruce Berman
New York City

PART 1

IP Business Models

CHAPTER 1

Out of Alignment—Getting IP and Business Strategies Back in Synch

BY DAN MCCURDY

PERSPECTIVE The desire to extract decisive returns on innovation is clouding many companies' judgment. In an environment, where inventions have greater impact and court cases and legislative reform are weakening the value of many patents, confusion reins about what constitutes the proper way for a CEO or board of directors to behave.

Dan McCurdy contends that most business executives are ill-equipped to use patent strategy or understand the IP marketplace. Often, they fail to deploy intellectual assets for their true value. He also believes that IP executives have done a poor job of conveying IP imperatives to senior management, especially those in the C-suite, and to shareholders.

"In virtually all other aspects of business, executives fully grasp the requirement to knit together various elements of business operations into a cohesive whole," says McCurdy, a licensing executive turned defensive strategist.

"They understand how to use a company's equity, its cash, real estate, human resources, global reach, supply and distribution chains, marketing prowess, customer relationships, personal relationships, banking relationships, and government relationships to advantage their business. But, curiously, they do not understand—or generally even have much

(continued)

curiosity about—how to use to their advantage perhaps their most valuable corporate asset—their intellectual property."

McCurdy suggests that better alignment (or realignment) of IP strategy with business objectives starts with people. It includes having IP and senior corporate executives communicate better by getting to know one another and understand the challenges they each face. McCurdy believes it is important they not fear each other—their company's future may depend on their ability to collaborate.

The CEO's Dilemma

The new millennium brought a flurry of activity and anxiety that has infused the global intellectual property community with both fear and opportunity. It is spilling over into the highest levels of corporate leadership. The anxiety is largely the result of mixed signals about how IP can impact business operations. Most business executives view intellectual property more as a problem likely to happen than an opportunity waiting to be unleashed. While there are a significant number of CEOs who have become aware of the profit-building business models of successful licensing companies such as IBM, Lucent, Philips, Thomson, Kodak and, more recently, Hewlett-Packard, a greater number of executives are becoming aware of the complexities and unpredictable outcomes that the licensing of intellectual property presents.

There was a time when companies that invested heavily in research and development and produced useful inventions that found their way into the products of others could collect significant royalties from infringers. Even then the battles were protracted and risks were present, but in the end the "first mover advantage" of a patentee seeking a royalty from a likely infringer was powerful and generally decisive. Thrown off balance by the attack, the potential licensee was frequently unable to regain its footing. After a few technical and business discussions that typically stretched across 12 to 24 months, the licensee caved and paid the aggressor a sum that was less than the royalty sought by the patentee, but much more than the tax expected by the licensee.

As this practice circulated around various high-tech industries for a couple of decades, old-time CEOs grew accustomed to it. However, entrepreneurial New Age CEOs of highly successful companies were not so accommodating. They viewed "expansionist" patent enforcement as a rip-off. The *modus operandi* of these executives was to hire exceptionally smart people who were in tune with market needs and who would create products that solved important problems confronting their customers. These engineers were not reverse engineering the products of competitors seeking to steal their innovations, but rather were independently solving important problems facing their customers through the creation of new technologies. They knew their solutions—novel in their minds—would drive huge sales of problem-solving products.

It is possible that the solutions they independently created would unknowingly share some of the concepts of an invention previously made by another. The fact that someone else had come upon a similar (or even nearly identical) idea first, and had patented that invention, now created an obstacle to the use of this similar, independently created idea. Indeed, *neither* inventor had copied the idea, but nonetheless the first inventor was in a position to disrupt the latter invention's use. This dynamic was particularly troublesome in high-tech companies, where hundreds—possibly even thousands—of inventions were synergistically combined into a system such as a laptop computer to provide a solution to a problem. Contrast this with a pharmaceutical innovation, where the discovery of a new molecule could cost as much as U.S. $1 billion but alone could create tens of billions of dollars in revenue—or nothing. Infringement of such a pharmaceutical discovery was also more difficult because any resulting product would be subject to a dense minefield of regulatory oversight that would discourage or even prohibit such infringement, at least in countries enforcing their patents.

With this backdrop, put yourself in the shoes of a CEO. On the one hand, shareholders would argue that Lou Gerstner and Marshall Phelps at IBM made nearly $2 billion dollars annually at the height of the IBM licensing program, most of which was pure profit, by offering IBM patents and technology to licensees (see Exhibit 1.1). But on the other hand, the world is increasingly littered with jury verdicts against significant product companies, ordering them to pay monstrously huge royalty payments to companies with smaller revenues, and with patent trolls, who successfully enforce their patents against the much larger "Goliath."

EXHIBIT 1.1 **SELECTED HIGH TECH PATENT LITIGATION AWARDS AND SETTLEMENTS, 2004-2007[1]**

Year	Plaintiff	Defendant	Amount ($US)
2007	TGIP	AT&T	$156 m
2006	NTP	RIM	$612 m
2006	Rambus	Hynix	$133 m
2006	Z4 Technologies, Inc.	Microsoft	$140 m
2006	Texas Instruments	Globespan Virata	$112 m
2005	EMC	Hewlett Packard Company	$325 m
2004	Eolas	Microsoft Corporation	$565 m
2004	Sun Microsystems, Inc.	Microsoft Corporation	$900 m
2004	Intertrust Technologies Corporation	Microsoft Corporation	$440 m
2004	Yahoo, Inc.	Google, Inc.	$328 m

[1]Patent Infringement Damages, Statistics & Trends, 1990–2004, Navigant Consulting; ThinkFire, Inc. research.

In the mind of a CEO bent on success, a modest amount of revenue and profit can be derived from adversarial IP licensing, versus the amount of revenue and profit that can be derived from the sale of successful products and services. And yet the risk of a counterclaim that could impose a significant tax, or shut down a major product line, is ever present. Moreover, the distraction to technical, marketing, sales, and operational staffs caught up in the discovery phases of patent litigation have a major impact on product operations.

For this reason some CEOs, such as Steve Appleton of Micron and John Chambers of Cisco, have long concluded that building a strong offensive patent position ensures that their executive and operational staffs are not disrupted by the tedious intricacies of patent litigation, enabling personnel to give their full attention to building valuable products that solve problems that will make their customers more successful. Others have reached the conclusion that their resources will allow them to build such products and services *and* obtain royalty revenues from the use of their most valuable inventions. The jury is out, both literally and figuratively, as to the correct decision. This is the CEO's dilemma. Over the past decade the actions of patent speculators have further magnified the risks that patents play in innovative business operations.

The Emergence of Patent Trolls, and Their Impact on IP Licensing

At the turn of the 21st century, patent speculators, sometimes called patent trolls (or worse) began to grow in number and expand in capability. Their growth was driven by a perfect storm of intellectual property made available by the bursting dot-com bubble, significant capital, and massive revenues to be taxed by speculators intent on buying patents and enforcing them against product-producing companies. Operating companies, awakened with a jolt from their détente, were suddenly confronted with an adversary that did not respond to the IP skills and knowledge they had honed over the prior decades. The formula these operating companies had developed to deal with patent disputes with other operating companies no longer applied. They were up against an enemy they did not know, that used tactics they did not understand, that struck without warning, and that was invulnerable to a patent counter-attack.

Those product-producing companies that had developed active patent licensing programs, such as the aforementioned IBM, Lucent, Texas Instruments, Kodak, Thomson, and Philips to name just a few, each in a sense a patent "hunter" seeking royalties from those who used their inventions, were now the potential prey of a new breed of adversary. The patent landscape was changing again, requiring companies worldwide to develop new mechanisms, tools, and techniques to adapt to this environment. While the companies exposed are screaming "foul," the fact is that this environment has exposed innovative companies since the patent laws were written into the U.S. Constitution more than 220 years ago. Charlatans of one sort or another have been exploiting the patent system ever since. The more things change, the more they stay the same.

The destabilizing impact of patent speculators has been, on the one hand, both significant and, on the other hand, potentially based on unfounded hysteria. There are now estimated to be more than 800 identified patent trolls, more than 200 of which are unaffiliated with one another. This excludes independent inventors and small companies pursuing patent enforcement of their inventions as a result of a failed attempt to produce and/or market a product embodying the invention. Operating companies almost universally agree that a patent troll is any entity that attempts to enforce a patent against them and is not vulnerable to patent counter-assertion because they have no or an inconsequential amount of product sales. In this broad definition, patent investors, law firms that accumulate and enforce patents, failed companies, individual inventors, research institutions, and even universities would largely qualify. Madey v. Duke adds an interesting twist to this debate.[1] Given this broad definition, there are clearly thousands of "patent trolls" worldwide that pose a potential threat to successful product-producing companies.

With the exception of research institutions, universities, and independent inventors, patent trolls generally are dependent upon purchasing or otherwise gaining enforcement rights to patents created by others as the weapons of their trade. In the case of most research institutions and universities, while their threat may be significant, their patent portfolios are generally "a mile wide and a millimeter deep," which is sometimes enough to pose a credible threat. With independent inventors, their patent portfolios tend to be a millimeter wide and perhaps a millimeter deep. Thus, while these latter potential adversaries are very real, they are somewhat more readily assessed and potentially easier with which to grapple. There are always exceptions, e.g., NTP's $612M settlement with RIM, or the recent $501 million dollar award to Dr. Bruce Saffran, who had sued Boston Scientific for infringement of a single patent.

In a Changing IP and Business Environment, What Is the Correct IP Strategy?

Until the emergence of patent trolls, the primary IP concern of CEOs of innovative companies was that their R&D, patenting activities, and overall investment in innovation was sufficient to produce an ample supply of intellectual property that would competitively differentiate the company's products from competitors and thereby drive higher revenues. At the same time, they would provide an adequately broad and deep IP portfolio such that if anyone tried to poke a stick in the company's marketing wheel, there were more than enough sticks available in the firm's patent portfolio to stop most patent enforcement strikes from other product-producing companies.

EXHIBIT 1.2 **U.S. UTILITY PATENTS ISSUED, 1980–2007**

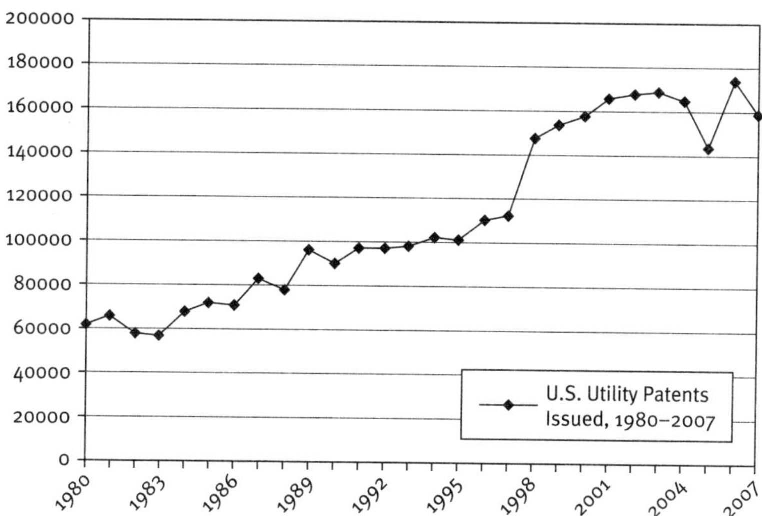

This philosophy led to an enormous increase in issued U.S. utility patents in the period from 1980–2007 as companies built a patent arsenal capable of "mutually assured destruction" (see Exhibit 1.2).

By the early 1990s, as potential licensees were becoming more knowledgeable and sophisticated in the business and legal aspects of defending against patent aggression by others, the most experienced would-be licensors (such as IBM) had come to the conclusion that they needed to evolve their IP strategy to transform from "win-lose" (taxing those companies who used their inventions) to "win-win" (providing value to the licensee, rather than simply a patent license). One approach was to focus on the transfer of valuable and differentiating technology to the licensee (together with a patent license). Such a strategy provided that the licensor's most talented engineers would teach engineers from the licensee how to adopt the licensed technology, thereby enabling the licensee to enter the market with products of improved performance and function sooner—and with less expense—than would have been possible without the transfer of the differentiating technology. The licensor received a higher royalty than they would have if they had licensed only patents without the know-how, and completed the transactions in less than a year, rather than the two to five years that would have been required to complete the average patent-only "win-lose" license.

While this strategy worked extremely well for the few companies that adopted it broadly, such as IBM, in more than 15 years it has failed to gain the level of acceptance it deserves. The primary reason is that the strategy is counter-intuitive, and there are an insufficient number of executives worldwide to lead the adoption and implementation of such a strategy. This formula requires that the licensor make available to any licensee its most valuable technology. This need not take place on the same day a product is introduced by the licensor to the markets, but within a short period—not more than perhaps a year. For many within an innovative company, such a strategy appears to be heretical. Why would any sane company enable its competitors by permitting full access to its most valuable competitive technology? The answer: because the competitor will ultimately discover it on its own, or find an alternative solution (design around).

There may be an extraordinarily rare exception to the rule, but sustainable businesses are not built on exceptions, but rather on repeatable actions. Believing your latest innovation can ensure your competitive success is a fallacy. What ensures your success is the *next* innovation, and the one after that, *ad infinitum*. Leaders of research and development, and business leaders funding R&D, scratch their heads over the idea that the licensing of their most valuable intellectual property can help them achieve stronger business performance, when their instinct tells them the opposite. But if they were to step back from the trees and observe the forest, they would understand that when their intellectual property strategy is tied to their broader business strategy they are fully utilizing one of the most valuable assets within their enterprise.

The Need to Tie Intellectual Property Strategy to Overall Business Strategy

In virtually all other aspects of business, executives fully grasp the requirement to knit together various elements of business operations into a cohesive whole. They understand how to use a company's equity, its cash, real estate, human resources, global reach, supply and distribution chains, marketing prowess, customer relationships, personal relationships, banking relationships, and government relationships to advantage their business. But, curiously, they do not understand—or generally even have much curiosity about—how to use to their advantage perhaps their most valuable corporate asset—their intellectual property. Techniques can be applied to fix this.

As observed earlier, most executives see intellectual property as a pending problem rather than an opportunity waiting to emerge. With rare exceptions, history has taught them that if the IP lawyer comes to visit, it is generally with bad news. Patents have long been thought of as the output of patent lawyers who sit buried in a company to codify the discoveries made within the company. Once a patent is issued, a technologist is frequently given a monetary reward for their discovery (an expense to the company), the patent is put in a drawer, and once a year the most innovative inventors are given an award presented by a senior business executive, delivered with words of encouragement to "continue the breakthrough technical work that drives the company's success. . . ." Occasionally, some other company pulls some patents out of its drawers and claims infringement. A long, expensive battle ensues, where everyone loses. This is IP 101 from the perspective of most business executives.

Curiously, most IP executives know almost as little about business operations as business executives know about IP. Until relatively recently, most IP executives were patent lawyers or litigators who see their function as minimizing risks to the company and protecting the company's products from copying by a competitor. They generally have never worked in marketing, sales, finance, product development, corporate strategy, or business development. Similarly, most business executives have never worked in IP or licensing functions. Moreover, since they do not share a set of experiences with most business executives, they may not even share an extensive common business vocabulary. What they worry about every day, or every quarter, is likely completely different. They have different performance metrics, with little or no intersection.

It should come as no surprise that if executives within a company are not regularly (at least monthly) talking about the issues they are facing and how the assets under one executive's management might be used to help solve the most pressing problem facing another executive, it is unlikely the executives will help use these assets to improve

EXHIBIT 1.3 **PATENT BROKERAGE TRANSACTION DATABASE SUMMARY**

Overall Summary Statistics	Value
Years covered	2002–2008
Quantity of deals	163
Total gross deal proceeds transacted	$447.35 m
Total US issued patent families transacted	1,083
Median sale price/ issued U.S. patent family	$110,000
Average sale price/ issued U.S. patent family	$413,000

Source: ThinkFire, Inc.

the company's performance. This is a simple way of saying that intellectual property is *not* an esoteric asset. It is, in fact, completely—and increasingly-quantifiable. Currently, the median open market price to buy a single, high-technology patent family (a patent and all of its related patents, such as foreign counterparts) is about $110,000. The mean is a little more than $400,000 (see Exhibit 1.3).

The true value for those patents useful in patent enforcement or defense (a small fraction of the total number, perhaps two or three percent), could be 10×, even 100 times, that amount.

Even at the median price, in a company with a patent portfolio of 5,000 patents (IBM has six times this number), the patent portfolio alone would be valued at more than half a billion dollars. The know-how that underlies it would be worth at least that, probably more. The value of the corporate brands could be worth hundreds of millions, and in some cases more. Examined in this perspective, there exists an asset worth conservatively more than a billion dollars and in many cases many billions of dollars as a direct reflection of an increased quantity of assets, even without lucrative licensing activities. This value could be increased substantially (albeit with much higher risk) through the "win-win" licensing of the commercially important patents and the technology that underlies them. If most business executives were approached with a group of corporate assets worth billions of dollars that they could use to build their business, this would get their attention. Several conclusions might be drawn (see Exhibit 1.4).

One is that business executives generally are unaware of the enormous value of their company's intellectual property portfolio. Another is that the company's intellectual property leaders are unaware of the value of the

EXHIBIT 1.4 **SIMPLIFIED VALUATION OF 5,000 PATENT FAMILY PORTFOLIO**

Assumption		Value		Comments
Patent Families		5,000		Exemplary Global 2000 technology company
	75th Percentile	**Median**	**25th Percentile**	
Sale Value/ Patent Family	$290,000	$110,000	$30,000	ThinkFire study, 2002–2008
Theoretical Portfolio Value	$1.45 billion	$550 million	$150 million	

Source: ThinkFire, Inc.

portfolio. This would be understandable, given the fact that this is a business judgment, not a legal or technical judgment. It is also possible that even if the business and IP professionals understand the value of the IP portfolio, they are uncertain as to how these assets can be put to work to advantage the company's operations and financial performance. Again, this would not be surprising, since too frequently the business professionals know too little about the IP and how it might be used to put the puzzle together, and the IP professionals know too little about the business, its strategies, and its most pressing problems to know how to apply the IP assets to move the business forward.

Using the Company's Intellectual Property to Improve Business Performance

Since the company's business strategy and objectives should always drive the IP strategy, and not vice versa, the first step in putting the company's IP to work is to open the line of communication between the company's business leaders and its IP executives. Without a strong relationship among these executives, the IP strategy will be necessarily misaligned with the company's. The question is whether with good guessing it might be close or, with bad guessing, a mile off with severe future market and financial consequences. No other critical function of a company where billions of dollars in value is on the line is left to chance. This critical function cannot be either. The line of communication required is not a one-time shot, but rather a true partnership, where IP is committed to helping their business colleagues solve their most pressing near- and long-term problems. Business leaders must learn to see their chief IP executive (some consider this executive a "CIPO") as a source of significant leverage to be used in every way possible to help them win. IP executives must see their job as a business leader, an integral part of every business leader's team, aimed at making the leader's team a success (and sharing in that success alongside them). Unless or until these deeply personal relationships are established, people will go through the motions, but the value will remain locked up.

To facilitate the relationship, it will be helpful for each side to provide a detailed introduction of where their functions are today, including their current perspectives on the business and the major business challenges they face. They should talk about key members of their team who can be drawn into the relationship, ensuring that working-level professionals are knit into the fabric of the relationship between the business and IP functions. The executives need to spend enough time together and find some common interests so they learn to like each other (like everything, people work best with people they like, and avoid the people they don't like).

The IP executive must be prepared to help bridge the gap by providing practical examples of how intellectual property might be used to open the bottlenecks confronting a business executive. For example, what if the problem confronting the business executive is that her competitors are achieving a 4% lower cost of goods sold than she is, and her increased cost is driving down her profitability, making it virtually impossible to meet her profit objectives. In the discussion, the IP executive learns there are two primary suppliers of components to the company who, together, make up a major portion of the cost of goods sold. With a bit of exploration, the IP executive determines that neither of the suppliers is licensed to her company's patent portfolio, and that both are selling products that infringe on that portfolio.

Working with the business executive's supply chain team, both suppliers are approached with an offer to take a license to the patent portfolio, and to also receive some differentiating technology from the company that will improve the suppliers' products. An agreement is reached that results in a royalty of 5% payable to the company. This is paid as a 5% discount in the price of the goods being sold by the suppliers to the company. Suddenly, the improved communication between the business and

IP leaders has led to a situation where the business executive now enjoys a 1% advantage in cost of goods sold over her competitors, and her profit objective can be realized.

There are an endless number of possibilities for the use of intellectual property to achieve meaningful business results. Most of them remain hidden because no one is looking. Most businesses and executives focused on IP exploitation tend to be fixated on royalties. Generally, they would do better to begin at a broader level, first seeking to discover business problems, then considering IP-based solutions.

One productive use of IP to rapidly find revenue and profit can be achieved through patent brokerage. As a result of the rapid accumulation of patents over the last several decades (see Exhibit 1.2), many companies have found themselves awash with patents that are both expensive to maintain and of limited value given that there are triplicates, quadruplicates, and more covering similar products. The result is that with this "over-coverage," the company is investing in assets that will not improve its licensing position and are unnecessary in the quantity held to protect a key product from infringement by others. It is likely that in most companies with a significant patent portfolio (greater than 1,000 patent families), at least 20 percent of the patent portfolio could be sold with no negative impact on the IP position, either offensively or defensively. With the sale, two things are achieved. First, patent maintenance costs are reduced. Second, in a period of months many millions of dollars (even tens or several hundred millions of dollars, assuming sufficient quantities of high-quality patents) in revenue and profit can be realized.

Selection of patents to be divested, however, is a critical project that once again is intimately tied to the company's business strategy. Too frequently, a company will reach a judgment to sell a group of patents in a business area they are no longer pursuing. Stock is not taken of the company's current and future patent adversaries given an ever-changing company product mix and strategy. After the sale, the company may come to determine there are several potential adversaries that have been identified with patents that impact a new product introduction that is key to the company's new business strategy, and that the companies holding these patents have major products that infringe the patents divested. The divestiture was obviously poorly planned; this is a mistake that must be avoided.

Understanding the current business and the emerging product roadmap, and identifying other operating companies that could present patent challenges to the company's current or future freedom to operate, are critical elements to a successful divestiture process. Moreover, a firm policy should be adopted to never divest all patents in any area regardless of their use within the company. Keep a handful or two of the best patents for a rainy day. Weather is unpredictable. Of course, assessing the risks posed by potential adversaries, as well as evaluating a portfolio to separate the wheat from the chaff—recognizing every good patent lot sold for fair value always has both—is a time consuming process. Luckily, firms such as ThinkFire are expert in such analyses, having performed them for corporations worldwide for M&A-related transactions, portfolio tuning and maintenance decisions, and for brokerage assignments.

Not Magic—Just Hard Work

The world of intellectual property is not particularly difficult to understand, nor are the solutions that use IP assets as a lever especially challenging to create. But finding and implementing these levers requires a commitment from IP and business professionals to learn much more about the issues and assets that each is responsible for managing, and how those assets might be applied to create shareholder value. So, with this as a prerequisite, the question is how to get these groups of people to spend more time together, to commit to a process that necessarily will take time to mature.

At a minimum, upon finishing this chapter, every business executive should reach out to the IP executive in their company and start the dialogue. And every IP executive should jump at the opportunity. Don't rush the conversation. Get to know one another. Don't spend more than an hour initially if you don't know one another. Do it over lunch if you can (food always helps). Each party should take a small task away from the meeting, and agree on the next meeting date. Starting the dialogue is critical. As you get to know one another better, as trust is established, as a common vocabulary emerges, the business exec will learn more about IP, and the IP exec will learn more about the business.

Every business exec should ensure that an IP exec is included in every important business strategy meeting and, every time a business crisis occurs that can have a material effect on the business, the IP exec should be brought into the circle. Maybe there won't be an IP angle that can help, but maybe there will be. Even if there is not, both will learn from the experience. The objective is clear: A corporate IP strategy is only useful if it supports the corporation's and each business unit's strategies. Lacking alignment, patents and other IP will be found in file cabinets, not on balance sheets. With alignment, it can put to work a wealth of assets that can mean the difference between winning big and just staying in the game.

ABOUT THE AUTHOR

Dan McCurdy is CEO of Allied Security Trust and Chairman of PatentFreedom, which helps companies manage their interactions with IP holders, including NPEs and patent trolls. Mr. McCurdy was cofounder and CEO of ThinkFire, Inc., a leading provider of intellectual property business strategy and advisory services. He has worked closely with senior corporate and IP executives and private equity investors. He was president of Lucent Technologies' Intellectual Property Business from 2000 to 2001, where he generated more than $500 million in annual revenues from the licensing of 26,000 worldwide patents developed by Bell Laboratories and Lucent. Prior to that, he was vice president of IBM Corporation, responsible for the creation of the IBM Life Sciences business unit. Prior to rejoining IBM in 1999, Mr. McCurdy was vice president of corporate development for CIENA Corporation, serving on CIENA's senior management committee and directing overall corporate merger and acquisitions strategy.

From 1982 to 1997 he served in a variety of business and intellectual property management roles in IBM, including director of business development for IBM Research and corporate manager of technology and intellectual property policy. Mr. McCurdy received his B.A. *summa cum laude* from the University of North Carolina, where he received the Mangum Medal in Oratory and was admitted to Phi Beta Kappa and the Order of the Long Leaf Pine. He is a frequent author and speaker on the use of intellectual property to improve business results, and was a member of the Intellectual Property Policy committee of the United States' National Academies.

NOTE

1. See discussion on this subject in McCurdy and Reynolds, "U.S. Universities Enter the Real World of Patents," *Intellectual Asset Management,* April/May 2004, issue 5. http://www.thinkfire.com/US%20UNIVERSITIES%20ARTICLE.pdf

CHAPTER 2

Evolution of the Technology Firm: IP Rights and the Business of Licensing

BY BRYAN P. LORD

PERSPECTIVE More innovative companies are using patent licensing not as a complement to revenue generation, but as a fundamental part of their innovation strategy. Some patent owners may choose not to manufacture products because of the high cost of capital and various barriers to entry, such as access to distribution channels. Having to go head-to-head with much larger and better-financed competitors also are impediments to selling products.

Despite these obstacles (and, perhaps, because of them) universities, biotech companies, and other technology based organizations have been able to create profitable licensing businesses and, in the process, improve innovation overall. These firms should not be confused with so-called patent trolls that do not sell products. Many licensing companies invest in research, secure valuable invention rights from some of the world's leading thinkers, and provide their customers with access to the technology developments they need.

Bryan Lord suggests in the following chapter that innovative businesses today come in many shapes and sizes. A licensing-centric business model is not right for every technology business or IP holder. Companies under pressure to demonstrate return on R&D and mastery of innovation assets often have felt it necessary to make licensing an integral part of their success.

(continued)

The promise of profit-laden revenue streams is attractive not only because of their immediate impact on a balance sheet, but because they can be understood broadly, i.e., in the C-suite and on Wall Street. While patent licensing can be a good motivator for some companies, it can obscure objectives for others. It is probably at best a secondary revenue stream for most high-tech companies, and probably should remain so. For the right business, however, it can be the key to a bright future.

Qualcomm, InterDigital, and a host of independent inventors and universities have made an attractive business out of technology development and a significant licensing program. Bryan Lord, an executive with semiconductor R&D company AmberWave Systems Corporation, which has licensed its inventions to Intel and others, discusses in his chapter how and why the technology firm has evolved in the past century and how it may continue to in the future. "The business of licensing is in its mere infancy," says Lord, whose AmberWave Systems focuses on licensing its inventions. "Robust business models incorporating technology development, intellectual property, and licensing will continue to emerge in the years and decades to come."

Introduction

Inventions play an important role in determining the nature of a technology-oriented firm. This chapter seeks to review the evolution of the technology firm past and present and looks ahead to business models for technology of the future. Throughout, it examines the important role of intellectual property in those firms, refers specifically to the changes underway in the modern semiconductor industry, and pays particular attention to the evolution of the business of licensing, which is beginning to embrace an open innovation model. Because sophistication, creativity, and experience with intellectual property are on the rise, impediments to new models that incorporate intellectual property into a technology firm's business are being reduced. The chapter concludes with predictions that the business of licensing is in its infancy and that more robust business models will incorporate technology development and intellectual property rights to generate a positive impact on innovation.

The Past: The Integrated Industrial Economy

The Nature of the Technology Firm

Patented inventions have served important roles in industrial firms since the industrial revolution. Colorfully named inventions such as the flying shuttle (John Kay, 1733), the spinning jenny (James Hargreaves, 1764) and the water frame (Richard Arkwright, 1769) improved the speed and efficiency of textile manufacturing. Eli Whitney's invention of the cotton gin in the early 1790s improved the speed and efficiency of processing freshly picked cotton. Together, these and other inventions built the foundation for the growth of the modern textile industry that changed the landscape of America.

For decades to follow, great companies and in some cases entire industries were built around breakthrough inventions. Some examples:

Date	*Inventor*	*Invention*	*Company*
1840	Samuel Morse	Telegraph	Western Union
1870s	Alexander Graham Bell	Telephone	AT&T
1880s	George Eastman	Rolled photographic film	Eastman Kodak
1890s	Wright Brothers	Three-axis aircraft control	Wright Company; later, Curtiss Wright Corp.
1890s	Herman Hollerith	Punch card data processing	Computing Tabulating Corp.; later renamed International Business Machines (IBM)

Industrial firms used their inventions to obtain and protect market power. Many became large and fully integrated firms. In northern Massachusetts and Southern New Hampshire, flying shuttle and spinning jenny helped the Boott Mills and Amoskeag Mills become some of the largest employers in the nation and the nucleus for entire cities. In Dearborn, Michigan, Henry Ford's invention of the assembly line helped establish the dominance of the Ford Motor Company. Ford's massive Rogue Rover manufacturing plant, which integrated the entire manufacturing process from refining raw material to final assembly, demonstrated the height of vertical integration. Companies like Western Union, AT&T, Eastman Kodak, Curtiss Wright Corp., and IBM became powerful market leaders on the strengths of their technological advances.

The Role of Intellectual Property

Vertically integrated industrial firms sought to build and defend market power. Patents, therefore, were used to exclude others from the right to manufacture competing products and, in some cases, to recover royalties for patent infringement. Eli Whitney, for example, found imitations to the cotton gin appearing in the market soon after its introduction. Whitney pursued a costly legal campaign to protect his business and combat infringement, tragically spending more on enforcement actions than his company made. The Wright Brothers brought suit against Glenn Curtiss and a number of other early aviators, challenging their use of ailerons as the equivalent of their patented wing warping techniques (see Exhibit 2.1). The Bell Telephone Company fought hundreds of challenges from the United States Government and firms which challenged the priority of the Bell telephone invention. In 1904, Henry Ford successfully defended against a patent on the "road engine" awarded to patent attorney George Selden. Much later, in 1990, Kodak was found to have infringed 12 patents assigned to Polaroid and ordered to pay close to one billion dollars in damages, the largest infringement award in history. Patent law issues in the industrial economy related primarily to the traditional patent infringement issues, namely establishing primacy of the inventor, proving validity of the patent, and combating infringement, whether to exclude competitors or to enforce the payment of a royalty to the inventor.

A Precursor to the Business of Licensing

While most patent holders in the industrial era sought to build a market-dominant firm around their inventions, a few exceptions existed. One of the era's most famous inventors, Thomas Edison, preferred ideas to widgets, so instead of a widget factory, he built an invention factory. The Smithsonian recounts:

> Thomas Edison approached the Western Union Telegraph Company with several inventions of his relating to the telegraph, especially the quadruplex telegraph system he had just completed. When asked how much he wanted for the inventions Edison thought of asking for about $2000, but instead he turned the question around and replied, "Well suppose you make me an offer." Edison was amazed when they offered

EXHIBIT 2.1 **U.S. PATENT #821,393, "FLYING MACHINE" GRANTED TO O. & W. WRIGHT, MAY 22, 1906**

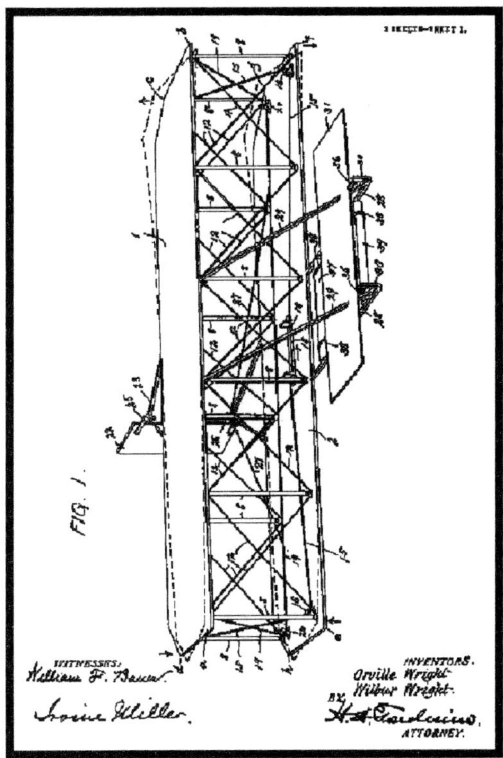

him $40,000! This was a lot of money for those days and it allowed him to fulfill his wish to become a full time inventor. Edison signed a highly profitable contract with Western Union, took the money to the New Jersey countryside, and built a laboratory complex at Menlo Park, nicknamed "The Invention Factory!"

To invent, you need a good imagination and a pile of junk.

—Thomas A. Edison (1847-1931)

Thomas Edison and his invention factory went on to invent the phonograph, the telephone transmitter, the electric pen and the electric light bulb, the motion picture camera, the electric battery, and many other wonders of the times. Edison was granted over 1,000 patents, more than any other inventor on record. His business model also foreshadowed a more sophisticated use of intellectual property—the business of licensing—which would become a new feature in the modern economy.

The Present: The Disaggregated Modern Economy

Transition from Industrial to Modern Economy

Harvard Business School professor Michael Porter offers a vivid description of the changes involved in the transition from the industrial economy to today's modern economy. He contrasts the industrial economy's "extensive vertical integration where, for example, in-house productions of parts, services or training were once the norm," with today's modern economy where "a more dynamic environment renders vertical integration inefficient, ineffective, and inflexible." Today's modern economy is a complex, specialized, and increasingly disaggregated system with "close linkages [among] buyers, suppliers, and other institutions [which] contribute importantly not only to the efficiency but to the rate of improvement and innovation."[2]

Economist Ronald Coase describes the economic reasoning behind the disaggregation of the modern economy. Coase argues that private parties can "internalize" inefficiencies and other externalities in economic exchange or production through negotiation.[3] Therefore, a consolidated operation whose sum of its parts is more profitable than the disaggregated entity can simply allocate these inefficiencies by contract to one or another of its disaggregated parts, so long as transaction costs in the negotiation are kept to a minimum.

During the industrial age, externalities were too great to justify a departure from the traditional vertically integrated technology firm. However, as the economy transitioned to the modern economy, modern management thinking evolved (as exemplified by the observations of Porter and Coase), and some significant changes in the law between 1979 and 1982 helped eliminate problematic externalities. First, a lack of independent, private risk capital was addressed by a seemingly innocuous change in the nation's labor laws. Second, a lack of incentives to advance federal investment in research and development was addressed by the Bayh–Dole Act in 1980. Third, uncertainty and inconsistency in federal patent law was addressed by the creation of the Court of Appeals for the Federal Circuit in 1982. Each helped pave the way towards disaggregation of the technology firm and is explained a bit further below.

The first externality, the lack of independent, private risk capital, was addressed by a U.S. Department of Labor ruling on the Employment Retirement Income Security Act (ERISA) in 1979. Professors Paul Gompers and Josh Lerner Harvard Business School explained,

> One policy decision that potentially had an effect on commitments to venture funds . . . is the clarification by the U.S. Department of Labor of the Employment Retirement Income Security Act's (ERISA) prudent man rule in 1979. Through 1978, the rule stated that pension managers had to invest with the care of a "prudent man." Consequently, many pension funds avoided investing in venture capital entirely: it was felt that a fund's investment in a start-up could be seen as imprudent. In early 1979, the Department of Labor ruled that portfolio diversification was a consideration in determining the prudence of an individual investment. Thus, the ruling implied that an allocation of a small fraction of a portfolio to venture capital funds would not be seen as imprudent. That clarification specifically opened the door for pension funds to invest in venture capital.[4]

Gompers and Lerner reported that $424 million was invested in new venture capital funds in 1978 prior to the new ERISA interpretation and that individual investors accounted for 32% of those dollars invested, more than twice the share of pension funds. Eight years after the new interpretation, more than $4 billion was invested in venture capital, and pension funds accounted for more than 50% of all contributions.[5]

The second externality, the lack of incentives to advance federal investment in research and development, was helped by the passage of the Bayh–Dole Act in 1980. In the late 1970s, U.S. patent issuance had steadily declined for more than ten years, investment in research and development was dormant, and small businesses were receiving a declining percentage of federal research funds. There was simply a dearth of investment and incentive to commercialize early-stage research technology.

Part of the cause was an insistence that patent rights derived from federally funded research remain the property of the U.S. government. As a result, incentives to transfer technology out of federally funded research facilities and into the private sector did not exist. With passage of the Bayh–Dole Act in 1980, title to patented technology based upon federally funded research became the property of the institution conducting the research. While a seemingly subtle shift, the Act was nevertheless controversial at the time. In fact, the Chairman of the Senate Finance Committee called the bill "the worse I had ever seen." But two decades later, *The Economist* declared Bayh–Dole "possibly the most inspired piece of legislation to be enacted in America over the past half century."[6]

> More than anything, this single policy measure (Bayh–Dole) helped reverse America's precipitous slide into industrial irrelevance.
>
> "Innovation's Golden Goose," *The Economist*, December 2002

The third externality, uncertainty and inconsistency in federal patent law, was addressed when Congress created the Court of Appeals for the Federal Circuit (CAFC) a few years later in 1982. Professor Susan Sell of George Washington University described the situation leading up to the CAFC's creation:

> The central problem . . . was uneven application of patent law in the various circuit courts. Some circuits favored infringers, whereas others favored patentees. For example, between 1945 and 1957, a patent was nearly four times more likely to be enforced in the Seventh Circuit than in the Second Circuit. Infringers scrambled to have their cases heard in the lenient circuit courts, whereas patentees fought to have their cases heard in the stricter . . . circuits. Forum shopping, and requests to have patent infringement appeals transferred to different circuits, injected considerable uncertainty into patent litigation. When 250 U.S. companies engaged in industrial research were surveyed by the Industrial Research Institute on the question of a single patent court, the vast majority of respondents indicated that the uncertainly, complexity, and inconsistencies in patent enforceability eroded the full economic value of the patent. In this convoluted legal environment patents could not be considered sufficient incentives to invest in research and development.[7]

After creation of the CAFC in 1982, technical and legal criteria for determining patent infringement and the level of damage and royalty compensation awarded to successful patent-owner litigation was increased.[8] The CAFC's rulings were also more "pro-patent" than the previous courts. For instance, the circuit courts had affirmed 62% of district court findings of patent infringement in the three decades prior to the creation of the CAFC, while the CAFC in its first eight years affirmed 90% of such decisions.[9] As a result, businesses were able to make better risk assessments and business judgments based upon a more consistent, informed, and strengthened patent regime.

These three changes had enormous impact and helped support the nation's transition from the industrial to the modern economy. Gompers and Lerner later estimated that by 1998, venture funding now accounted for about 14 percent of U.S. innovative activity.[10] At the peak of the venture capital market in 2000, PricewaterhouseCoopers Money Tree survey reported venture investment of over $1 billion in close to 9,000 deals.[11] The Association of University Technology Managers (AUTM) reported that in 2005, $42 billion was spent on research and development in U.S. academic centers. This led to 527 new products, and 628 new spin-off companies introduced to the market in one year alone. Since 1980, over 5,000 spin-off companies have been created from university research.[12] Venture capital investment in university and federally funded research and development has spurred the development of such wide-ranging industries as telecommunications, semiconductors, software and the Internet, biotechnology, medical devices, and alternative energy, and become an economic driver for multiple regions of the country.

The Nature of the Technology Firm

As the modern economy became increasingly disaggregated, firms sought to exploit their market specialties and entered into transactions with other firms similarly focused on their unique market offering. Complex, interdependent supply chains resulted, and the number of participating firms increased dramatically.

An example of this transition can be seen in the semiconductor industry. In the late 1950s, the silicon integrated circuit was invented. Jack Kilby and Texas Instruments received a patent for "miniaturized integrated circuits," and Robert Noyce received a patent for a "silicon-based integrated circuit" and later co-founded Intel Corporation. Although

Texas Instruments and Intel are today large, successful technology firms, their nature differs from the totally integrated Rogue River operation of the Ford Motor Company. While they are integrated in part, they still rely upon a complex set of external suppliers and they sell their goods to a complex set of customers. Gas companies such as Praxair and Air Products & Chemicals supply these chipmakers with specialized semiconductor gasses. Silicon manufacturers such as MEMC and Shin-Etsu Handotai supply them with precisely engineered silicon wafers. Equipment manufacturers such as Applied Materials and Novellus supply them with sophisticated manufacturing equipment. Semiconductor manufacturers purchase these goods with investor capital, build and operate semiconductor manufacturing plants, and hire technical and management expertise to design and manufacture semiconductor chips. They do not sell their products to consumers (as did the Ford Motor Company) but to other technology firms such as Dell Computer, Hewlett-Packard, and Nokia, who in turn incorporate the semiconductor chips into other products such as computers, peripherals, or cell phone handsets, which are then marketed and sold to consumers. Simplified, the value chain with

EXHIBIT 2.2 **VALUE CHAIN WITH INTEGRATED DEVICE MANUFACTURER**

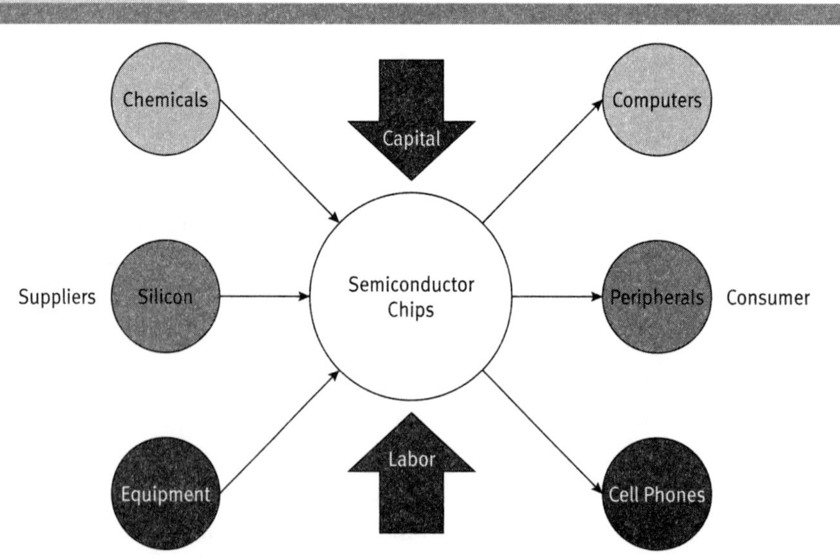

the integrated device manufacturer (IDM) Intel or Texas Instruments in the center looks as shown in Exhibit 2.2.

Although the semiconductor manufacturing supply chain is already disaggregated in comparison to Ford's Rogue River operation, further disaggregation can and does occur at virtually any component of the supply chain. For example, a "fabless" semiconductor model is challenging the IDM model and decouples the function of semiconductor design from the function of semiconductor manufacturing. Semiconductor foundries, the largest being Taiwan Semiconductor Manufacturing Corporation (TSMC) in Taiwan, provide semiconductor manufacturing services for hire. In parallel, semiconductor chip designers, often called "fabless" semiconductor manufacturers, focus their efforts on designing advanced chip architectures using sophisticated design techniques and computer software, then outsource the manufacturing to the foundries. Examples of "fabless" semiconductor manufacturers include Xilinx, Nvidia, and Broadcom. The chips they design are manufactured and sold to many of the same customers and at times in competition with the integrated device manufacturers. The foundries rely on many of the same supply relationships as the integrated device manufacturers. The designers often rely upon supply of an intangible sort—outsourced services, designs, and intellectual property—as their inputs. Some designers, for example, purchase or license design services and design "cores" from companies such as ARM or MIPS. These cores serve as building blocks in a chip design, avoiding costly duplication of effort for standardized functions. A more complex "fabless" value chain is depicted in Exhibit 2.3.

Simplifying then, whether it is an integrated device manufacturer or foundry/"fabless" semiconductor manufacturer which sits at the middle of this model, suppliers provide inputs of goods, services, and intellectual property; chip manufacturers add their own internal or outsourced capital and labor, and the output is semiconductor chips for a variety of customers, who in turn incorporate those chips into consumer products. The simplified model appears as shown in Exhibit 2.4.

Further generalizing, virtually any position on the supply chain can be disaggregated into smaller subcomponents of specialization where inputs, application of capital and labor, and outputs provide business opportunities. Broadly speaking, these inputs of goods, services, and intellectual property are advanced by a firm, and in turn become outputs of goods,

EXHIBIT 2.3 **MORE COMPLEX VALUE CHAIN**

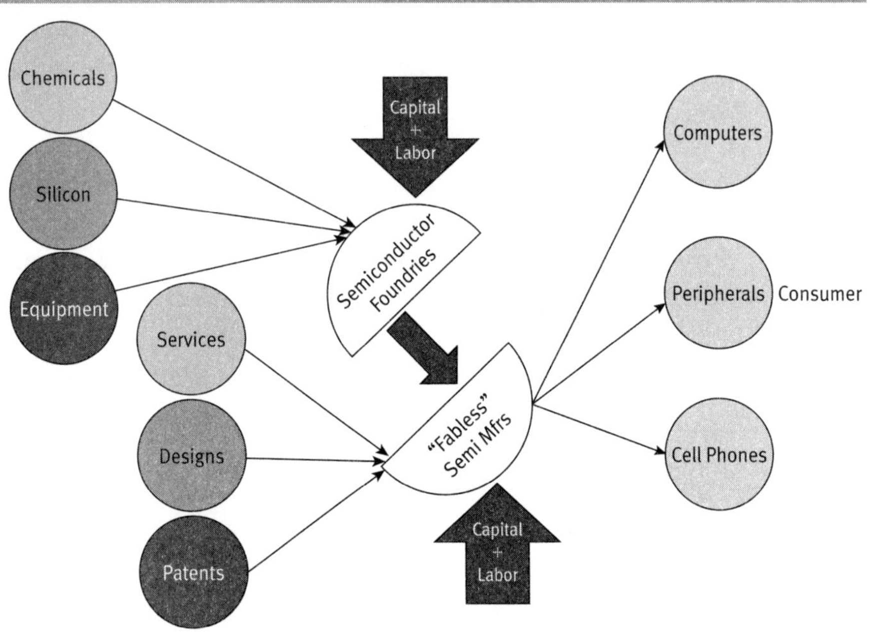

EXHIBIT 2.4 **SIMPLIFIED VALUE CHAIN**

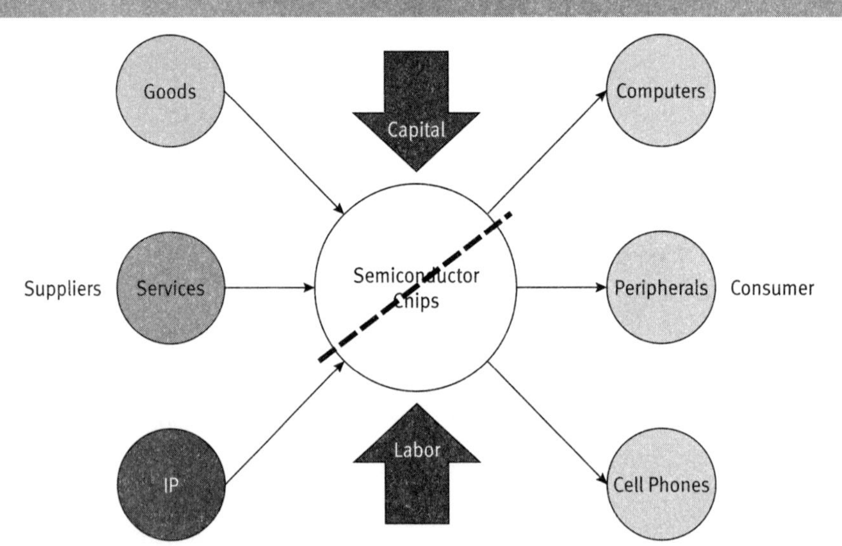

EXHIBIT 2.5 **MODERN TECHNOLOGY SUPPLY CHAIN**

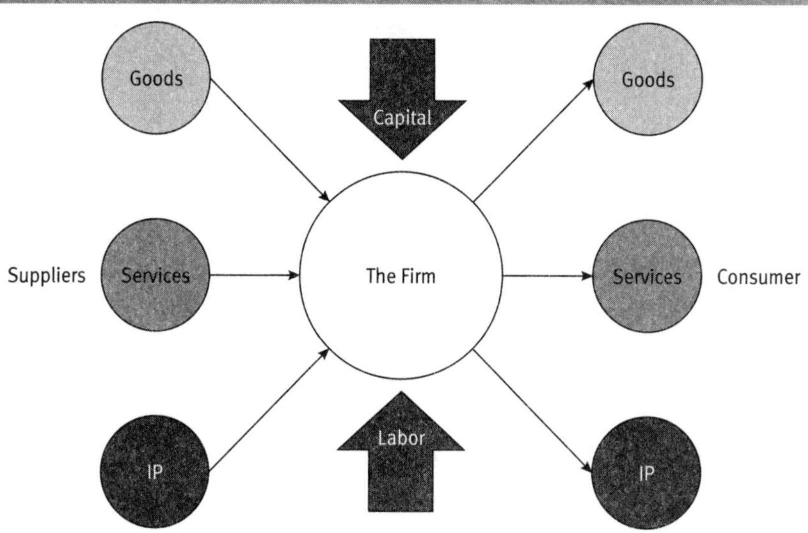

services, and intellectual property to the next step in the supply chain. Most generally, a component in a modern technology supply chain can be modeled, then, as shown in Exhibit 2.5.

Within this disaggregated supply chain, a variety of business models proliferate. For example, in the semiconductor industry alone, a matrix of business models varying inputs and outputs can be summarized as shown in Exhibit 2.6.

And from this diverse disaggregation, opportunities arise for a wide variety of smaller, specialized firms. As a byproduct, their emergence

EXHIBIT 2.6 **MATRIX OF VARIOUS INPUTS AND OUTPUTS**

Business Model	Input	Output	Example
IDMs	Goods; IP	Goods	Intel, Texas Instruments
Foundries	Goods; P	Services	TSMC, UMC
"Fabless" manufacturers	Services; IP	Goods	Nvidia, Broadcom
Design core providers	Services	IP	ARM, MIPS
Technology development firms	Goods; IP	Services; IP	AmberWave, Tessera (see discussion in next section)

accelerates the pace and broadens the scope of the nation's technology development. A recent study by the Small Business Administration found that "Small firm innovation is twice as closely linked to scientific research as large firm innovation on average, and so substantially more high-tech or leading edge." These small firms add to the nation's technology diversity, create jobs, and stimulate economic activity and, according to the SBA, "maintain the diversity in our country's innovative capacity, which is a source of economic strength over the long-term." In some cases, these small firms stay small. In other cases, small firms are acquired by larger firms and provide for important strategic synergies for the larger firm. And in still other cases, those small firms grow into large firms which become future anchor employers in regions across the country.

The Role of Intellectual Property

As was the case in the industrial economy, patents maintain an important role in the market economy to defend market position and protect inventive products against infringement. In addition, as the modern economy disaggregates, cooperation among firms becomes paramount. Patents therefore serve also another critical function in the modern economy. They are an important vehicle for coordination, exchange, and allocation of value among technology firms. Professor Scott Kieff of the Hoover Institute explains:

> Coordination . . . refers to the process by which many diverse individuals interact with each other for a particular activity to be achieved effectively. Coordination helps them achieve that common goal. And the availability of coordination helps them to be more specialized in the skills and resources they each can bring to a collective enterprise than they would have been without the ability to coordinate. In the context of IP, for example, the process of bringing a new invention to market after that invention has been made—a process called commercialization—often requires the coordination of inventors, financiers, labor, management, advertisers, and marketers. [See generally Kieff, *Commercializing Inventions*, supra note 14, at 707–12 (discussing role of patents in commercialization of inventions]. That is, without the ability to coordinate, in the case of an invention for example, the inventor hoping to achieve commercialization would need to serve simultaneously as financier, laborer, manager, advertiser, and marketer. The recognition of this problem

> was indeed one of the motivating factors behind the present U.S. patent system, which focuses on the importance of coordination to achieve invention commercialization.[13]

Modern intellectual property law facilitates coordination between a patent holder and the ultimate beneficiary of the patented technology. Consistent with Coase's observations, it allows the patent holder flexibility to negotiate patent licenses with the commercial entities that ultimately benefit from its value and fairly assigns payment of that value to the commercial entities that practice that patent. As a result, intellectual property assumes a featured position in the business strategies of technology firms in the modern economy.

The Business of Licensing

At a minimum, intellectual property strategies must be integrated with more traditional business models such as those previously described. But in many cases, intellectual property becomes central to a firm's business strategy and licensing of intellectual property can become a business in and of itself. For example, large IDMs such as Intel and Texas Instruments accumulated a significant storehouse of patented technologies for the traditional purposes of gaining and sustaining market power. They realized, however, that by licensing their technologies to other firms they could achieve important business objectives. Texas Instruments is believed to have earned over $1 billion in revenues from licensing its patented technologies. Intel, on the other hand, has entered into broad cross-licensing agreements with multiple industry players, establishing an intellectual property détente between firms, and in some cases encouraging interoperability between its products and the products of other firms.

> *We can't live any more in a world which is based on stuff and not ideas.*
>
> —DEAN KAMEN, INVENTOR OF THE SEGWAY HUMAN TRANSPORTER

At the other end of the spectrum, independent inventors mirror Edison's invention factory model and relied upon intellectual property to protect breakthrough inventions and facilitate the licensing of their rights to manufactures. For example, Dr. James Fergason invented the liquid crystal display in the early 1970, and licensed his technology to numerous makers of LCD TVs, projectors, and notebook computers, including Epson, Panasonic, Sharp, and Samsung. Another, inventor Dean Kamen, invented the first insulin pump, an all-terrain wheelchair called the iBOT, and the famous Segway human transporter. Instead of commercializing these inventions, Kamen chooses for his inventions to be commercialized by other corporations, while maintaining his ability to work on new ideas and new research through his DEKA Research and Development Corporation.

Licensing can also close gaps in the technology supply chain. While the commercialization of many university and federally funded technologies has flourished under Bayh–Dole, and venture capital investment has increased exponentially over the past decades, some technologies take years to properly develop and gaps arise between the distance a university researcher can take a technology development project and the maturity of a technology needed to attract venture capital funding. Because this gap is a place where many promising technologies die, technologists call it the "valley of death." Intellectual property licensing provides a vehicle to fund research in the valley of death. For example, this author's employer, AmberWave Systems, in-licenses promising early-stage university technologies as inputs, dedicates research and development resources to advancing the technology, and out-licenses higher-value, later-stage technologies as outputs. Not unlike the traditional model where lower-value goods are purchased as inputs and higher-value goods are sold as outputs, the AmberWave model simply does the same with patented technologies and uses licensing as its mechanism. The company has raised close to $100 million in venture capital funding, operates a state-of-the-art research facility in southern New Hampshire, has in-licensed technologies from the Massachusetts Institute of Technology, AT&T Bell Laboratories, and the University of California, and has out-licensed its technologies to major semiconductor manufacturers worldwide.

Intellectual property licensing also permits firms to transition their business models from less- to more-productive strategies. For example, San Jose-based Tessera Technologies transitioned from a semiconductor packaging company to a specialized technology firm that focuses on developing and licensing its patented packaging technologies to other semiconductor companies. While it once struggled as a manufacturer, today Tessera has licensing relationships with over 60 companies, its wafer-level packaging technologies are used in semiconductor products worldwide, and it is a publicly-traded company with a multi-billion-dollar market capitalization.

Intellectual property licensing also permits firms to employ multiple, complementary business models. Much like Texas Instruments' licensing business works in parallel to its manufacturing business, San Diego-based QUALCOMM Inc. is a prime example of complementary, intellectual property-oriented business models. QUALCOMM is the leading developer of advanced wireless technologies, which it licenses to telecommunications and consumer electronic manufacturers worldwide. At the same time, QUALCOMM is also the world's largest "fabless" semiconductor manufacturer. Intellectual property protects its technologies and licensing helps in the coordination of the rights needed to manufacture QUALCOMM chips through semiconductor foundries. Intellectual property, therefore, is not only at the heart of QUALCOMM's technology licensing business, but it also supports its product manufacturing business. Founded in the den of a San Diego home in 1985, today QUALCOMM holds over 6,000 patents and has a market capitalization of over $60 billion.

Finally, the business of licensing technology and the significant role of intellectual property in the modern economy have provided opportunities for intellectual property "middlemen" to offer services to the players in the technology marketplace. Numerous intellectual property consulting firms have emerged to add business strategy services to the traditional legal services provided by patent attorneys. Other middlemen help facilitate "liquidity" in the technology marketplace by providing IP brokerage, M&A advisory, auction, or technology exchanges. Each helps connect buyers with sellers of patented technology.

In addition, specialized sources of capital have emerged that offer experience and expertise in intellectual property commercialization and a willingness to invest in or even acquire patented technologies from inventors. Some of these sources of capital invest as traditional venture capital investors would invest by investing in the potential of a future promising technology. Others will lend against intellectual property royalty streams, providing new sources of capital to successful inventors. Still other sources of capital recognize value in intellectual property which is believed to be infringed in the marketplace and will provide financial backing to protect against the infringement in court in exchange for some financial return.

There are some who object to the entry of these new market players into the intellectual property marketplace. Much of the objection, like those who defended the trust giants in the early 1900s, stems from those who benefit from an inefficient intellectual property market with large barriers to entry and for whom liquidity and efficiency in the market for patented technologies are threats rather than opportunities. And yet, the addition of new capital and expertise, coupled with creativity, interest, and an ability to calculate and accommodate risk, brings new opportunities to the technology market. In fact, in much the same way that prior changes in the law served to minimize externalities—by increasing incentives to commercialize research technology, by increasing the strength and predictability of the intellectual property regime, and by making available more risk capital—these new intellectual property middlemen also serve to lower externalities in the marketplace by adding liquidity to the market and by reducing inefficiencies by bringing together willing buyers and sellers. These middlemen therefore support the business of licensing and help facilitate a more robust technology economy.

The Future? The Interrelated "Open" Economy

Transition from Modern to "Open" Economy

Authors Dan Tapscott and Anthony Williams describe a new promise of technology collaboration in their recent book, *Wikinomics*.[14] They describe our economy encountering a new "perfect storm" which combines three forces: the Internet, a new generation of people experienced in collaboration, and a global economy coming together to enable new forms of global economic collaboration, which he predicts "will drive deep changes in the strategy and architecture of firms." The idea, called "open" innovation envisions technology development conducted by networks of innovators collaborating to solve problems and come up with new ideas. Open innovation contrasts to the series of disaggregated, but sequential relationships which are the hallmark of the modern technology supply chain.

Tapscott and Williams also trace their observations to Coase. Tapscott and Williams postulate that "a firm will tend to expand until the costs of organizing an extra transaction within the firm become equal to the costs of carrying out the same transaction in the open market. As long as it is cheaper to perform the transaction inside your firm, keep it there. But if it is cheaper to go to the marketplace, do not try to do it internally." The Internet, they say, in effect turns Coase's Law upside down. "Nowadays firms should shrink until the cost of performing a transaction internally no longer exceeds the cost of performing it externally." They contrast Ford Motor Company's Rogue River plant, which "drew rubber and steel into one end and pushed finished cars out the other," with today's wiki-economy, where steel comes from China, rubber from Malaysia and glass from Kansas, all coordinated via online clearinghouses and delivered just in time via a global shipping service.[15]

If successful, open innovation would continue the advancements made in the transition from the industrial economy to the modern economy. In transitioning from the modern to the open innovation economy, disaggregation would further accelerate, specialization would increase, and the "perfect storm" of the Internet, demographics, and globalization would provide opportunities for coordination and integration that would exceed even those of the fast-disaggregating modern supply chain. Tapscott and Williams predict that "old, ironclad vessels of the industrial era will sink under the crashing waves" of change, while "firms that create highly nimble and networked structures and connect to external ideas and energies will gain the buoyancy they require to survive and win important advantages in their industries."[16]

The Nature of the Technology Firm

Larry Huston, a senior fellow at the Wharton's Mack Center for Technological Innovation, says, "Innovation networks are people, institutions, and companies that are outside the firm . . . They are intellectual assets that companies can link up with to solve problems and find ideas, while beginning to think about those assets as an extended part of their organization—and therefore quickly create top-line growth and bring new things to the marketplace."[17] Modifying previous representations of the disaggregated supply chain, an innovation network might look as shown in Exhibit 2.7.

EXHIBIT 2.7 **AN INNOVATION NETWORK**

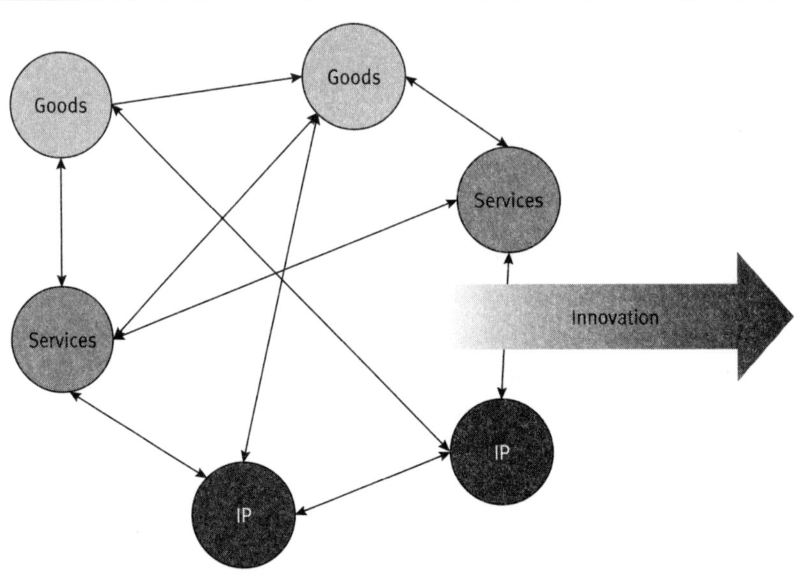

From a competitive-advantage standpoint, I think [open innovation] is going to be a really big deal.

—Larry Huston, managing partner at 4INNO and senior fellow at Wharton School of Management

Huston explained innovation networks as an opportunity for large companies, citing Procter and Gamble's success in extending the company's innovation process to include 1.5 million people outside the company. He also describes open innovation as further opportunity for small businesses:

> [M]any of the most innovative people out there are in small companies. They were leaders. They were technologists in big companies. They didn't like the environment in big companies and so they went and became a small company. And so they're out there, and they're doing highly innovative work, but what they lack is market access, scale. . . . That's the kind of thing a Microsoft or a Procter & Gamble or Eli Lilly

> or companies like that can do. It's because they have scale, and the small company has the agility and the entrepreneurship to think, 'I've got to do this well. I've got to do it at low cost.' And, you know, they have some advantages that big companies don't have. So what you do is marry the scale advantages of the big company and sort of the hungry attitude and agility of a small entrepreneur, and that's what you get.[18]

Large, or small, then, open innovation provides a promising model for the firm of the future.

The Role of Intellectual Property

However promising the concept, the role of intellectual property in the open innovation model remains a work in progress. Champions of open innovation often cite the wonderful success of "open source" software as an example of the power of open innovation. Because the contributors to the open source project do not retain intellectual property rights to their work, some conclude that intellectual property rights are at best unnecessary, and at worse, impediments to innovation. For example, John Kao, author of the book *Innovation Nation*, explores the promise of open innovation but spends precious little time exploring the role of intellectual property in technology development. What little attention he does grant intellectual property in his work he uses to dismiss intellectual property laws as "impediments to openness and invention" and argues that they "stand in the way of the United States' efforts to reignite its innovation engine."[19] In essence, Kao describes intellectual property as an externality which ought to be reduced in order to increase innovation.

To treat intellectual property itself as an externality takes Coase's observations and turns them on their head. Coase argues that where externalities and transaction costs can be allocated among negotiating entities and reduced, new structures arise and disaggregation increases. He does not argue the inverse, namely that where new structures and disaggregation can be created, legal protections (whether externalities or not) ought to be blindly reduced. To do so reverses cause and effect. In fact, as has been shown, strong legal protection has served as a necessary element of a well-functioning technology economy which itself helped reduce externalities in the process of developing new technology. The reduction or elimination of intellectual property rights which support innovation would not be advisable simply to facilitate novel collaboration configurations in the name of a new kind of innovation.

Beyond that, instead of standing as an example of reasons to reduce intellectual property protection, open source software stands as an example of how maintaining a strong, predictable intellectual property regime can support open innovation. The GNU public license (GPL) which governs the legal regime of many open-source software projects, including the well known Linux kernel, by contract (a public license) subordinates the intellectual property rights of any one individual to the collective rights of the group. Participants who contribute source code to the open source project agree that their source code when contributed to the project becomes part of, and subject to, the terms of the GPL. The GPL, in turn, ensures that the works of the collective effort remain available free of charge to all, subject of course, to the terms of the GPL. As a result, while open source software may be "free" in the monetary sense, it is not "free" in the liberation sense.

To make the point, instead of calling the software "freeware," many cleverly refer to open source software as "copyleft," contrasting but also analogizing to the copyright protection protecting traditional closed system software. This structure is consistent with Coase's observations and economic justification disaggregation. The GPL allows private parties (in this case, contributors to the open source project) to "internalize" the externalities in their economic exchange through negotiation. Here too, then, this license properly addresses the ownership of the relevant intellectual property rights, reduces transaction costs, and facilitates coordination in keeping with the objective of the open source project.

Implications for the Business of Licensing

Disaggregation and new collaboration structures, therefore, should not be viewed as ends unto themselves, but as the byproducts of business and policy decisions that reduce externalities which are impediments to innovation and maintain those structures (whether externalities or not) which increase innovative activity. And where innovation can be encouraged and profit derived, firms will deploy the structures of open innovation.

In doing so however, firms will need to increase, not decrease, the strength and predictability of their intellectual property regime. This will become even more critical as the volume and means for mass collaboration increases. Former U.S. Diplomat James Lewis notes, "IP protection is part of the infrastructure of rules and laws that make economies more productive and more innovative. IP protection reduces the risks associated with innovation—an inventor takes a gamble in creating a new product, whether it is a new soda or a new semiconductor that requires immense R&D investment. Without IP protection and the incentives they provide, fewer people will accept the risks required for innovation."[20]

Lewis supports the notion of "openness" within a strong IP regime. "Transparency is crucial," he says. "The beauty of the patent system is that the ideas behind an innovation are made public. This openness accelerates innovation and eliminates the risk of monopoly. Patent disclosure requirements diffuse technology and allow competing products to be developed. A well-designed and -enforced patent system is crucial for innovation."[21]

Licensing firms are well-positioned to embrace the benefits of open innovation should it advance as a future model for the technology firm. Creative collaborative licensing agreements can and will be structured to achieve the business purpose of the collaboration in much the same way that the GPL does for the copyleft movement. In doing so, the opportunities in business of licensing will increase under open innovation, as will opportunities and vehicles to develop new and exciting technologies.

Conclusion

It has been said that good fences make good neighbors. Patents are like fences. The more neighborhood cooperation occurs, the more one needs to know, at the end of the day, where one's property begins and where it ends. Clarity brings confidence and a willingness to cooperate. Ambiguity brings the opposite. As our market economy, which once transitioned from an industrial to a modern economy, transitions to an innovation economy—in whatever form it may take—this truism will continue to be an important guidepost, and strong intellectual property will continue to be an important feature of all technology economies.

As we have seen, increasing incentives to commercialize research technology, supporting a strong and predicable intellectual property regime, and encouraging the availability of risk capital are examples of positive changes in the law that reduced externalities and improved opportunities for the technology firm. The business of licensing is in its mere infancy, and more robust business models incorporating technology development, intellectual property, and licensing will continue to emerge in the years and decades to come. New intellectual property middlemen will also serve to facilitate a more robust technology economy by reducing transactional externalities. New systems for encouraging collaboration will emerge, and new forces will create new "perfect storms" which will provide challenge and opportunity for the globally integrated economy. And above all, new inventions will continue to create new business opportunities, new technologies, and new ways to improve the quality of life for mankind.

ABOUT THE AUTHOR

Bryan P. Lord is Vice President of Finance and Licensing, General Counsel for AmberWave Systems Corporation, a research and development corporation in Salem, New Hampshire, that licenses its advanced semiconductor designs to Intel and others. Mr. Lord is responsible for AmberWave's financial, legal, and public policy matters. Previously, Mr. Lord was a corporate and venture capital attorney at, Testa, Hurwitz & Thibeault, LLP in Boston, one of the nation's leading high-technology law firms. He earned his B.A, *magna cum laude*, from Concordia College in Moorhead, Minnesota, and his J.D. from Notre Dame Law School in South Bend, Indiana, where he was an editor of *The Notre Dame Law Review.*

Mr. Lord lives in Manchester, New Hampshire, with his wife and three children.

NOTES

1. http://invention.smithsonian.org/centerpieces/edison/000_story_02.asp
2. Michael Porter, *On Competition* (Boston: Harvard Business School Publishing, 1998)
3. Ronald Coase, "The Problem of Social Cost," *Journal of Law and Economics*, 1960
4. Paul A. Gompers and Josh Lerner, "What Drives Venture Capital Fundraising?" (January 1999) at p. 8. Available at SSRN: http://ssrn.com/abstract=57935

5. Paul Gompers and Josh Lerner, "The Venture Capital Revolution," *The Journal of Economic Perspectives* 15, No. 2 (2001):145–168.
6. "Innovation's Golden Goose," Technology Quarterly, *The Economist*, December, 2002.
7. Susan K. Sell. *Private Power, Public Law: The Globalization of Intellectual Property Rights* (Cambridge: Cambridge University Press, 2003), 68.
8. Ibid at 69.
9. Josh Lerner, "The Patent System and Competition," 2003. www.ftc.gov/opp/intellect/lernerjosh.pdf
10. Paul Gompers and Josh Lerner, *The Venture Capital Cycle* (Boston: The MIT Press, 2002), 306
11. www.pwcmoneytree.com
12. http://autm.org/about/dsp.licensing_surveys.cfm
13. Scott F. Kieff, "Coordination, Property & Intellectual Property: An Unconventional Approach to Anticompetitive Effects & Downstream Access" (Washington University School of Law Working Paper, June, 2006 No. 06-06-01) Available at SSRN: http://ssrn.com/abstract=910656
14. Don Tapscott and Anthony Williams, *Wikinomics: How Mass collaboration Changes Everything* (West London: Portfolio, 2006).
15. Ibid at 56.
16. Ibid at 63.
17. "Innovation Networks: Looking for Ideas Outside the Company," Knowledge@Wharton, November 14, 2007. http://knowledge.wharton.upenn.edu/article.cfm?articleid=1837
18. Ibid.
19. John Kao, *Innovation Nation: How America is Losing Its Innovation Edge, Why It Matters, and What We Can Do to Get It Back* (New York: Free Press, 2007) 180.
20. James Lewis, "Inside Views: An Argument for IP and Innovation Boosting Development," *Intellectual Property Watch Monthly Reporter*, May 29, 2007. www.ip-watch.org/weblog/index.php?p=635
21. Ibid.

CHAPTER 3

Reengineering the IP Ecosystem

BY KEVIN RIVETTE

PERSPECTIVE Profit means one thing to most companies: a positive impact on the bottom line. However, a patent's contribution toward the profitability of a product or business is not so easily measured, especially if that patent is strategic and its role poorly delineated. Good patents often have less to do with the cash flow they generate and more to do with the valuable freedom to sell products and the competitive advantage they provide.

Outspoken *Rembrandts in the Attic* co-author Kevin Rivette believes that overemphasis on simplified IP tactics is potentially dangerous for companies with significant patent portfolios. Forsaking long-term business strategy for short-term profits, he says, can be dangerously shortsighted.

"The drive for quarterly EPS from IP revenues frequently overshadows the larger business benefits that can be derived from a well-shaped and -executed IP strategy . . . A strategy needs tactics to come alive. In the patent world this typically means that a strategy will anticipate potential use of litigation and licensing. However, litigation and licensing are not the only tools of the IP trade and should only be used when the potential trade-offs are understood and worthwhile. In short, not very frequently."

Former head of IP strategy at IBM and an IP management expert with Boston Consulting Group, Rivette advises senior executives and boards. He believes that few senior managements "get it" when it comes to deploying their companies' most valuable and complex assets. Rivette suggests that patents can be more effectively and efficiently used by

(continued)

some companies for strategic advantage in innovative ways, such as in facilitating "open" innovation networks, supply chain relationships, and collaborative inventing, or pooling to establish standards that save participants time and money, and can help get products to market faster.

Strategy Before Tactics

Books have appeared in recent years that offer insights from which both business and IP professionals can benefit. Much of this writing is strong on how to achieve "results," and conspicuously weak on why they are appropriate for a particular business. Not until Bruce Berman conceived the book in your hands, *From Assets to Profits*, and gathered a group of battle-scarred IP veterans to contribute to it, was there a counterbalance to an abundance of prior works that tended to place tactics ahead of strategy. The IP business has entered a period of what Europeans might call "deconstruction," a period of intensive analysis of structure and context. This period is less about what IP rights are and how they can be used, than about who needs to use them and why. The substance of much IP discussion to date has dealt with the means by which the IP industry monetizes intellectual property and the ways various types of IP owners generate the best return. Good stuff without a doubt, but too often this approach overlooks and undervalues the bigger innovation picture, the one that allows observers to see the forest for the trees.

In *Rembrandts in the Attic* (HBS Press, 2000) I discussed a number of issues relating to patent strategies and how they could be integrated into a corporation's thinking process and business objectives. However, when I hear people talk about *Rembrandts* today, it seems to me that many readers focus too narrowly on the tactics of patent licensing or litigation, the "how to," that were enumerated in the book. What I hear less about is the patent strategies that form the foundation for these activities or tactics.

A strategy needs tactics to come alive. In the patent world this typically means that a strategy will anticipate potential use of litigation and licensing. However, litigation and licensing are not the only tools of the IP trade and should only be used when the potential trade-offs are understood and worthwhile. In short, not very frequently. The drive for quarterly EPS from IP revenues frequently overshadows the larger business benefits that can be derived from a well-shaped and -executed IP strategy. In this chapter I plan to articulate some ideas I have been developing that potentially update the strategy issues laid out in *Rembrandts in the Attic.* To this end, I would like to introduce the concept of using an IP strategy to reengineer a business ecosystem, an environment for generating ROI.

Ecosystem Reengineering—What Is It?

Wikipedia defines an ecosystem as "a natural system consisting of all plants, animals and microorganisms (biotic factors) in an area functioning together with all the non-living physical factors of the environment (abiotic)."[1] The business equivalent of the biological ecosystem is a reflection of how all companies live in a world made up of customers, suppliers, distributors, and competitors that could be seen as the biotic factors in the Wikipedia definition. When I think of the products businesses sell, the features that drive the product sale, the technologies that enable these features, and the competitive technologies that potentially can disrupt sales, can all be considered as the abiotic factors making up our business or industry ecosystem. In addition, there is a kind of connective tissue that ties these two factors together and animates the system. This connective tissue is made up of the business models that each member of the system uses to gain advantage for themselves. An IP strategy that aligns the needs of the ecosystem members and helps orient the business models in the system to a company's sustainable competitive advantage is a powerful force. This strategy should be identified and evaluated before a management team reverts to a default revenue generation mode. This realignment of the ecosystem is the basic concept of ecosystem reengineering. The reengineering can be seen as having three basic elements or concepts, they are: Profit Pool Positioning, Advantaged Networks, and Collaborative Innovation.

Profit Pool Positioning: "Show Me the Money"

This strategy is for determining where the profits are made in an industry or value chain. A company needs to be at the center of profit generation and competitors should be as far from that position as possible. With better profits you can increase investment in programs like R&D, sales, P.R., etc., and enjoy more satisfied shareholders. Your competitors will just have to do with less. It doesn't get any better than that, does it? In most cases management looks to restructure whole businesses to achieve this simple result. These restructurings and subsequent business dislocations are usually costly and typically carry high levels of risk. Can IP strategy offer another tool to achieving this result at lower cost and risk?

The profit pool concept, the approach of looking for who is making the most profit and where in the value chain these profits are being generated, was put forth by Orit Gadiesh and James L. Gilbert, both consultants at Bain & Co., in their *Harvard Business Review* article, "Profit Pools: A Fresh Look at Strategy" (May 1, 1998, article reprint # 98305).[2] According to the Value Based Management.net website (http://www.valuebased management.net/methods_profit_pools.html): "Although the concept is simple, the structure of a profit pool is usually quite complex, the pool will be deeper in some segments of the value chain than in others, and depths will vary within an individual segment as well. Segment profitability may, for example, vary widely by customer group, product category, geographic market, and distribution channel. Moreover, the pattern of profit concentration in an industry will often be very different from the pattern of revenue concentration." Where and who is making the money in your industry is one of the best places to start when developing an IP strategy. "Show me the money" gets management's attention every time.

If you know where your industry and competitors make their money then the trick is to shift or reposition where the profits are made to your company's advantage. This can be achieved with the right patents and other IP in the right place and time. (Given the recent Supreme Court cases involving patent, most notably Medimmune, Inc. v. Genentech, Inc., and eBay, Inc. v. MercEchange L.L.C., it makes the most sense to think about developing designer IP portfolios to achieve desired results, which may include patent acquisitions in addition to organic IP generation.) In a case with which I am familiar a service company controlled a set of industry-based models or tools that determined how the company's client's technology needs should be addressed for a desired outcome. The company's business was not in developing these sophisticated models, but in providing the technologies to satisfy the client's needs based on results generated by the tools. The company had developed these tools only to forecast and justify what technologies the client needed to purchase. However, this was a fairly new industry and the problems and technological solutions were not well defined, so the tools provided a real benefit to the client in defining the issues it faced and also in determining what technologies it needed. Having developed the right diagnostic tools for its products and industry appears to have been enough for success.

When the industry was analyzed, it turned out that a number of competitors had similar, but inferior, tools and their profits were actually being made at the definition or diagnostic stage of the process instead of at the technology acquisition and integration stage, as would benefit our company. The other tool providers were making most of their profits from the sale and use of their proprietary diagnostic tools.

Should the company shift its business to mirror its competitors' while giving up its core competency in developing and supporting the technological solutions? Should the company invest more in the tools and services end of the business, giving up potential R&D funding for better technologies? Luckily the company had the foresight to properly protect its IP in these new tools from the beginning. This permitted the company to develop an IP strategy for draining the profits around the diagnostic stage of the value chain and relocating them to the technology acquisition and integration portion of the industry.

Exhibit 3.1 was developed as a simple example of how to visualize a profit pool by the makers of the WEPSS tool which can be found at www.mepss.nl.

This repositioning strategy is not one of "let's sue the bastards," but an approach of let's "help the industry." The strategy was fairly simple, with only a couple of elements. The first action was to standardize the problem definition so that our technologies were in demand. Many times the problem definition is the key to the sale and, in fact, this is why our company and its competitors had developed the tools in the first place. To help encourage this standardization our company could offer a no-cost patent license on the tools. Any competitors or clients could then use the tools without liability. However, to ensure that the industry knows where these tools came from and to be sure that our company is recognized as an industry leader that must be considered when seeking potential solutions, the non–revenue generating license would require a simple trademark and service mark designating the developer of the tool would be required.

EXHIBIT 3.1 **VISUALIZING A PROFIT POOL**

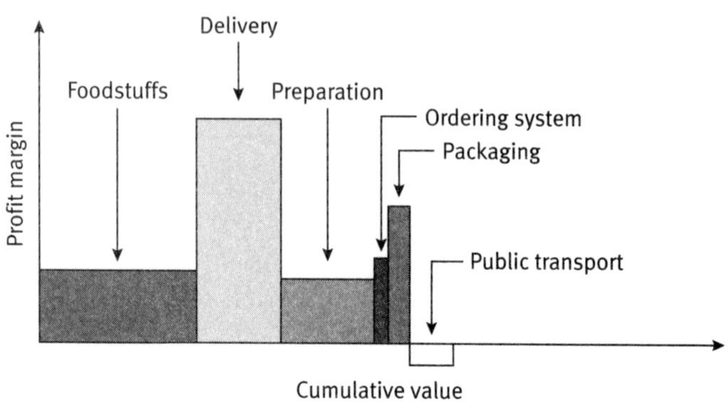

Imaginary profit pool for a meal delivery. Several actors in the pool add value. Each activity has a different value creation and operational margin. *The ordering system* brings just a small turnover, but a high margin. Thus, this may be a profitable service to add.

With the price of the tools pegged at zero, the profits being made selling these tools dissipates—the new focus is now on the solution, right were our company wants it to be with little cost and risk. The company needs to innovate in the tools and the technologies, but they were doing that anyway. Now they have the industry seeing their logos on problem definition proposals all across the industry while effectively draining their competitors' profit pools and shifting the pool for their own swimming pleasure. I have oversimplified this example for brevity, but, it does highlight that an IP strategy that involves non-recurring revenue streams can, and many times is, what is strategically called for. It can drive sales and profits in ways that pure revenue licensing cannot.

Advantaged Networks: "Who Do I Want to Play With?"

How can a company follow up shifting profit pools so that they play to its advantage? By defining who it wants to play with. Which companies are the ones which it would like to work with on a daily and industry-wide basis? Many companies take it for granted that their partners in the value chain are predetermined. However, companies like Toyota, IBM,

Microsoft, and others clearly do not play by these rules. Using IP strategies, some revenue-producing and others not, they can and have defined and redefined with whom they want to work in different parts of their industries.

I will suggest that in such instances these types of companies have created Advantaged Networks of IP (ANIP). These networks typically reduce the transactions costs inside the network while increasing the cost of accessing the same IP for non-network members. A simple network map in the wireless telecomm space is shown below. The map in Exhibit 3.2 is generated by a proprietary BCG IP networking tool known as N-Compass that I helped develop with Ralph Eckardt and Mark Blaxill, among others, while we were all at BCG and running the IP strategy practice. This tool provides a visual means to understanding how competitors, inventors, and the patents relate to each other over time, technologies, industries, markets, etc. This type of information is critical in defining how to influence the players' relationship to your advantage.

The best examples of this type of IP strategy can be seen in the open source software (OSS) community. The IP strategy around OSS provides very high IP costs outside the community, such as the requirement to donate innovation back into open source for the right to use the copyrighted work, while the transaction costs inside open source are zero. In addition, many of the large companies that fund and rely on OSS platforms have even gone beyond the copyright licenses and have set up patent-free zones for likeminded members, as well as patent protection groups such as the Open Innovation Network (OIN), to support members sued over alleged OSS patents. The companies working in the OSS community have an alignment of purpose to create open platforms to enhance interoperability while seeking competition in other areas of the technology market.

Similarly, Toyota for many decades had an IP strategy that would have rivaled the OSS community. Much of the work of the strategy was, and in many cases still is, done through its joint patent holdings with its suppliers and distributors. Again, the strategy translated into lower transaction costs for Toyota partners using this patented technology and higher costs for the non-partners. Just ask Ford and Nissan, who are currently paying Toyota for access to Toyota's patented hybrid technology even while they develop their own unique hybrid solutions. Toyota didn't develop all of

EXHIBIT 3.2 **N-COMPASS NETWORK MAP**

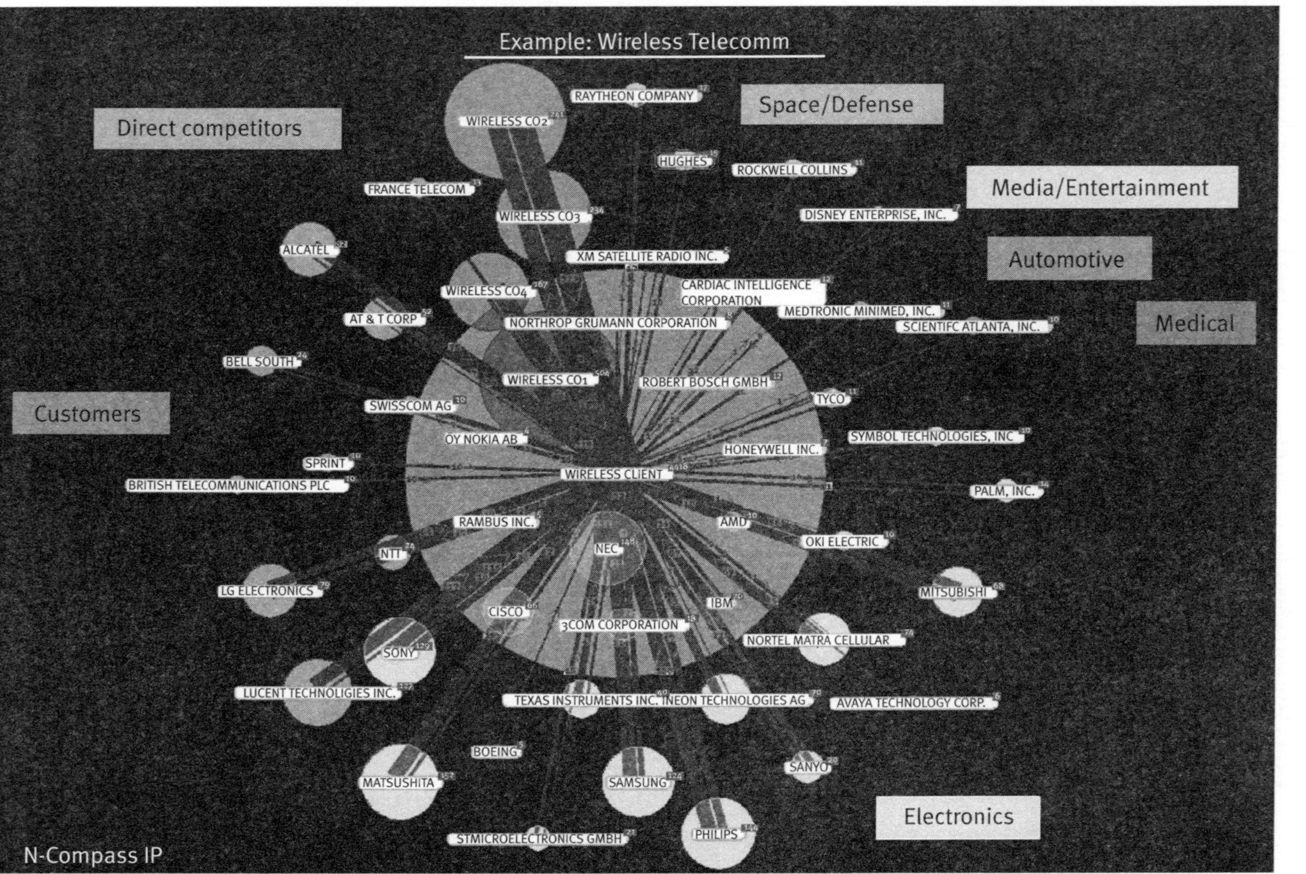

N-Compass is a visual tool that is designed to show how competitors, inventors, and patents relate to each other over time and technologies

this technology itself, but its network did. Toyota reinforced its business relationships with its partners using an Advanced Network patent strategy.

Another example of the strategic use of IP to effect the network of business partners can be seen in the efforts of many companies to join together to offer a new Open Document Format (ODF) as an alternative to Microsoft's OOXML format.[3] This ODF strategy aimed at the Microsoft Office near-monopoly can be seen, in part, to be working due to IBM's patent strategy of non-assertion pledges around specific documents, such as medical records. The ODF strategy, since 2005 when the state of Massachusetts adopted it, has put into question Microsoft's prior dominance in office tools and allowed companies like Novel, IBM, and Sun to redefine a market once thought to be locked up by Microsoft. Now there is Open Office and Lotus Symphony available, while Google seems to be eyeing this new space also. With regard to whom a company wishes to work with, the right IP strategy may be a key component (see Exhibit 3.3).

EXHIBIT 3.3 **ALIGNING IP STRATEGY AND TACTICS**

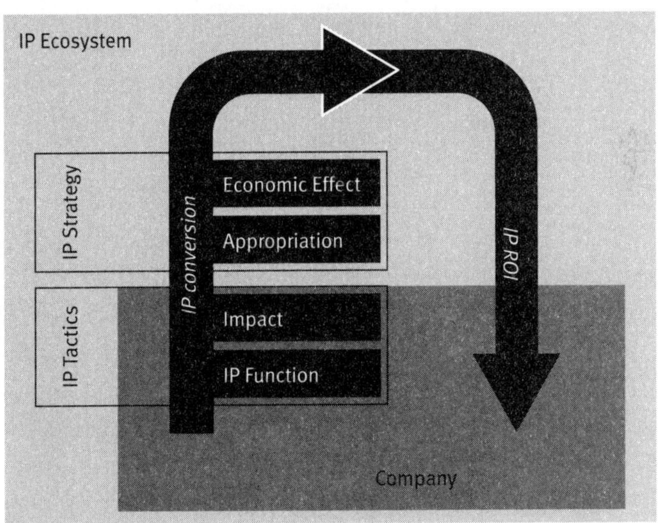

Mechanisms for appropriating return on IP rights must be strategically aligned with a patent holder's business model. IP strategies are optimized when they are consistently conveyed and supported by relevant tactics.

Source: PATEV

Collaborative Innovation: "How to Avoid Looking Over Your R&D Shoulder"

Next to profits and selecting your partners "with whom do you want to work?," the success of a company's R&D program ranks as one of the most important issues facing the organization. Historically, R&D programs can be some of the most risk-sensitive investments any company can make. Huge amounts of money as a percent of revenue are at risk, and in addition, once the project is underway the trajectory of the program and technology choices are almost impossible to change. Can an IP strategy help protect this investment and open space for premium pricing of a company's products? For Procter & Gamble, the answer is "Yes."

Here are the facts that P&G was facing: About a decade ago they would develop new futures for their products and bring them to market only to have them emulated by their competitors. Typically, the timeline went something like this: P&G would do years of development on a feature technology and launch the new product/feature into the market. By the end of the first year the competitors would normally decide if the new feature was a sales driver. If it was, the competitor would initiate its own development program to incorporate the feature into their product. This emulation of course would reduce the premium pricing that P&G was experiencing by commoditizing the feature. The return on the R&D was reduced and P&G's management was not happy.

With an unhappy management, patent lawsuits inevitably followed. The industry became involved in a nuclear spiral of patent suits, increasingly expensive R&D programs, and commoditized prices. P&G's CEO called in Jeff Weedman. Jeff, who is responsible for External Business Development (EBD) at Procter & Gamble, put together a strong solution with a new patent licensing program. Jeff's program was simple. P&G would license its technology at a reasonable cost three years after it began selling the product or five years after a patent was issued on the technology—and Jeff let all of the competitors know this.

This simple strategy all but put an end to the industry-wide frenzy of patent lawsuits. It shifted competitors' R&D programs away from P&G

programs and extended P&G's premium pricing for its products. It comes down to understanding the business issues. The first component of the plan is the 3/5 year licensing terms. These were determined based on industry timelines. It will vary by industry and product, but in this case the competitors typically waited one year to start their own R&D programs and another year to bring the feature to market. Thus, the new feature would only provide a two-year premium pricing advantage; after that, commoditization pricing would start. The three-year period before P&G would grant a license was designed to extend this premium pricing time by at least a year. Next, the low cost of the license was determined to force a buy/build decision by the competitors. The question in competitors' mind is, should they accept the low-priced license and have a comparable feature one year later than they would normally, or should they pay for the re-creation of the feature and enter the market sooner knowing that they will probably face a patent suit immediately, with all that additional cost and uncertainty.

Added to this is the component that if competitors try to emulate the features and spend their R&D on that technology, other non-P&G competitors are likely to participate. These non-P&G competitors could leap-frog the direct competitors by investing in another technology while taking the low-cost, certain, P&G license. An added benefit of this strategy is that the competitors will typically become reliant on the technology, and will come to expect that the next versions of that technology will effectively provide a protection for the P&G R&D program. Again, the strategy is not the high reoccurring revenue type, but may have much longer-term advantages for protecting product pricing as well as R&D expenses.

These are just a couple of the ecosystem reengineering IP strategies that should be clearly understood and evaluated in business contexts before any revenue-based licensing program is established. The examples have been simplified to make a point. Clearly, there is a huge amount of work and business modeling that goes into developing any successful strategy based on the specific facts and industry dynamics. New and innovative IP strategies are reshaping return on R&D and its cousin, IP rights. They can and will drive business success in our companies today and in the future.

ABOUT THE AUTHOR

Kevin Rivette is Managing Director of 3LP Advisors, an innnovative IP advisory. He most recently served as Vice President for IP Strategy for IBM. Mr. Rivette was appointed in 2006 by the U.S. Secretary of Commerce to act as the Chairman of the Patent Public Advisory Committee, a position he still holds. For three years he was Executive Advisor for Intellectual Property Strategy at the Boston Consulting Group (BCG), one of the leading management consulting firms. Rivette founded in 1993, and was CEO of, Aurigin Systems (SmartPatents), the first company to develop and commercially market visualization technologies for analyzing the competitive patent landscape. Aurigin Systems was subsequently sold to Thomson Scientific.

Mr. Rivette has been awarded over forty patents worldwide and is the author of the *Rembrandts in the Attic (*Harvard Business School Press), which the *New York Times* called the "textbook" on Intellectual Property strategies. He was voted into the Intellectual Property Hall of Fame in 2007. Mr. Rivette, a recovering patent attorney, lives with his family in Palo Alto California.

NOTES

1. http://en.wikipedia.org/wiki/Ecosystem
2. http://harvardbusinessonline.hbsp.harvard.edu/b01/en/common/item_detail.jhtml;jsessionid=1C2DKMR1FWQSOAKRGWDSELQBKE0YIISW?id=98305&referral=7855
3. www.openxmlcommunity.org

CHAPTER 4

IP Investing: Catalyst for Return or Recipe for Pain?

BY BRUCE BERMAN

To achieve satisfactory investment results is easier than most people realize; to achieve superior results is harder than it looks.

—BENJAMIN GRAHAM

PERSPECTIVE Intellectual Property investors are more diverse and prevalent than some of their detractors would lead us to believe. The transactions they engage in may typically be off of the radar but their impact on company performance frequently is not.

Patent investing is still in the process of being defined because returns on IP rights, while substantial, are extremely difficult to measure. Several types of IP investor have emerged, some more apparent than others. Not coincidentally, they all seek success in terms of earned profit, indirect value creation, or return on IP (ROIP). How an IP investor achieves results depends on its particular industry, business model, timeframe, tolerance for risk, and ability to access the capital markets. Non-practicing (i.e., non–product selling) patent owning entities (NPEs) are by definition IP investors, but they are not all guileless predators as some would have us believe. Nor are they necessarily in direct conflict with operating companies and their shareholders.

(continued)

IP investors include R&D-oriented businesses such as biotech companies and semiconductors designers, universities, private equity and venture capital firms, governments, and independent "garage" inventors, among others. The bulk of the mix, are large, strategic IP holders, who in a flatter, more global economy must now rely increasingly on external sources for invention flow. The most obvious or direct investors are forcing some patent owners to revisit their IP strategy to determine how and when less contentious options can better serve their needs and which returns are most meaningful to their business. Businesses are learning that it takes innovative management to manage innovation assets.

"Licensing can work well for some companies at certain times in their IP and business life cycles," I note in the following chapter, "but it is becoming apparent that it is not an appropriate permanent business model for most. Licensing is only one measure of IP management skill and business performance. . . . For the majority of strategic patent owners the economics of patent enforcement do not add up. Strangely, this rent in the fabric of innovation has encouraged speculators to secure and capitalize rights as they might other business assets. The challenge for strategic owners is to identify innovative ways to monetize huge investments in R&D without necessarily generating licensing cash flows or engaging in litigation."

Has today's more contentious, bottom-line approach for managing IP rights improved innovation, patent quality, or increased shareholder value? Probably. But you won't hear most strategic IP owners admitting that. In *IP Investing: Catalyst for Return or Recipe for Pain?* chapter I attempt to put into perspective who are the different types of IP investors are how they operate. I also consider the ironic dependency they have on each another. It *IS* an innovation jungle out there. A range of IP holders with an appetite for return, however, are helping to maintain a precarious and necessary balance.

Agreeing to Disagree

Irony is at the very core of innovation. Patents that permit companies to sell more products and generate higher profits by temporarily excluding others can provide businesses a competitive advantage. It sounds simple, except that patent value is poorly reflected on financial balance sheets, and there is anything but agreement on what IP rights cover, which patents are assets, and how best to manage and measure them.

Patents are not inventions. It's easy to confuse them because they coexist in a kind of symbiosis. Patents provide holders with the negative right to exclude others from practicing an invention for a period of time. This is not just semantics. Holders have to do their own enforcement, and policing patents is both expensive and risky. Their rights permit them to hire an army of expensive lawyers and valuation experts to enforce what may be unenforceable. As a result, the right to practice an invention, today, is worth more to some parties than others. For most companies, patent rights are enablers, a means to achieving a business goal. For other parties, they are the end itself.

U.S. companies spent $219 billon on research and development in 2007. Total U.S. R&D spending (including universities) is estimated at $338 billion.[1] There is no argument that generating a return on a business's investment in R&D is essential. However, identifying an invention, or successfully commercializing and selling it, does not mean a company has secured the right to practice. Inventions frequently are not covered by any of a company's thousands or even tens of thousands of patents. Perhaps in the course of commercialization an invention has morphed into something slightly different from the original idea and the patent or patents necessary to practice it have already been secured. Perhaps, too, the claims, extensive and specific as they may appear, do not actually pertain to the product sold. Yet another possibility is that prior art (the body of published work predating the invention) has rendered the invention obvious and not novel, and therefore not patentable. Patents issued by the USPTO that are challenged are found invalid approximately 40% of the time.[2] Identifying and securing a patent that may eventually form the basis of an intellectual asset is an arduous and unpredictable enterprise.

Investors of all types are becoming better acquainted with the difficulty associated with monetizing IP. Innovation in the U.S. is at a crossroads and so, too, are the rights associated with it. The debate continues as to what are the most efficient methods for a particular owner to extract value from R&D and the patents and know-how (trade secrets) associated with them. There also is the question of what is best for innovation? After a number of court decisions in 2006 and 2007 that diminished the strength of patent holders, and in light of the payout in recent years of a number of large damages awards, the pendulum has swung in favor of product sellers and away from patent holders. The immediate impact is that patents have less value because holders now may not have the leverage to enforce them. Lower patent value means that significant patent infringement wins are more difficult to secure and settlements more likely.[3]

The courts are weakening patents rights for numerous reasons. They include a general perceived lack of patent quality and the relative ease with which patents can be secured. The IRS and USPTO have a lot in common. Like the IRS the USPTO is a severely understaffed government agency, prone to budgetary and bureaucratic limitations. Decisions issued by inexperienced examiners under time constraints cannot always be relied upon. It is not that difficult for a filer to get a patent to issue, just as it is not difficult for an accountant to engineer a favorable tax return on a 1040. Spot checks catch only some abusers. In the case of the IRS, filers who are subjected the scrutiny of an audit, may have to pay penalties and interest, or even serve jail time. Similarly, not all patent infringers (or asserters) get a free ride, but many gamble and do. In most arts the reliability of an issued patent (validity) can be called into question, especially when there is a dispute, and enforcing a patent can be a painful road to nowhere.

The courts' and the United States Congress's suspicion of "too strong" patents have cast a spotlight on the complex role of the IP investor. A message has been sent: Patents deployed for direct financial return, and the entities that own them, are likely to be subjected to a higher level of scrutiny. Whether this is net-positive for investors, innovation, and the general public good is still unclear. The immediate results are better positioning for some defendants, mostly larger ones, and several lingering questions:

- What is IP investing?
- Who engages in it?
- Is it appropriate to use IP rights as business assets?
- How and when is it most effective to do so?

This chapter will address these and other questions affecting IP managers, shareholders, and senior corporate executives. As you will see, when it comes to discerning the quality of IP returns and balancing them with broad business objectives, one size seldom fits all.

IP Comes In Many Shapes and Sizes, So Does IP Value

The most blatant embodiment of IP investing is the "patent troll." Trolls have been labeled outlaws because they frequently acquire patents of dubious quality for the sole purpose of litigating them. Some believe that acquiring and enforcing good patents is another matter entirely and should not be confused with illegitimate assertions. Few think patent speculation is what the Founding Fathers intended. They established the patent system early in the United States Constitution. This article is actually enumerated before the right to raise an army, wage war, or coin currency.[4]

So-called trolls acquire rights from bankrupt companies, brokers, and inventors who can not afford to assert them or are unwilling to do so. The trolls produce no manufactured products and have no incentive to cross-license with other companies, making them invulnerable to countersuits. As Non-Practicing Entities, or NPEs, patent trolls often are configured much like real estate businesses—as holding companies, with no other assets than rights. To some, this is a blatant abuse of the patent system and a threat to operating businesses; to others, it is a viable if not arduous way to generate return. I prefer not to use this space to debate the merits of patent speculators and who qualifies as the more legitimate IP owner. Suffice it to say that trolls and other types of IP investors appear to have had a lingering impact on innovation. For many, including the courts and some operating companies, trolls represent the embodiment of an unsavory and wasteful byproduct of modern commerce. To others, they are among several types of IP investors that are vital to the innovation ecosystem and the nasty, but apparently necessary, natural selection process that accompanies it.

Intellectual property rights are finally being recognized as business assets. For S&P 500 companies, the estimated market value of intangibles is 70 to 80%. IP rights play a highly significant role in the success of almost every business, including those less obviously dependent on innovation and technology, such as consumer product giant P&G, which holds tens of thousands of patents worldwide. Given companies' commitment to R&D and to capturing the value associated with it, IP plays a key role in achieving performance objectives. R&D spending for companies in 2007 included $8.03 billion for Microsoft, $10.61 billion for Pfizer, and $7.17 billion for Daimler-Chrysler AG.

Explosive technology and science growth in the 1980s, coupled with record damages awards for patent infringement and the high cost to defend against them, have fueled interest in IP rights. But investing in IP conjures a shadowy image of outsiders speculating on grants of exclusivity some feel they have no right to. It challenges us to look at what is expedient for shareholders and society, and at what constitutes an ethical business practice. Today, there are many different kinds of IP investors, representing a wide range of expectations. They all require some form of ROI, but they differ radically on how they achieve it and the footprint they leave behind. IP investors, legitimate or otherwise, and their strategies for success are being taken more seriously today than at any time in history.

Speculating on IP rights and asserting them against risk-adverse operating companies, nonpracticing owners—whatever some may think of the practice—have served as catalysts for change. Such entities question what are the most efficient ways for businesses to secure rights and turn them into productive assets (see Exhibit 4.7 towards the end of this chapter) IP investors come in many shapes and sizes and even those that create pain can serve a purpose. The right IP rights, especially the right patents, have increasingly been seen as valuable resources, even if they cannot be readily captured and valued like real estate and other tangibles. Not everyone agrees that using patents for direct return and measuring their performance in terms of revenue generated facilitates innovation or longer-term business objectives. The framers of the U.S. Constitution had unusually high respect for the rights of innovators, such as inventors and authors. While they could not foresee the complex financial engineering that would take place starting in the late 20th century, they did anticipate the impact that rights could have on a broad range of innovative businesses and how that could affect America's competitiveness.

Patent speculators aside, the jury is still out on whether the returns on direct IP investing justify the investment (see Exhibit 4.1). On the other hand, strategic IP investors are still without a clear way to measure return on IP (ROIP). R&D, legal costs, and filing fees do not come cheap. Which IP owners are better off licensing their best patents to others, even competitors, while they still can, rather than using them for freedom to sell products? These are difficult calls, and, unfortunately, decisions that senior

EXHIBIT 4.1 PROMINENT DIRECT IP INVESTORS

Investor	Founded	Capital (mill.USD)
Intellectual Ventures	2000	1000+
Acacia Technologies	2001	400
Rembrandt Group	2003	150
Ocean Tomo Capital Fund	2005	200
Altitude Capital Partners	2005	250
Deutsche Bank Patent Fund	2006	32
Paradox Capital	2006	280
Coller Capital	2006	200
IP-Com (Fortress)	2006	???

Source: Corporate Deal Maker and Brody Berman Associates

managements are loath to make. Company executives tend to play a passive role in IP decision making, sometimes to the detriment of shareholders. IP is abstract, context-dependent, and ever-changing. CEOs are trained in business schools to manage resources, such as products, people, and tangibles (e.g., real estate), which can be identified on balance sheets and scrutinized by shareholders. They are at a loss when it comes to dealing with intangibles like IP rights, of which a rare few are considered assets. With the advent of senior IP executives like Marshall Phelps at Microsoft and Joe Beyers at HP, effectively "CIPOs" or Chief IP Officers, the picture is slowly improving. Their direct and regular contact with senior management is helping to move patents out of the file draw and onto the balance sheet.

Fewer Than 5% of Patents Are Assets

C-level execs and Wall Street consistently fail to realize that only a small handful of patent rights are financial assets. For a patent to be an asset, strategic or otherwise, a galaxy of stars and planets must align. In a high-tech company with some 10,000 patents, fewer than 5%, by most estimates, and perhaps as few as 2%, have discernable value. Perhaps 45% of the rights are necessary for bargaining leverage (cross-licensing or counter-assertion, should it be necessary) and future uses, and the remaining 50%, or more, have no value and are typically allowed to lapse. Two out of every three patents lapse because of failure to pay fees. It is not that the owners lack the funds to pay the renewals, or forget to. At a point it makes little economic sense to do so. Pharmaceutical company patent portfolios are much smaller than those in the high-tech industries, such as semiconductors, telecom, computer hardware, and software. Typically, a formulation will be covered by a single patent or a few patents, eliminating the need for a lot of filing or cross-licenses. Also, patent validity is much less of an issue for most bio-pharma patents. Finally, it is relatively easy for small companies or individuals to invent, file, secure, and even buy high-tech patents. It is a different matter in the pharma industry if you do not have access to a modern laboratory and significant capital.

In real estate it is all about location; with IP rights, context is king (see Exhibit 4.2). A patent is 100% of something. Rarely is this as grandiose as it sounds. Mostly, the "something" that a patent provides the exclusive right to is worth nothing. It's like owning a 100-square-mile tract in Siberia. Yes, you may hold the title to a large expanse of land, but unless a lot of oil is found there, and it can be accessed, it has no financial value. Hence, "location, location, location." Fifty square feet in Manhattan, London, or Tokyo is another matter. A patent is not unlike a mining claim. It is all about knowing where and when to place the stakes. Stake

EXHIBIT 4.2 **"CONTEXT, CONTEXT, CONTEXT"**

Weak Patent A Reads on
Strong Patent B Reads on

Intel Pentium® D Processor
2005 Sales = $2 billion

Strong Patent C Reads on

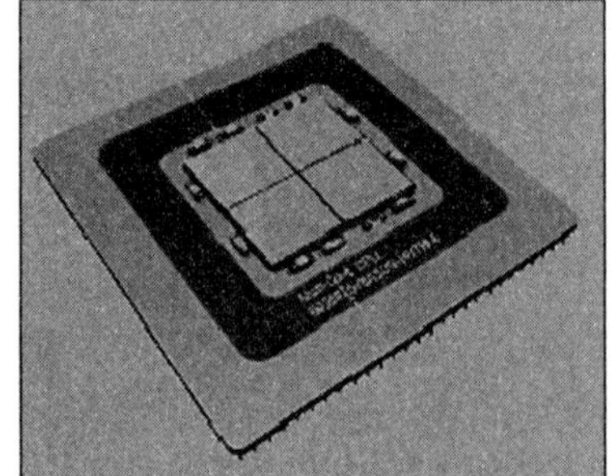

Brand "Y" Processor
2005 Sales = $100K

Location significantly influences value in real estate; with intangible assets like patents it is all about context.

it too broadly and it will be difficult to defend; too narrowly and it may not cover anything worthwhile; too early and it may go unnoticed. A few miles (and sometimes a few meters) can make all of the difference in the world.

For a patent to have licensing value it not only needs to be well configured and prosecuted, one or more of its claims typically needs to actually "read" on an invention that generates significant revenue. Simply put, it needs to be valid and infringed. A beautifully rendered patent that reads on a product with little or no sales is not very meaningful; nor is a poorly researched and configured patent that reads on a successful product. What has meaning is a patent (better still, a family of patents) whose claims read directly on an invention whose products have been successfully commercialized selling well in the market place. However, even for patent holders who are able to establish a strong fact pattern, there is substantial cost, time, and risk required to prove infringement. At a median cost of $4.5 million (for cases with $25 million or more at stake), and as high as $62 million for an unusual and protracted case, such as the $1.4 billion trial won in 2005 by Kirkland & Ellis for Karlin Medical Technologies, patent suits require a substantial investment of the infringed patent owners' time and money. They are a viable investment for some, the operative word being "some." To prevail regularly in patent litigation you need to be selective, deep-pocketed, lucky, and patient—no matter how strong the patent or how obvious the infringement.

Building a portfolio of thousands of patents, as many high-tech companies do, is no assurance that any of them will read on the products they sell. In fact, frequently they do not (see Exhibit 4.3). This leaves operating companies vulnerable to patent suits and damages awards. Some nonpracticing entities and others attempt to exploit these weaknesses. The question is whether an NPE's patents are (1) valid and (2) actually are infringed. The complexity is compounded by USPTO pendency: it can take as long as five years for some patents to issue and, when they do, they are often of dubious reliability. Patent examination cost, manpower, and other issues are factors. The value of a patent may diminish significantly or even disappear by the time the invention it has been filed to protect goes to market. As inventions evolve into products the patents filed originally to cover them may become less relevant or even irrelevant. The claims contained in a patent filed on the original invention may differ from those necessary to protect the product actually sold. This can leave even conscientious companies vulnerable and frustrated. Wise IP holders need to keep their perspective regarding not only what coverages they have secured through patent filing and in-licenses, but which ones they may need and do not have. Burying your head in the sand will only take a good business so far.

The pharmaceutical industry is somewhat ahead of high-tech companies in terms of using capital and other resources. Pharma companies learned decades ago that spending, say, \$3 billion in annual R&D expenditures to ensure a pipeline of blockbuster drugs is a lot but nowhere near enough. Even \$30 billion would not do it. Hence, drug companies tend to use their research dollars efficiently, identifying areas of interest, inventions they may need to in-license, and which patents or companies it makes sense to buy. They know they cannot survive without partners. High-tech companies today have been less resourceful in this area.

Whether or not the approach of early independent patent enforcers like Jerome Lemelson (who filed seemingly endless continuations), Eugene Lang (an early "extortionist") and Robert Kearns (inventor of the

EXHIBIT 4.3 **ANATOMY OF A (HIGH-TECH) PATENT PORTFOLIO**

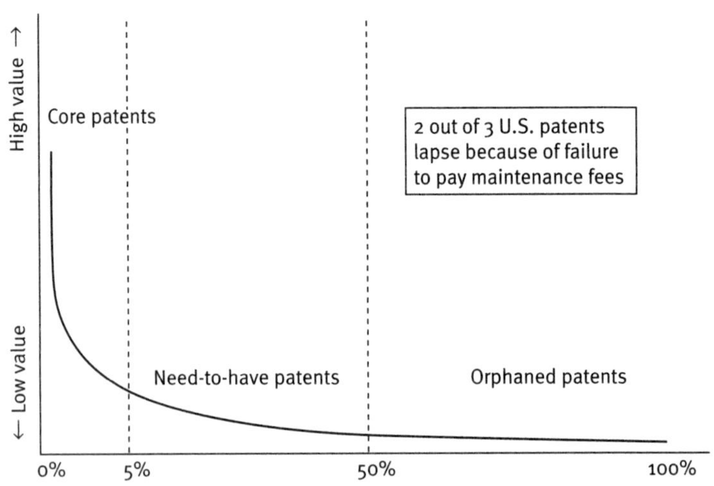

Fewer than 5% and as few as 2% of a high-tech company's patents have discernable value to a company; 50% or more are unnecessary.

intermittent windshield wiper) was fair or pleasant, it was expedient and, for the most part, lawful. Unlike an IP operating company that sells products or services, IP holding companies have no fear of counter-assertion. Patent suits certainly existed in the time of Bell, the Wright Brothers, and Edison. Edison used patents not only to promote himself but to attract investors. He inadvertently created what was in fact the first modern IP company—an organization whose business and assets revolved around the creation and commercialization of inventions through a variety of strategies.[5]

Not until the mid-1980s was there desire on the part of a large portfolio-wielding operating company to act in an assertive manner toward other large businesses or customers. The high profitability of patent licensing royalties and potential return on damages awards was sufficient incentive to turn some strategic IP investors into direct ones. Cash-starved Texas Instruments blazed the trail with its dynamic random access memory (DRAM) patents. Those who took a modified page from TI included IBM, whose IP portfolio under Marshall Phelps, now head of IP for Microsoft, grew to significantly exceed $1billion annually. Most of this revenue, 95% by Phelps' estimate, was profit.[6] IBM's achievement was all the more remarkable because it engaged in surprisingly few patent suits to generate a very substantial income stream. Its presence in the IP world was so large and intimidating it was able to secure partners and valuable cross licenses rather than notch victims.

"TI has since made billions of dollars from this policy," said Mike Hatcher, editor of *Compound Semiconductor,* a UK-based magazine, "which has reportedly netted the firm $1 billion over 10 years with Hyundai alone. Similarly, IBM initiated its own licensing program in the early 1990s and increased its annual royalty revenue from just $50 million in 1988 to around $2 billion by 2002."[7]

Over the past couple of years the courts have been less sympathetic to income-hungry patent owners. As a result, significant damages awards have become rarer, costlier, and more unpredictable. The Supreme Court and U.S. district courts via *eBay Inc. v. MercExchange, L.L.C.* and other cases have made it harder to secure revenue-threatening injunctions, claim willful infringement (triple damages), and prove that a combination of inventions is not obvious. While infringement today is more difficult to prove, it has not stopped many patent holders from trying to do so.

Diverse Patent Holder Motives and Expectations

IP investors come in many shapes and sizes; so, too, do IP stakeholders. Companies that conduct research and development (R&D) are by nature IP investors. Research on behalf of U.S. companies attempts to identify new inventions and processes that, when commercialized, will result in products that can be sold in significant volume for a good profit. To maintain their freedom to operate in this commercial manner, most companies file patents well before an invention has been commercialized. While these patents are in most cases used strategically to discourage threats from potential infringers, they often fail to achieve this objective. A strategic patent portfolio is a semblance of what IP attorneys and managers believe their company needs or will need to discourage infringers at a given time. The needs of most innovative companies, however, are constantly changing and so is the relative value of the inventions they "productize" and the patent rights they require. Until relatively recently, senior managements at high-tech companies expected their IP execs to generate internally a sufficient number and type of patents from internal R&D and patent office filings to provide the necessary freedom to sell their products. In practice, this is seldom the case. Most high-tech portfolios are in constant need of pruning, cultivating, and transplanting. Businesses are becoming more resourceful about portfolio management. Shoring up weaknesses by cross-licensing with other high-tech companies is not a new strategy, but buying patents a business might need generally is; so is buying a company that owns the right patents or has secured the right licenses.

Not all IP investors have the same motives or objectives, nor do they have the same strategy and expectations for return. Direct investors may wish to take advantage of a slow-moving business's strategic IP misjudgment and launch a suit. All IP investors expect a return on their investment. Relatively few expect it to come in damages awards, royalty streams, or settlements. But just because someone is an innovator, not a manufacturer, does not mean their invention rights should be ignored or not enforced. Until the mid-1990s there was a scarcity of capital available to patent owners who sought to enforce their rights. Many top tier law firms were reluctant to represent them. Today, there are specialists vying to support them. There are primarily three types of IP investors:

EXHIBIT 4.4 **WAYS STRATEGIC PATENTS GENERATE ROI**

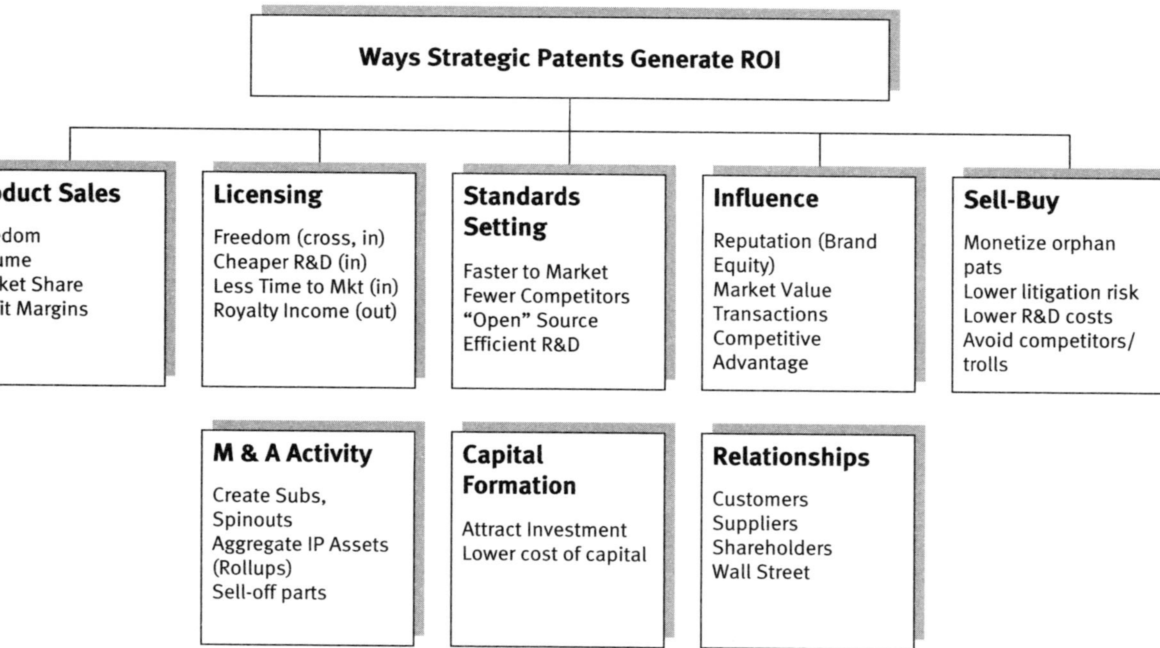

Source: Brody Berman Associates, © 2008

- **Strategic IP Investors:** Large companies that use patents primarily as a defensive "shield" to permit them to sell products without interference and generate a return on their sizable investment in R&D. When necessary, strategic investors will use patents as "swords" to dissuade some infringers from messing with them. Out-licensing and royalties comprise a relatively small part of strategic investors' apparent income (see Exhibit 4.4).
- **Direct IP Investors:** These investors acquire and then deploy patents to generate licensing royalties and infringement damages awards or settlements. This group includes private equity funds, patent trolls, and other speculators who like to buy low and either generate a return through licensing and litigation, or "flip" the patents to, or partner with, those who can do so. Foundations, pension funds, and hedge funds are starting to make direct IP investments. Some IP investors, like Rembrandt Group and Acacia, invest specifically in patent litigation (see Exhibit 4.1).
- **Passive (Indirect) IP Investors:** This fast-increasing segment is a subset of direct investing. Many in this group distance themselves from the frontlines of direct litigation. They include private equity investors who do not buy individual patents, but make equity investments in IP-centric companies. They also include research and development companies who feel they are more competitive and can return better value to their shareholders or stakeholders by employing a licensing-centric business model.

  Passive IP investors are unable to, or choose not to, manufacture, especially in capital-intensive industries like semiconductors. Universities, research institutions, hospitals, some biotech companies, and others who license also are part of this group. Lawyers who will take patent litigation on a contingency basis should also be considered investors, as would those brokers who provide due diligence for a possible future commission on a sale or other IP-based transaction or liquidity event. Both direct and passive IP investors are what can be considered NPEs or Non-Practicing Entities, because they do not sell products.

It still is unclear if direct IP investing is a business. Some IP rights speculators have raised significant capital, especially Intellectual Ventures (IV), which as I write is raising its second billion dollars of capital. IV's investors reportedly include Sony, Google, Microsoft, and Nokia, as well as pension funds, private equity investors, and public foundations. Some direct IP investors such as IV, have put their money to work purchasing a broad range of patents. Others have taken a position in patent litigation (Rembrandt Group), invested in young IP-centric companies (Altitude Capital Partners), and collateralized IP-based loans (Paradox Capital). Still, the viability of these business models has yet to be determined. What all of these investors have in common, in addition to seeking a return, is a need to understand the changing marketplace, courts, and specific risk scenarios, all of which are context specific.

Strategic owners lack the metrics to quantify the complex role their patents play in the success of specific products. They are finally realizing that it is not enough for a business to achieve superior profit margins or market share; it is necessary to determine how the patents figure in. In the bio-chem-pharma space, where one patent tends to read on one product, performance is easier to track. Because there is little impetus to value these patents internally, and little methodology to do so, the value of strategic patents is often unrecognized. Indeed, GAAP accounting makes it difficult to capture the impact of strategic patents on the bottom line. Only when a business unit is sold (under FASB 141 and 142) is the market value of the patents recognized and impairment of value considered. Lack of transparency associated with IP transactions, difficulty determining the value of rights, and the inability to identify their precise role in competitive advantage, hamstrings C-level execs and tongue-ties otherwise articulate financial analysts. Whether it is revenues generated or costs saved, managers need to do a better job of understanding and articulating the role specific patents play in supporting overall objectives.

The inability of strategic owners to measure and convey performance plays right into the hands of direct IP investors, especially patent trolls and other NPEs who focus on cash returns. Many shareholders have the impression that it is the direct investors, not strategic ones, who are most adept at monetizing IP when, in fact, strategic owners may be doing a more effective and business model-appropriate job of deploying their assets (see Exhibit 4.5) Without the ability to codify and articulate relative IP value, even informally, strategic owners are at a disadvantage. IP measurement and metrics are growth industries that will receive a great deal of attention over the next decade, especially as monetization models

EXHIBIT 4.5 **BENEFITS OF DIRECT/INDIRECT INVESTING**

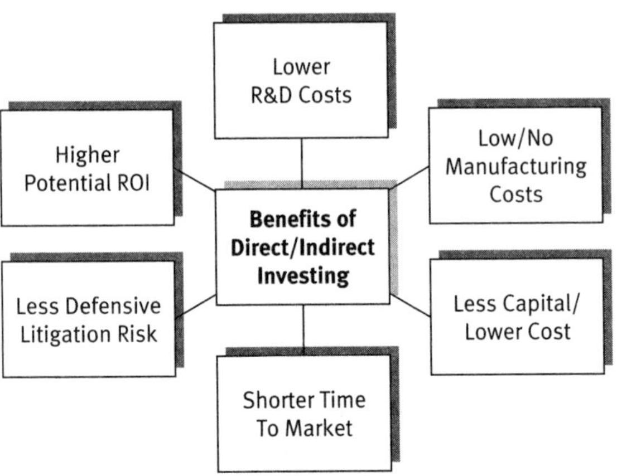

proliferate. IP management needs to help company management step up and do a better job conveying the impact of their IP strategy and their role in value creation. Some CEOs will do a better job than others. This is an enormous opportunity for those willing to step up.

IP in Context: Toward a Broader Interpretation of ROIP

Monetizing IP is rarely a literal "cashing in" on a patent's value. Copyrights and trademarks may enjoy sustained royalty streams, but most patents need a wider perspective to generate return. Patent success means converting assets into performance, however interpreted by a given rights holder, and, ultimately, into profits. Performance need not be cash flow in the form of a royalty stream, as credit rating agencies Moody's and S&P would have us believe. Performance can mean competitive advantage, first-mover advantage, a likelihood of a standard, or any number of difficult-to-identify-and-convey attributes. (See Exhibit 4.4) While extremely attractive to some because of their high margins, royalties are not all things to all patent-owning entities. Licensing may be attractive to CEOs, boards of directors, and Wall Street, but as Harvard Business School's Willy Shih and others point out elsewhere in this book, they can become a dangerous dependence and ultimately harmful to a company's health. Patents that allow a product to be more profitable for a longer period of

EXHIBIT 4.6 **SEARS' IP ASSET ENGINEERING**

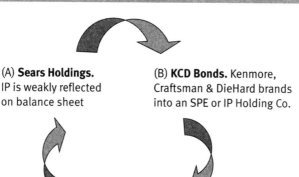

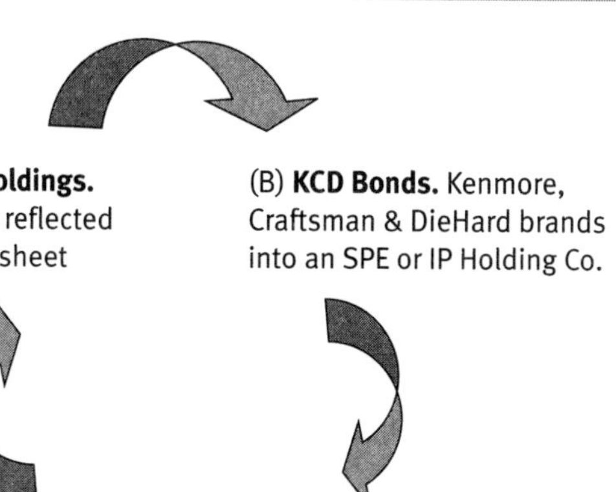
(A) **Sears Holdings.** IP is weakly reflected on balance sheet
(B) **KCD Bonds.** Kenmore, Craftsman & DieHard brands into an SPE or IP Holding Co.
(C) **Sears' Bermuda Insurance Captive.** $1.8 billion in IAs are now visible.

Sears' Kenmore, Craftsman, and DieHard brands ("KCD") are worth more on its captive's balance sheet, $1.8 billion according to a 2007 debt financing which was rated by Moody's, than on Sears' own, where they would likely be bundled into "good will."

time are worth more to some owners than the high-margin cash flows emanating from out-licensing. Quantifying their role in company profitability, however, is another matter. In 2007, beleaguered Sears licensed its top Kenmore, Craftsman, and DieHard brands to an insurance subsidiary for $1.8 billion. The IP transaction, really a bit of financial engineering, served to unlock the value of otherwise illiquid trademark assets, which clearly are worth more on Sears' insurance subsidiary's balance sheet than on its own (see Exhibit 4.6).[8] Now the parent can more readily leverage those assets. I would not be surprised to see a strategic family of patents similarly repackaged and deployed.

Direct and passive IP investing can be catalysts for innovation. They force greater scrutiny of patent quality, performance, and relative value. Much like the U.S. auto industry beset by higher quality Japanese imports in the early 1970s, a variety of nimble independent IP investors have been putting companies' IP portfolios to the test. Some have fared better than others. Patent quality, many large portfolio owners are finding, can be finessed only so much. If an operating company does not have the patents it needs to run its businesses properly, it had better gain access to them or invent around those who do. Patent thickets are less reliable than in the

EXHIBIT 4.7 **DIRECT & PASSIVE IP INVESTORS**

Patent Buyers & Lic Partners
UTEK
Acacia Technologies
General Patent Corp
Intellectual Ventures
Coller IPCapital

R&D Businesses
Chiron (biotech)
Columbia U., Stamford
Qualcomm
InterDigital
Independent Inventors

IP-Centric Equity Investors
Bessemer, Sequoia, Bechmark
Cerberus, Silver Lake
Altitude Capital
Deutsche Bank
Goldman Sachs

IP Securities
Royalty Pharma
Paul Capital
Paradox Capital
Newlight Capital

Litigation Investors (time)
Kirkland Ellis
Robins Kaplan
Weily Rein
McCool Smith

Litigation Investors (capital)
Rembrandt Group
Oasis Legal Finance
IP Finance
IP-Com

Patent Brokers
Inflexion Point
ThinkFire
IPotential
Ocean Tomo

past. Many direct and indirect IP investors have the patience, experience, and capital to confront them now that the playing field has leveled. Until recently, companies had many patents and little awareness of their role at a given time. A Director of IP could be fired for insufficient patent count, quality be damned. There was little certainty about which were producing needed results or providing a return, and many companies were willing to take their chances with a patent infringement suit.[9] It was enough to have a large number of patents; quantity implied a semblance of quality. Patented products were rarely challenged by competitors and seldom by independents who lacked sufficient capital, counsel, and will. When damages awards skyrocketed, patent holders were forced to become more mindful of their portfolios' relevance to products they sold, or planned to, and of which rights were indeed assets.

Even Microsoft can feel the impact of having to repeatedly pay patent infringement damages. Companies that spend billions of dollars on R&D and hundreds of millions on patent filings and legal fees may look well prepared to compete against other IP holders. Often, they are not. Smart businesses are learning to admit—internally at least—that when they do not have the IP assets they need, they must consider if, how, and when they need to rectify the situation. Constantly improving their position through patent portfolio fine tuning is no longer seen as a failure, but as a healthy and adaptive response to changing company needs and market conditions. It also presents an opportunity for them to (dare I say it) speculate in future IP value. Smart businesses are learning the advantage of engaging in a sort of IP risk arbitrage, using IP rights to hedge positions, much as investors do with futures contracts. Acting like independent IP investors, when necessary, includes using any reasonable manner to secure the rights a company may need to achieve business goals at the right price and with the appropriate level of anonymity. This includes buying patents in anticipation of possible future needs through third parties like brokers, or joining with other companies in pools, trusts, or networks to secure rights.

The CEO Challenge: Recognizing and Maximizing IP Assets

Inventing today is faster, more global, and more essential than in Edison's time. Autonomous proprietary research centers like Lucent's Bell Labs or IBM's Watson may no longer be the best sources of business innovation. Some argue that the days of those once revered invention factories are numbered. In what Tom Friedman calls a "flatter" world, with outsourcing and more facile communications, innovation can be organized and secured more readily from diverse sources for less cost, especially from nations such as India and China. Large companies, even those that actively license, have a very different way of looking at rights than do smaller companies or independent inventors. They have to be careful about who they enforce against because of possible counter assertion and because they are loath to mistreat customers who may be infringing. But being mindful of assertion does not mean they can be glib about where to secure the rights they need or think they might.

One of a business's greatest strengths today is to be able to recognize when intellectual rights (their own and others') become intangible assets. There is a disconnect between relative patent value, which is its meaning to its owner, and market value, which is what a buyer is willing to pay for it. The market for transacting IP rights is still highly fragmented and inefficient, but it is improving daily. The threat of costly litigation on an injunction still is an inducement for settling disputes, but recent court decisions and patent reform are making other solutions attractive. In all likelihood it will continue in that direction. This creates opportunity for those with capital and vision. Active, well-capitalized buyers like Intellectual Ventures, borne out of ex-Microsoft and -Intel execs, are taking advantage of market inefficiencies and a strong cash position by buying up practically any patent that owners are willing to sell. At first IV was able to secure decent rights for a fraction of the R&D, filing, and legal fees that went into securing many of them. But with much of the low-hanging fruit already picked, and the practicality of acquiring invention rights better established, prices are starting to rise. This is likely to benefit both strategic and direct IP investors as well as independent inventors. Currently, IV owns between 15,000 and 18,000 patents that cover a broad range of inventions and technologies. In addition, they have secured scores number patents from their own original filings.

While IP investors are here to stay, the future of IP investing as an industry is less clear. Some of those who invest directly in patents such as Acacia, Rembrandt, and IV have succeeded in affecting occasional settlements or damages awards. They all have attracted capital from private equity and other sources, including, in some cases, pension funds and foundations. None have established a sufficient pattern of ROI to determine their long-term viability, yet they still play an important role in the IP ecosystem.

Those who invest in patent litigation have affected some settlements, but it is unclear if the settlements are of sufficient frequency or magnitude to generate ROI comparable to that of strategic users. Columbia University has generated some $1.4 billion over more than 20 years of licensing activity, magnificent returns even for private sector innovators. But Columbia is one of only a few universities that have benefited on this level, and it is willing to enforce its rights, when necessary. On the public company side, companies that use their R&D and patent portfolio primarily to license as opposed to manufacture include InterDigital, Rambus, Tessera, and Qualcomm. Out-licensing can be an acceptable and prudent business model. Many R&D based companies have done quite well with a strategy that relies significantly on licensing, but it is unclear if their successes will endure over time. Some are under intense pressure to show they can be consistent performers. How well they succeed long term is certainly important, but so is the impact they have had. If nothing else, IP investors with narrower goals have made patent portfolio managers more circumspect about identifying IP rights and intellectual assets they do and do not own.

Companies large and small are focusing on rights' performance. IBM, Intel, HP, and GE have improved their patent portfolios and regularly attempt to rid them of unnecessary rights. They also are quietly acquiring and sometimes asserting patents, or, at least, threatening to. They employ a wide range of techniques to secure, manage, improve, and monetize their portfolio. As a result, a new type of IP investor is emerging. She is less a patent speculator with an eye on licensing and assertion than a prudent risk taker willing to place broad bets on a variety of relevant patents at the right price. TI and other large companies have shown that strategic deployers are not beyond cashing in on their patents directly, engaging in litigation against competitors or even customers. In reality, however, few companies can afford to follow in their bloody footsteps (see Exhibit 4.8).

Better measures of patent performance and understanding of their role in product sales, profit margins, and company performance will relieve some of the pressure from Wall Street and others on IP management and company executives to generate royalty income. While out-licensing patents certainly can be attractive, it frequently is accompanied by costly and painful litigation. It also is a huge distraction for those running an operating business. Recent court decisions have made litigation even less

EXHIBIT 4.8 **IP PROFIT IN PERSPECTIVE**

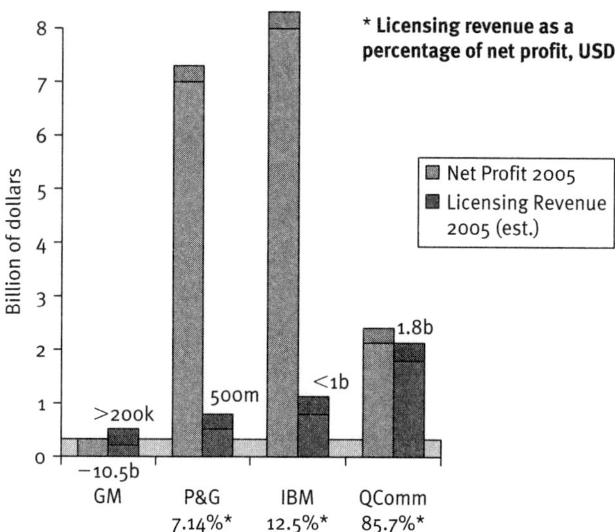

Some companies rely on patent licensing for net profit more than others. How much is the right amount depends on business objectives, particular invention rights, and timing.

predictable. Licensing can work well for some companies at certain times in their IP and business life cycles, but it is becoming apparent that it is not an appropriate permanent business model for most. Licensing is only one measure of IP management skill and business performance. Other measures that should be applied are not always readily apparent. They include the determination of patents' role in achieving or maintaining market share (freedom of action), profit margins, product sales, customer relationships (sales), M&A activity, shareholder or market value, reputation, and capital formation.

For the majority of strategic patent owners the economics of patent enforcement do not add up. Strangely, this rent in the fabric of innovation has encouraged speculators to secure and capitalize rights as they would other business assets. The challenge for strategic owners is to identify innovative ways to monetize huge investments in R&D without necessarily generating licensing cash flows or engaging in litigation. This approach, while less dramatic, more readily supports most patent holders' long-term objectives and shareholder value. While there is intense competition among all types of patent owners, it appears for now they can and even should coexist. At the end of the day, it is about the meaning and quality of innovation. Without a level of reliability a rational notion of patent performance, and a competitive market to facilitate the pricing if not policing of IP rights, innovation is destined to take longer to produce and cost more to procure.

ABOUT THE AUTHOR

Bruce Berman is CEO of Brody Berman Associates in New York, a communications and management consulting firm that focuses on innovative businesses and intellectual assets. Mr. Berman works closely with IP-based businesses and their advisors, to enhance patent and brand values, win disputes, and facilitate transactions. In addition to this book, Mr. Berman is responsible for, *Making Innovation Pay—People Who Turn IP into Shareholder Value* (John Wiley & Sons, Inc., 2005). He also edited and contributed to *From Ideas to Assets—Investing Wisely in Intellectual Property* (John Wiley & Sons, Inc., 2002), a widely acclaimed book about the business of IP. His articles, reviews, and book chapters have appeared in many publications, including *Nature Biotechnology*, *The National Law Journal*, and *The Book of Investing Rules* (Financial

Times, Prentice Hall, 2003), which The Motley Fool called one of the all-time best investment books.

Mr. Berman has guest-lectured at Columbia University School of Business, and chaired panels and organized IP business conferences for IncreMental Advantage, The Wall Street Transcript, the Intellectual Property Owners' Association, and, in 2005 and 2007, the Center for Intellectual Property Studies (CIP Forum) in Gothenburg, Sweden. He has donated his time and expertise in support of the International Intellectual Property Institute (IIPI), the Brookings Institution, and other leading foundations. Mr. Berman's column, "IP Investor," appears regularly in *Intellectual Asset Management (IAM)* magazine, and he serves on the editorial advisory boards of *IAM* and *Patent, Strategy & Management*. He is an honors graduate of The City College of New York (CCNY) and holds a master's degree from Columbia University.

Notes

1. "US Corporate R&D Spending To Reach $219 Billion This Year." *Metrics 2.0, Business & Market Intelligence*, January 2007. www.metrics2.com/blog/2007/01/25/us_corporate_rd_spending_to_reach_219_billion_this.html
2. Paul M. Janicke and LiLan Ren, "Who Wins Patent Infringement Cases?" *American Intellectual Property Law Association Quarterly Journal* 34, (2006):1; John R. Allison and Mark A. Lemlley, "Empirical Evidence on the Validity of Litigated Patents," *American Intellectual Property Law Association Quarterly Journal* 26 (1998): 185.
3. Paul M. Janicke, "Patent Jury Verdicts: Myths and Realities." *Intellectual Property Today*. July, 2007. www.iptoday.com/pdf/2007/7/Janicke-July2007.pdf
4. Bruce Berman, *Making Innovation Pay* (Hoboken, NJ: John Wiley & Sons, 2006), 141.
5. Pat Choate. *Hot Property* (New York: Knopf, 2005), 75-6.
6. Conversation with Marshall Phelps and the author, February 11, 2006.
7. Mike Hatcher, "Rising Patent Awards Hint At a Future Increase in Litigation." *IP Frontline.com,* July 13, 2005. www.ipfrontline.com/depts/article.asp?id=4830&deptid=3&page=1
8. Bruce Berman, "IP Bonds 2.0," *IAM Magazine*, June-July 2007. http://brodyberman.com/articles/IAM_24%20IP%20Investor%204.pdf
9. Mark A. Lemley, Only about 1% of all patents are ever litigated, and only 0.1% of all patents actually go to trial, "Rational Ignorance at the Patent Office," *Northwestern University Law Review* 95, No. 4, February 2001.

CHAPTER 5

Making Sense of Recent Trends, Court Decisions, and Attempts at Patent Reform

BY IRVING RAPPAPORT

Technological creativity is rooted in a country's institutions, as well as its people's ingenuity. The rules that govern a society must police ideas just enough to reward innovation, without stifling diffusion and collaboration. Governance is itself a kind of technology . . .

—DANIEL ROSEN, CHINA STRATEGIC ADVISORY

PERSPECTIVE Information technology has dramatically altered the amount, quality, and importance of innovation. Some companies fear that patent holders now enjoy too strong a position and are actually impeding innovation and shareholder value. Others believe that only with strong patents will inventors and businesses have the necessary incentive to create new solutions and provide better alternatives.

Irving Rappaport has served as chief IP counsel at companies like Apple and National Semiconductor. He is a patent attorney, former patent examiner, entrepreneur and an inventor with 18 patents. Rappaport believes that "patent trolls" are largely a myth perpetuated by typically

(continued)

large companies who may be forced by courts to pay them licensing fees or infringement damages.

In "Making Sense of Recent Court Decisions and U.S. Patent Reform," Rappaport discusses emerging IP business models, recent U.S. court cases that are affecting them, and ways patent reform could affect the future of innovation and the U.S. economy "Eliminating the injunction," he argues, "takes the teeth out of patent infringement suits and effectively provides a compulsory license and a lower royalty." He feels that this reduces both innovation and competition, which is ultimately bad for business.

Rappaport concludes: "My ultimate concern with the current environment impacting our patent system is that it will result in less innovation, less investment in pursuing innovation, fewer patents, less patent licensing, and more patent litigation with less predictability. These conditions will significantly weaken the U.S. economy, which has been built upon the three I's—Inventors, Innovations, and Investments."

Too Much Litigation, Too Many Big Awards

More fundamental changes to the U.S. patent laws have occurred in the recent two years than in the preceding fifty. Overlaying these changes are several new IP-based business models that have emerged to challenge traditional methods of using patents. These legal changes and new business models are together changing the U.S. business landscape. The concern is that these legal changes may have serious adverse affects on the U.S. economy by discouraging investment in innovation. Many of these legal changes are being driven by the largest high tech companies that already enjoy unfair competitive advantages in their businesses. These companies do not want to pay for others' inventions, but do not seem concerned whether the changes are good for the patent system. I will briefly examine some of the new IP-based business models and discuss the effects these recent changes are likely to have on the U.S. patent system and the overall U.S. economy.

Patent Competition

- What Is It?
- How Has It Changed?
- How Does It Impact Business/Innovation?

What Is Patent Competition?

There are many forms of competition, two of which are "market competition" and "patent competition." Market competition is simply where firms compete in the market place based on quality of products or services, marketing acumen, price, performance, and all the other factors that can provide competitive advantage. Patent competition, however, is where firms compete in a market based on patent and other intellectual property rights they have been able to develop and/or acquire. Firms can grow to dominate a market without patents. On the other hand, it is patents that allow new ideas to flourish and new wealth to be created based on inventive activity, where the inventor may not have the funds or inclination to pursue the innovation by manufacturing products or offering services directly. The impetuses that patents can provide to stimulate the growth and development of a new technology are enormous. One example that comes to mind is the invention of Kevlar, a material used in body armor, and many other applications. Two rivals, DuPont and Dutch-based Akzo, for years went head to head competing in patenting new developments and improvements in Kevlar, improving the product and its applications. Patent competition of this kind pulls the entire industry, stimulating innovation and benefiting the public.

How Has Patent Competition Changed?

Thirty years ago, patents were used primarily as defense tools by companies to ensure their freedom to sell exclusively their own products and services. Patent licensing was a rather small industry. Because U.S. firms dominated most industries until the 1970s, patents played a fairly insignificant role. However, in the 1970s, European and Asian technological development began to mature. In fact, by the 1980s consumer electronics, automobiles, and other industries previously dominated by the U.S., were fast becoming the province of Asian and European companies. Patents then started playing a more significant role. The establishment of the Court of Appeals for the Federal Circuit in 1982 resulted in greater predictability in patent infringement cases, with increased holdings of patent validity through a common view of what constituted "obviousness" under 35 U.S.C. 103.

These shifts caused patents to be in- and out-licensed to a much greater extent. Patent licensing grew from a few billion dollars per year to an annual business of hundreds of billions of dollars. Globalization and the change from the industrial era to the knowledge era helped drive this growth. In the knowledge era, intellectual capital and intellectual property, particularly patents, have become greater determinants of corporate valuation than the older bricks and mortar financial models. This is why today, so much of a company's market capitalization stems much more from its intellectual capital or intangible assets, and less and less from its tangible assets. Economists for at least a decade have claimed a firm's market cap to equal 80% intellectual capital and only 20% tangible assets. As associate general counsel at Apple in the late 1980s, I believed the company had two strategic assets—its people and warehouses full of nearly-obsolete inventory or tangibles.

Recently, some enterprises are based entirely on intellectual capital and intellectual property, where the company makes no products and offers no services, but directs all its efforts to developing and patenting technology and licensing that technology to manufacturers and service providers. With the high U.S. labor costs, this is not an unreasonable model. The U.S.'s technological innovation capabilities make this model a springboard for a knowledge-based economy.

"Dark Pools" of Competitive Information

Every business seeks competitive advantage. Some businesses lend themselves to seeking patents, while others maintain certain information in secret. Hedge funds are an example of the latter. Some financial commentators refer to *dark pools of liquidity*, where price and trading information is hidden. As soon as a fund identifies a pricing inefficiency in the markets, it becomes in everyone's interest to exploit it. This results in everyone chasing after the same opportunity, which quickly disappears. The advantage is lost when everyone has it. With patents, companies are valued on those characteristics that make them unique and different from their competitors, not on their similarities. Public data, processes, and knowledge in the patent system are quickly assimilated into products and services in the marketplace. But patents and private data allow the market to place a unique value on a business as the business continues to develop and adapt to new opportunities that have not been yet identified. Patents and private data allow businesses to slow the commoditization of their value.

What Patent Competition Means for Business and Innovation

The shift in the value and importance of patents requires businesses to continually develop and patent "better, cheaper, and faster" products and services. Innovation becomes the key to business success and survival. A strong patent system is critical in attracting investment and controlling the companies that will manufacture the products. Innovation comes at a faster and faster pace. Ray Kurzweil, a tech inventor and entrepreneur, theorizes that we live in a time of "accelerating returns." Because innovation is accelerating, he claims that the amount of technological innovation achieved in the 20th century will be realized in only 20 years in this century. He believes that by 2025 computers will be more intelligent than humans. Observe the speed with which new products and services are coming to market and you may agree with him. This accelerating rate of change requires a strong and flexible patent system.

Myths Fostered by Those Claiming the Patent System Must Change

There are a number of myths in the market parroted by today's media, claiming that the U.S. patent system is broken and in need of drastic change.

Some believe there are too many patents being issued today. Considering that there are more scientists and engineers working today than the total in all recorded history, this belief seems absurd. Because of this innovation explosion, the world benefits from an acceleration of technological growth.

Some believe the Patent Office is totally broken. Sixty months to a first Office Action in the most highly technical art units is way too long. But the path to fixing this is to employ more technology to make the patent examiners more efficient. Weakening patents or making them more difficult to obtain will not fix the USPTO's problems or help the U.S. economy. A strong patent system is dependent on an efficient and technology-driven patent examination system.

Many claim we have too much patent litigation today. Actually the ratio of patent infringement suits to new patent applications filed annually shows a decrease in the last 40 years.

Many, including Supreme Court Justices, have been misled into a false belief that "patent trolls" are a huge cancer on our system. Except in a very few instances, the whole notion of patent trolls is a figment of one lawyer's fertile imagination. Every issued patent has had work and money spent in conceiving and transforming the invention to practice. Purchasing patents to pursue infringers falls within Article I, Section 8 of the Constitution. Nothing requires an inventor to manufacture or sell anything. In fact, the patent gives no right to make the invention, but simply allows exclusion of others from making, selling, or using the claimed invention. The patent owner may require rights of prior patent holders to make her invention. The only instance of abuse is a patent owner suing others while knowing that the patent is likely to be held invalid or not infringed. Such abuses represent a small percentage of infringement suits. Rather than viewing the patent system as having overcorrected as suggested by some, I believe the patent system has reached a point where there is a much more level playing field between the behemoths and the smaller entities in most industries.

Some believe the patent system has tilted in favor of the patent owner. Certain companies have gained monopolies in the marketplace without the need for patents and don't want to pay others for using their patents. Greed is the true impetus for those clamoring for radical patent reform. While this view may benefit a few companies, the vast majority of companies gain competitive advantage from their patents under the current patent system.

Some believe patents are stifling innovation. There is no industry where patents stifle innovation. In fact, just the opposite is true. Valid patents force competitors to design around and improve on existing patents, giving those competitors bargaining position with the owner of the fundamental patent and benefiting the public and the industry. True innovation would be stifled under a weakened patent system, as the dominant companies can muscle competitors to prevent new developments, and smaller entities would have much less chance of succeeding.

The following is a discussion of some of the new emerging IP-based business models.

Emerging New IP-Based Business Models

A number of new IP-based business models have emerged in recent years. Many serve as intermediaries between the owners of patents and either infringers, licensees, or potential buyers of the patents. These intermediaries treat patents as strategic assets, with liquidity and greater profits for the owner and themselves. These are new ways to enter a market, assuming a reasonable level of predictability as to how these rights are treated in our legal system.

Patent Search, Software, and Analytic Services

Some firms are focused on providing specialized software and services with respect to patents.

Patent Search Services Several services focus on patent searching of worldwide patent databases. These include Delphion, Questel Orbit, and PatentCafé. Most are based on Boolean searching, whereas PatentCafé uses primarily semantic-based, natural language searching. Both types of searching have useful benefits.

IP-Based Analysis and Advisory Services Several firms offer services beyond just searching, providing in-depth organization, analysis, and interpretation of search results related to R&D, business development, investment, and merger and acquisition activities. These include IP Checkups, Ocean Tomo, Innovation Assets, Analytic Capital, Blueprint Ventures, Inflexion Point, and Pluritas. Some offer project-based pricing and others operate in a traditional investment banking role, earning fees determined by the value of the deal or the patents in the deal.

Patent Analytic Tools Some firms specialize in licensing software tools for patent analytic functions. Thomson Publishing, Lexis-Nexis, and Patent Café offer such software.

Patent Ratings Services A couple of companies offer software that allows patent owners, investors, attorneys, and others to rate individual patents based on criteria that gauges the strength, quality, and scope of a patent. PatentRatings, The Patent Board, 1790 Analytics, and PatentCafé offer these services.

Buying and Selling Patents

Patent Brokers Several companies are in the business of buying and selling patents, essentially serving as patent brokers. They seek to bring buyers and sellers of patents together to consummate a sale and passage of title. They work both the buy and sell sides of a transaction. Inflexion Point, IPotential, Ocean Tomo, ThinkFire, and Iceberg are such brokers.

Online IP/Technology Exchanges Online IP and Technology exchanges are Web sites, started in the late 1990s, that function in a business-to-business role. Their Web sites are focused on offering patents and other intellectual property as an online classified listing. They include Yet2.com, Tynax, and the Dean's List.

Auction Houses These firms conduct live auctions offering a number of individual patents, patent portfolios, and other IP assets, such as music copyrights with an ongoing royalty stream. They provide a marketplace, making it easier to sell what historically have been illiquid intangible assets. The sellers list their IP according to preset terms and conditions for which the auction firms charge listing fees, buyer's premiums, and/or seller's commissions, and attendance fees. Ocean Tomo, IPA GMBH, and ipAuctions are representative auction firms.

Patent-Based Licensing Firms

There are several different species of patent-based licensing firms, including licensing agents, patent licensing and enforcement companies, and patent aggregators.

Licensing Agents Licensing agents serve as go-betweens or intermediaries between patent owners and parties interested in licensing patents. "Technology transfer," "IP management," or "IP advisory," are terms used by these entities in describing their functions. They all require a retainer and/or success fees for assisting the patent owner in finding and signing license agreements. Generally, these entities do not get involved in litigation. They serve as a resource for companies that do not have licensing departments or otherwise choose not to perform these functions in-house. Examples of licensing agents are ThinkFire, IP Value, and General Patent Corporation.

Patent Licensing and Enforcement Companies (PLECs) A related form of licensing agents is the company that both licenses and enforces patents. Some people have, wrongly referred to these firms as "patent trolls." This model relies on buying patents from parties that either do not have the money or are otherwise unable to manufacture and sell their patented products. Usually, the patents are purchased for a small upfront payment, coupled with a percentage of 15 to 20% of the return that the buyer is able to extract from licensing or suing infringers of the patents. This model requires litigation based on a belief that the patents will ultimately be held valid and infringed. Although attempts to grant non-exclusive licenses are made, litigation follows. Companies practicing this model include the Lemelson Foundation, LPL, and Acacia Technologies, Inc.

Litigation Finance and Investment Firms

These firms are a hybrid of PLECs and funds that acquire patents. They operate as general partners of a limited partnership. Money raised from large institutional investors and high-net-worth investors is used to acquire a financial interest in patent portfolios being asserted by the owners of the portfolios.

Altitude Capital is a fund that raised over $200 million dollars for the purpose of making IP-based investments. To date the firm has primarily made investments in companies owning patents that require financing to address complex capital structures, later-stage equity, or litigation. Altitude provides cost-effective financing tied to the value of intellectual property, or to partial or full monetization of an IP asset. This type of financing can allow a business to continue to operate effectively during litigation or licensing programs. It can also enable new product development or provide sufficient time for a company to reach critical mass with existing products. Altitude does not take a controlling position in a company, but rather, assists the company in solving IP portfolio problems. Their focus is to realize the inherent value of the intellectual property and to add value to their partners through both capital infusion and intellectual property expertise.

Another company, Rembrandt Management IP, LLC, has raised about $150 million. It has acquired patent portfolios and is engaged in various stages of litigation. This model requires litigation with a belief that its patents are valid and infringed. Rembrandt acquires ownership in the patents and asserts the patents in its own name. Acacia also follows this model.

NW Patent Funding (NWP) is a fund started in 2005 by Canadian-based Northwater Capital Management, with seed capital of about $60 million to make IP-based investments. NW's goal is to allow patent owners to derive value from their patent portfolios in the form of licensing royalties. NW provides patent expertise, management time, or finances to launch a successful licensing program for patent owners. After assessing the patents, NW provides financing for the patent owner to license and collect royalties and, if necessary, litigate. Royalties are shared between NW and the patent owners on a net-revenue basis, allowing the patent owners to realize "new-found, no-downside money." Generally, NWP hires and works directly with the patent owner's law firm, but any litigation is filed by the patent owner and not NWP.

IP Financial Firms

Royalty Securitization These firms provide advice and capital to patent owners by performing IP securitization transactions. These transactions resemble mortgage-backed securities. The IP-based company lends money to the patent owner at a favorable interest rate. The loan is secured by the patent portfolio, so that if the patent owner defaults, the patent ownership passes to the lender.

In such loans, the patent owner sells the patents underlying the transaction to a bankruptcy remote entity (BRE), and the BRE grants a license to the patents back to the original patent owner. The BRE in turn issues notes (i.e., IP-backed securities) to investors to raise cash to pay the original patent owner the agreed-upon purchase price. The notes are then backed by the expected future royalties to be earned from licensing the underlying patents (to the original patent owner and/or third parties). At the end of the transaction, the original patent owner has essentially raised funds much more cheaply than a loan backed by its traditional assets. These firms include alseT IP and UCC Capital.

IP-Backed Financers Two companies, IP Innovations located in North Carolina, originally funded by Principal Insurance Company, and Paradox Capital, follow this model. These firms provide financing for IP owners, either directly or as intermediaries, usually in the form of loans (debt financing), where the security for the loan is either wholly or partially IP assets (i.e., IP collateralization). These firms act as intermediaries between borrowers and commercial lending institutions, such as banks.

If the patent owner successfully monetizes the patents, the lender gets a good interest rate. If the patent owner goes bankrupt, the lender obtains ownership of the patents. IP Innovations and Paradox Capital provide credit enhancement to banks, credit providers and other financial institutions for royalty and non-royalty generating patents, trademarks and copyrights used as collateral in commercial financing opportunities. The IP provides lenders with the ability to expand their customer base and affords IP owners access to lower cost, non-dilutive capital.

Developing, Patenting, and Enforcing Inventions (DPEIs)

One model that has developed is what I refer to as DPEI. These firms perform R&D and produce IP (including both patents and know-how), much like traditional operating companies. The difference, however, is that the developed technology is not used to make products, but rather, the IP derived from the technology is licensed by these entities to one or more operating companies which bring products and services employing the technology and IP to the marketplace.

Examples of this model include Qualcomm, Rambus, AmberWave, Tessera, MOSAID, and InterDigital. Qualcomm develops inventions related to CDMA wireless telephone technology, and Rambus develops inventions related to dynamic random access memory (DRAM) that communicates with a computer's microprocessor at a much faster rate than conventional memory. Qualcomm was formerly in the business of supplying semiconductors and other telephone-related equipment to its customers but decided to manufacture less and focus on more profitable patent licensing operations. The company has been quite successful in making this switch. Rambus never manufactured products but developed and licensed its technology to semiconductor manufacturers.

Although these companies have been successful, this business model has involved worldwide patent and other litigation. This model depends on a strong patent system with reasonably predictable results from litigation.

IP Acquisition Aggregators

A couple of firms buy and aggregate large numbers of patents and patent portfolios. They operate somewhat like a private equity fund. Generally they are general partners of a limited partnership, raising capital from either large technology companies or from the capital markets. The investors are promised above average returns based on specific patent portfolios or patent purchases on a grand scale. Typically, the goals are to continue developing the inventions in a portfolio, undertake licensing programs and/or employ arbitrage strategies of various types. Intellectual Ventures and Coller IP Capital are examples of this model.

Other than the search and analytics firms, the IP-based business models discussed above generally focus on some form of licensing or assertion of patent rights. In a less litigious environment, such as Japan, a licensing approach can work well. However, companies in the United States. companies seem much less inclined to willingly enter license agreements. So these models ultimately require the patent holder to bring costly and drawn-out litigation. The future success of these business models is highly dependent on a strong patent system.

Countries around the world are increasingly demonstrating the same technology competencies that exist in the United States. Much of chip fabrication has been moved outside the United States. China and India are providing engineering resources to replace development previously done in the United States. Large amounts of manufacturing have been moved overseas. The U.S. dollar has been in a steady decline in value.

The United States, however, continues to enjoy one asset that is distinctly American: startup companies funded by venture capital. The United States has consistently been the top innovator, dating all the way back to such founding fathers as Franklin and Jefferson. This tradition of innovation has continued through the fields of electronics, computers, software, pharmaceuticals, biotech, and countless others. The U.S. patent system, despite its flaws, has supported all of these innovation fields and startup companies.

However, recent patent decisions and reform efforts are having a large and perhaps chilling impact on the system.

Recent Supreme Court Decisions' Impact on Business

The decision in *KSR v. Teleflex* leaves the U.S. patent system without a clear definition of "obviousness." Many phrases are used in the decision trying to describe obviousness—"predictable results," "common sense," "combination of known elements," "obvious to try"—but without truly defining what is "obvious." This creates less predictability for patent owners involved in patent acquisition, licensing, and/or litigation.

MedImmune v. Genentech has made licensing negotiations a much more difficult process. Any communication from a patent owner may be interpreted by a potential licensee as a hostile act, giving rise to a declaratory judgment action. A patent owner has to file an infringement suit to engage in licensing negotiations. This clearly forces more litigation.

eBay v. MercExchange has made it more difficult for patent holders to obtain injunctive relief. Potential injunctive relief brings the infringer to the negotiating table. As a result, we now have more or less a de facto compulsory licensing system where infringers can drag out litigation, forcing patent holders to spend millions in litigation and years before any return can be received on their patents, if ever at all.

These decisions have significantly weakened the U.S. patent system. With obviousness simply a matter of common sense, declaratory relief available at the drop of a hat, and injunctions less likely, the patent system has suffered serious setbacks. Less licensing, more litigation, and less predictability in the litigation outcome, reduce the value of patents. This begs the question of whether recently proposed changes to the U.S. patent system are redundant or even harmful at this time.

Patent Reform Legislation

Patent reform legislation proposes several very significant changes to patent law. The changes, some of which could still be adopted, include:

- Unnecessarily limiting infringement damage recoveries
- Limiting choice of venue for patent suits

- Changing to a first-to-file, rather than a first-to-invent, system
- Making willful infringement more difficult to prove
- Providing post-grant review of patentability in Patent Office oppositions

Patent reform proposes to limit infringement damage recoveries solely to the value of the patented component, even though the value of the component to the performance, reliability, and benefit of the final product may be the true measure of the invention's value. The current law allows for this "entire market rule" to be applied when appropriate. Reasonable damages should be based on the value delivered to the user by the end product containing the invention, not necessarily a small percentage of a component cost. This change would make be the most adverse to the patent system and economy, and would make the newer forms of patent competition and business models much less attractive.

The recent cases and reform proposals are being driven by the misinformed Supreme Court and reform supporters' beliefs that there is "too much patent litigation" and that awards have been "too high." This reminds one of the movie *Amadeus*, where Mozart plays his newly composed symphony for the king, who responds—"too many notes." The reality is exactly contrary to that belief. From 1970 through 1986 there was an average of 916 new patent infringement cases filed each year, with an average of 67,000 patents issued annually. From 1987 through 2005 there was an average of 1,952 suits filed each year, with an average of 123,000 patents issued annually. Of those cases, about 100 go to trial each year and the remaining cases settle. In my opinion these numbers suggest the system is in balance and working. In 1970 the number of infringement cases brought represented about 1% of the applications filed and 1.4% of the patents issued. In 2005 those percentages were down to 7/10 of 1% of the applications filed and 1.6% of the patents issued[1] If anything, the number of litigations has declined 30 percent as a proportion of new patent application filings, and risen only slightly on patents issued. An examination system will never be perfect and yes, many patents that issue have little or no economic value. However, our free-market system ensures that the valuable ones will rise to the top.

As for damage awards being "too high," 35 U.S.C. § 284 provides that the patent holder is entitled to "damages adequate to compensate for the infringement, but in no event less than a reasonable royalty." In my opinion, that should mean compensation based on the value delivered to the user by the end product containing the invention, not a small percentage of a component cost, if the end product's performance, features, and benefits are primarily due to that component. The following exhibits[2] show the actual statistics on patent infringement awards. Some 66% of the cases and 69% of the dollars were in the non-tech arena, involving companies generally opposed to the patent reform proposals. Only 17% of cases and 16% of dollars involved companies from parties opposing patent reform. Although the Senate has removed from a floor vote in this session of Congress, it is likely to be reintroduced again by the proponents in the next Congress. (see Exhibit 5.1).

Exhibit 5.2 shows the list of companies with >$100 million patent settlements from 2000–2005, and provided in the reference by testimony supporting the proposals.

Patent Office Streamlining Initiatives

The USPTO proposals to limit both the number of claims and the ability to argue for claims might be acceptable if the U.S. had a central claiming practice as in Europe, where the inventor is not penalized if every "i" is not dotted and every "t" not crossed in the claim. Since U.S. case law has no

EXHIBIT 5.1 LARGE PATENT INFRINGEMENT AWARD FACTS

- Awards of › $100 Million from 2000–2005
  - The Pro-Bill testimony references list 33, not 21, cases
    - 3 are listed as being reversed, leaving 29
- 66% of awards were in industries AGAINST the Bill
  - Biotech, pharmaceuticals, chemical, etc.
- 34% of awards were in computer/high tech industries
  - Only 2 companies are in the Pro-Bill coalition: Intel and HP
    - Just 17% of settlements
- Not one case involved a patent troll

Technology companies supporting patent reform do not have a strong argument when it comes to the number of "troll" cases brought which awards they have had to defend aganist.

Source: Courtesy of Steve Perlman, President and CEO of Reardon Companies.

EXHIBIT 5.2 **COMPANIES WITH >$100 MILLION PATENT SETTLEMENTS FROM 2000 TO 2005**

Group	Amount	Year	Companies	Industry	Pro-Bill
Tech: 34% of cases, 31% of dollars	$115,000,000	2000	Farouda ← DWin Electronics	Electronics	
	$200,000,000	2000	Gemstar ← Motorola	Electronics	
	$400,000,000	2001	Pitney Bowes ← HP	Software	Pro-Bill
	$420,000,000	2001	Litton Industries ← Honeywell	Electronics	
	$114,000,000	2002	Internet Magic ← Netex	Software	
	$150,000,000	2002	Intergraph ← Intel	Electronics	Pro-Bill
	$300,000,000	2002	Intergraph ← Intel	Electronics	Pro-Bill
	$453,000,000	2002	InterTrust ← Sony, Philips	Software	
	$225,000,000	2004	Intergraph ← Intel	Electronics	Pro-Bill
	$325,000,000	2005	EMC ← HP	Computers	Pro-Bill
Non-Tech: 66% of cases, 69% of dollars	$100,000,000	2000	Chiron ← Hoffman-LaRoche	Biotech	
	$100,000,000	2000	Abbott ← Cephalon	Drugs	
	$169,000,000	2001	Boston Scientific ← Medtronic	Medical	
	$170,000,000	2001	Gilead Sciences ← OSI Pharmaceuticals	Drug	
	$187,000,000	2001	OSI Pharmaceuticals ← Genentech/Roche	Drugs	
	$135,000,000	2002	Gertis ← Aventis	Drugs	
	$158,000,000	2002	Guidant ← Medtronic	Medical	
	$175,000,000	2002	Boston Scientific ← Medtronic	Medical	
	$325,000,000	2002	Amylin Pharmaceuticals ← Eli Lilly	Drugs	
	$380,000,000	2002	Immunex ← Schering AG	Drugs	
	$424,000,000	2002	Medical Instrument ← Elekta	Medical	
	$500,000,000	2002	City of Hope Nat Med Center ← Genentech	Drugs	
	$505,000,000	2002	Igen International ← Roche Holding	Drugs	
	$295,000,000	2003	Eli Lilly ← Galen Holdings	Drugs	
	$330,000,000	2003	Identix Pharmaceuticals ← Novartis	Drugs	
	$130,000,000	2004	Elan ← Eisai	Pharmaceuticals	
	$134,500,000	2004	Masimo ← Tyco Nelcor	Medical	
	$1,350,000,000	2005	Karin Technology ← Medtronic	Medical	
	$475,000,000	2002	SpinBrush Inc. ← Procter & Gamble	Mechanical	

Pro-Bill: 17% of cases, 16% of dollars

Source: Courtesy of Steve Perlman, President and CEO of Reardon Companies.

such flexibility and validity and infringement may hinge on a single word, or misplaced comma, limiting the number of claims and number of applications related to an invention unfairly hurts the patentee. Many inventions are very complex, having many ways of describing them, just like an MRI making thousands of scans through the body. Besides, Congress is the only authority that has the power to change the substantive provisions of Title 35 U.S.C., not the USPTO. The Federal District Court for the Eastern District of Virginia heard a motion to throw out the USPTO's proposed rule changes. The Court granted the motion on April 1, 2008 on the grounds that the USPTO did not have the authority to enact substantive changes to the U.S. Patent Laws, only Congress has that authority.

The U.S. Patent Office is doing a reasonable job, despite all the naysayers, and particularly given the explosion of information and innovation in recent years. Sure, the USPTO could use more funding and better technology for processing applications. From 1965 to 1987, the number of new utility patent applications filed annually rose steadily and slowly from

95,000 to 128,000, or about 35%. By comparison, in the last 20 years the number has more than tripled to 426,000 annual filings in 2006.[3] However, the allowance rate (the percentage of applications allowed and issued of total applications filed) has fallen from a high of 70% in 2000 to just 44% in the first quarter of 2008 (see Exhibit 5.3).[4] This dramatic decrease in the allowance rate shows that the USPTO is indeed tightening the examination process and is already making it more difficult to obtain patents, making further substantive changes in the patent law unnecessary and, probably, unwise at this time.

Some have pointed to the dramatic filings increase as proof enough that the system is out of control. However, those decades showed a similar acceleration in the growth of the economy. From the mid-1960s to the mid-1980s, the S&P 500 more or less doubled. Since the mid-1980s it has increased nearly eightfold. Furthermore, there are more engineers and scientists alive today than in all of recorded history, and more U.S. patent applications are being filed annually from outside the U.S. Science and technology employment zoomed from about 200,000 people in 1950 to almost 5.5 million in 2000, as shown in Exhibits 5.4 and 5.5. It should

EXHIBIT 5.3 **PATENT ALLOWANCE RATE**

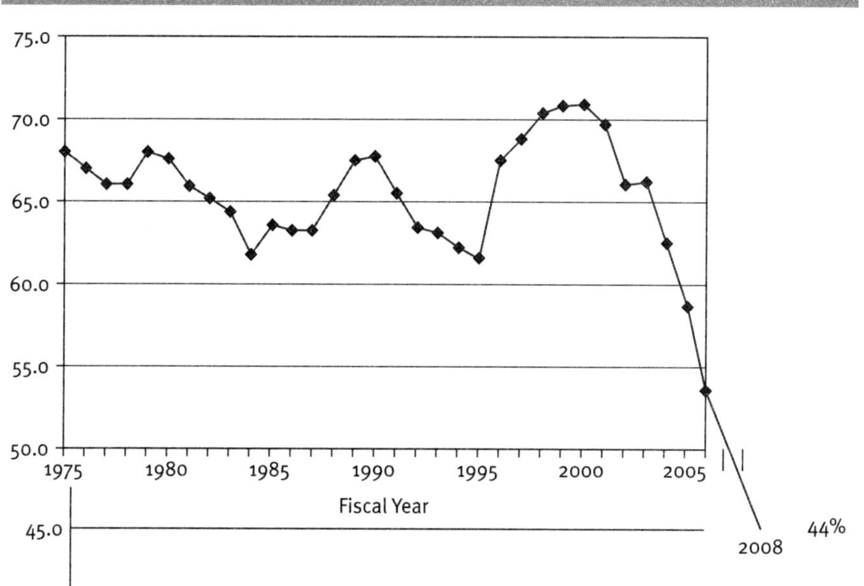

Source: USPTO

EXHIBIT 5.4 **FIRST UNIVERSITY DEGREES IN S&E, BY REGION: 1995 OR MOST RECENT YEAR**

Field	Three-region total	Asia	Europe	North America
First university degrees, all fields	5,208,205	2,043,677	1,713,423	1,451,105
Science & engineering	2,146,648	926,426	732,263	487,959
Natural sciences	764,820	301,877	309,837	153,106
Social science	642,777	280,775	138,896	223,106
Engineering	739,051	343,774	283,530	111,747

NOTES: The requirements for first university degrees in S&E fields are not comparable across or even within the countries included in these three regions, particularly for European universities. For example, Germany includes both university degrees (with an average duration of 7 years) and Fachhochschulen degrees (polytechnics of 4.5 years' average duration) as first university degrees (level 6 in UNESCO classification). Work has been under way for several years at UNESCO, EUROSTAT, and the U.S. Department of Education to refine the levels of higher education for better comparability across countries. See, for example, U.S. Department of Education and National Science Foundation, *Mapping the World of Education: The Comparative Database System(CDS)* (Washington, DC 1994). A new UNESCO survey will be designed and implemented by the end of this decade.
Source: Science & Engineering Indicators 1998.

be no surprise based on this rapid growth in the number of scientists and engineers, that more inventions are being made and filed as patent applications, as opposed to the idea that the USPTO is granting too many patents.

More funding and better technology could go a long way in fixing the current complaints about the quality of patent examination, without changing the substantive underpinnings of the U.S. patent system.

Conclusions

Recent Supreme Court decisions have already weakened the U.S. patent system. Patent reform may not only be redundant, but, together with rapidly falling allowance rates, could further weaken the system by creating many more hurdles for patent seekers and investors to overcome. I believe the effects are already being felt in decreased licensing and increased high-risk litigation.

EXHIBIT 5.5 **SCIENCE AND TECHNOLOGY EMPLOYMENT: 1950–2000**

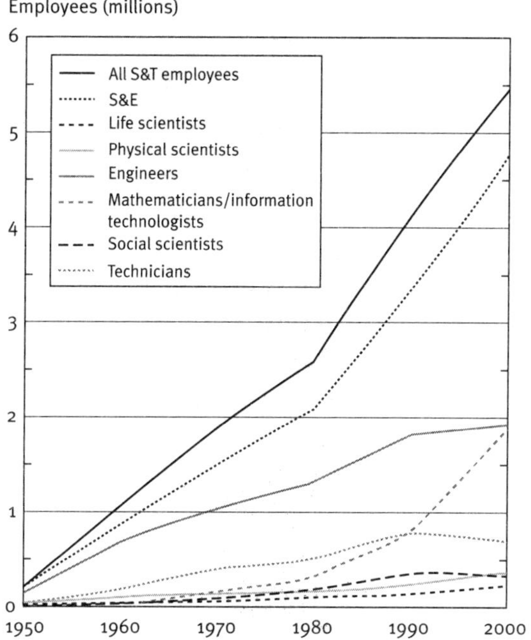

S&T = science and technology

NOTE: Data include those with bachelor's degrees of higher in science occupations, some college and above in engineering occupations, and any education level for technicians and computer programmers.

Source: B.L. Lowell, Estimates of the Growth of the Science and Technology Workforce, Commission on Professionals in Science and Technology Workforce, Commission on Professionals in Science and Techonology (forthcoming). *Science and Engineering Indicators 2006.*

The net effect of all these changes will result in less innovation and less investment in new ideas. Both innovation and business are likely to suffer. These changes are disguised attempts to delay the cycle of creative destruction that results from new patented inventions in our current system, a dangerous reason for change. So called "patent trolls," if they exist, seem to have been the catalyst for the jurisprudence, legislation, and regulations purportedly aimed at "reforming" the system. Indeed, there are those who are using the legal system to obtain money from risk-adverse and lose defendants with a lot to loose. But those few are not to be confused with those who assert strong patents that read on successful products. By weakening patents, the playing field is becoming less level, and small companies and inventors less consequential in the process. And the newly emerging IP-based business models are likely to suffer.

Eliminating the injunction takes the teeth out of patent infringement suits and effectively provides a compulsory license and a lower royalty. Legitimate asserters, independent investors, and companies with large portfolios, are catalysts for patent and innovation quality, and for competition. They help to establish market value and encourage improvement of patent portfolios, rather than acceptance of the status quo. Without asserters, innovation would be less likely to be challenged or improved. The whole point of Article I, Section 8 of the U.S. Constitution is to encourage inventors to make their inventions public. Inventors are not required to make products, nor to make them public. The quid pro quo of the right to exclude others from practicing one's invention for a limited time in exchange for making the invention public has made the U.S. patent system and our economy very successful for over two centuries.

A concern with the current environment's impact on our patent system is that it will result in less innovation, less investment in pursuing innovation, fewer patents, less patent licensing, and more patent litigation, that is less predictable. These conditions will significantly weaken the U.S. economy, which has been built upon the three "I"s – Inventors, Innovations, and Investments. Why should inventors waste their time creating new inventions and investors invest their money in U.S. enterprise, if the chance for a significant payback for a limited time is greatly diminished under a hobbled patent system? The U.S. should not willingly give up its competitive advantage as the world's leading innovator to economies enjoying much cheaper labor costs and growing numbers of scientists and engineers.

Patent experts in China and India have published articles suggesting that U.S. patent reform is good for infringers.[5] It is important to keep the U.S. patent system strong. It has been a foundation of the U.S. economy for more than 200 years and it has enabled the economy to be competitive in ways that other nations can only wish to emulate.

ABOUT THE AUTHOR

Irving S. Rappaport has been a patent attorney for more than 40 years. He is also an entrepreneur, inventor, and provides expert testimony witness in IP-related disputes. He is a co-founder of IP Checkups LLC, located in Berkeley, CA, which provides competitive patent portfolio landscape analysis services to companies and investment firms. Previously he cofounded Aurigin Systems and served as head IP Counsel to Apple 1984–1990, National Semiconductor, Medtronic, Data General Corporation, and Bally Manufacturing.

Mr. Rappaport is a coinventor on at least 18 U.S. patents and was elected to *Who's Who in America* in 2007. He serves on the Advisory Boards of Altitude Capital and PatentCafé. Mr. Rappaport received a degree in electrical engineering from Washington University, a J.D. degree with honors from George Washington University Law School and an M.B.A. from Boston University. He has served at the request of three U.S. Secretaries of Commerce on the U.S. Government Advisory Committee that led, among other accomplishments, to the adoption of the IP sections of both the North American Free Trade Agreement and the World Trade Organization.

NOTES

1. Administrative Office of U.S. Courts, Annual Reports
2. Courtesy of Steve Perlman, President and CEO of Reardon Companies.
3. www.uspto.gov/go/taf/appl_yr.htm
4. http://unitedstates.promotetheprogress.com/dudas-first-quarter-allowance-rate-at-about-44/644/
5. Yongshun Cheng and Li Lin; "Patent reform is friendlier to the infringers than to patentees in general as it will make the patent less reliable, easier to be challenged, and cheaper to be infringed. It is not bad news for developing countries that have fewer patents.... This bill will keep the companies from developing countries more freedom and flexibility to challenge the relative U.S. patent for doing business in U.S. and make it less costly to infringe." *China Intellectual Property News*, July 7, 2007.

PART 2

IP Performance

CHAPTER 6

Patent Valuation Contexts: Navigating Murky Waters[1]

BY JAMES D. WOODS

PERSPECTIVE For assets like real estate, receivables, and shares of stock, valuation is a direct function of market dynamics. What a willing buyer will pay for a particular asset at a given time determines price. For intellectual and other more esoteric, illiquid, and context-driven assets, valuation is fraught with a higher level of uncertainty. In the past, most companies and investors have thrown up their hands in frustration at patent values. But patents today are so integral to the value and success of companies that their meaning can no longer be forsaken, even if they are poorly reflected on most companies' balance sheet. Patents need to be understood not only for their market and relative values, but measured for their contribution to product and company performance.

James D. Woods is an economist who specializes in understanding the importance of designated patents in different contexts. In this chapter he looks at the accepted approaches to valuing patents and suggests which ones are most reliable. He also examines the various contexts in which patent valuation is necessary or useful.

"Because valuation deals with expected or future cash flows," observes Dr. Woods, "it must take into account the preferences and concerns of investors in accessing the timing and likelihood of receiving those benefits. He reviews the three basic approaches to valuation—income, cost, and market—as they relate to patents. He also discusses

(continued)

the challenges inherent in valuing strategic patents, which may be associated with product sales but not with licensing revenues.

"The value of patents used for strategic purposes is difficult to measure because you cannot easily determine the cash flows generated by the patents. That does not imply the cash flows are small. The cash flows could be substantial, but they are embedded in the profits from the sale of products covered by the cross licenses. Disentangling these profits is complicated by the fact that often no single patent can be identified as critical to the strategy."

Dr. Woods argues that "the patent investor can arbitrage between the value of the patent to the investor and the value he or she can achieve in raising the stakes for the potential corporate licensee. At times, the patent value realized by the patent investor closely approximates the value that would be negotiated between two manufacturers, one licensing to the other. However, the reality that the threat of a patent infringement suit and the cost associated with the defense of such actions is substantial and can be leveraged by some patent investors into settlements that have little or no relationship to the patent value negotiated between manufacturers."

Sounding the Shoals, Plumbing the Depths

MCI/Verizon agreed in 2007 to a settlement with a patent owner who had filed suit alleging infringement of two of its patents.[2] Does the amount of the confidential settlement shed light on the value of the patents? Maybe not. Another defendant in the suit, AT&T Corp., refused to settle and pleaded its case in a two-week trial. The jury awarded the patent owner $156 million in damages against AT&T Corp. for willfully infringing the patents. Did the jury verdict of $53 million (one-third of the trebled damages of $156 million) shed light on the value of the patents? Probably not, since the federal judge presiding over the case overturned the jury's verdict and vacated the award. Does this mean the patents are worthless? Probably not, since the federal judge's ruling can be appealed.

Patent valuations, regardless of the method used to arrive at the indication of value, are fraught with a high level of uncertainty. Just what does the patent cover? Will it withstand legal challenges? In the words of leading patent scholars, "most patents represent highly uncertain or probabilistic property rights."[3] We explore the implications of this reality and offer a framework for articulating and understanding the relative level of uncertainty associated with identifiable categories of patents. In an uncertain world even a crude map can be comforting.

The marketplace provides the best information about the value of most assets. If you want to know what a share of IBM stock is worth, you simply log onto a brokerage account and receive a quote from someone willing to buy or sell at a stated price. No analysis is required. If you want to sell a car, there is no single source of information about the current market price for that car, but you can search various information sources, the Kelley Blue Book, for example, and learn the price that others are asking for similar cars and then can determine a reasonable asking price for the car. In contrast to the IBM example, there is a market for used cars, but no two used cars are exactly alike. Therefore, you must take the information provided by the market and make adjustments to reflect the condition of a particular car. There is a similar process for valuing real estate and many other assets.

As you begin to examine assets used in commercial enterprises to generate wealth, the asset being valued becomes more differentiated from assets with market-provided information. When estimating the value of a business unit or subsidiary, analysts often develop detailed financial projections and create models to estimate the future profits based on these forecasts. These estimates are necessary because the asset being valued is significantly different from assets with known value in the marketplace, or because there are no known values of similar businesses. While the analyst may be able to refer to the market value of companies that are similar to the unit or subsidiary, his opinion will be primarily supported by his models and reasoning, rather than by similar transactions in the marketplace. Since by definition a patent is unique, unless there is a market sale of the patent prior to the valuation date, a patent valuation analyst will not have access to market data for a patent identical to the subject patent. Therefore, the patent valuation must rest upon the forecasts, estimates, and models created.

Valuation Techniques

Quantifying Value

The value of a patent can be defined as:

- The cash-equivalent
- of all expected cash flows (or benefits) from commercialization of the invention
- forecast over the remaining life of the patent
- adjusted to today's dollars through application of an appropriate discount rate.

This conceptual model is well established in the financial and valuation literature.

The economic principal of substitution underlies this concept of value. Analytically, you are attempting to balance a hypothetical set of scales. On one end is placed the ownership rights to a particular patent. The question to be answered is how much money is required to be placed on the opposite side of the scale (the *cash-equivalent*) to balance the scale. When an economically rational decision maker would be indifferent between owning the patent and possessing the cash, the *cash-equivalent* quantifies the value of the patent.

Our practical concern is limited to cash that will flow to the owner of the patent in the future. Any cash that was received by the patent owner prior to today (or an alternative measurement date) is irrelevant—it will not flow from transferring ownership of the patent today. While historical analysis is important, it is only relevant in forming reasonable expectations for the future. Because the future is unknown, it is necessary to *forecast* these expected cash flows. *Expected cash flows* created through the commercialization of the patented technology are the economic benefit of ownership of the patent. However, patent rights exist only for a limited time. As a result, only expected cash flows for the *remaining life of the patent* accrue from patent ownership. Therefore, in determining the value of a patent you can substitute the expected cash flows over the remaining life of the patent for ownership of the patent (see Exhibit 6.1).

Because valuation deals with expected or future cash flows, it must take into account the preferences and concerns of investors in accessing the timing and likelihood of receiving those benefits. Investors have a

EXHIBIT 6.1 REASONS TO VALUE A PATENT

Typical reasons to determine the value of a patent or portfolio of patents include the following:

- Decision making regarding investment and/or commercialization opportunities
- Outright sale
- License of rights to practice the invention
- Mergers and acquisitions
- Loan collateralization and securitization
- Litigation or arbitration disputes
- Charitable donations
- Transfer pricing and intellectual property holding company transfers (tax-based activities)
- Bankruptcy and reorganization
- Financial statement reporting

preference for a dollar today over receiving that dollar tomorrow—this is referred to as the *time value of money*. Not only is the future unknown, but any forecast of the future is inherently uncertain until viewed in retrospect. Our intuition tells us that while all forecasts are uncertain, some are more likely to be realized than others. We use the term *risk* to describe this notion—the higher the risk, the greater the uncertainty and *vice versa*. A tenant of finance is that investors/purchasers are risk-adverse and, therefore, they place a price on uncertainty. In a valuation, the analyst derives a *discount rate* to reflect his or her estimate of the hypothetical investor's expected adjustments to the expected cash flows to reflect consideration of the time value of money and risk. The mathematical adjustment of the expected cash flows through a discount rate results in the *present value* which is the value in today's dollars.

This conceptual definition of a patent's value can expressed mathematically as:

$$\text{Value} = V_0 = \left(\frac{CF_1}{(1+r)^1} + \frac{CF_2}{(1+r)^2} + \frac{CF_3}{(1+r)^3} + \cdots + \frac{CF_n}{(1+r)^n}\right)$$

where:

V_0 is the value of the patent today
n is the remaining life of the patent
CF_1 through CF_n are the expected cash flows (benefits) to be derived from ownership in periods 1 through n
r is the discount rate that adjusts future dollars to present value.

This is the basic *discounted cash flow (DCF) model.*

Approaches to Valuation

There are *three basic approaches to valuation*—the income, cost, and market approaches. While there are multitudes of valuation methods and procedures, they all are simply different ways of implementing one or more of the three basic approaches. These approaches can generally be defined as:

1. The *income approach* measures the economic benefits accruing from the ownership of the patent. Computation of the discounted cash flow model is a method under the income approach.
2. The *cost approach* measures either: 1) the historical cost incurred to create the invention and obtain the patent; or, 2) the cost to reproduce or replace the patent (e.g., research and development personnel and expense, legal and other professional fees related to patent prosecution, application/registration fees, etc.) or to reproduce or replace the functionality that the patented invention provides.
3. The *market approach* measures the prices at which patented technologies considered to be comparable to the patented invention to be valued have changed hands in the marketplace.

Synthesizing and Reconciling Values Derived from Alternative Approaches

The valuation analyst often quantifies value using more than one of the three approaches and/or multiple methods. Common sense, informed judgment, and reasonableness are required to synthesize and reconcile these alternative value indications into either a single point estimate or estimated range of value. For example, assume that the limits of a patented invention are such that a *noninfringing alternative design* is available to a hypothetical buyer to obtain the functionality/benefits offered by the patented invention. In this instance, the cost of obtaining, developing, and practicing that alternative design (determined using the cost approach) may be the ceiling above which an economically rational party would not pay for the patent. So even if the value of the patent determined using the discounted cash flow method (an income approach) exceeds the value determined using a cost approach, common sense requires that we recognize that the reasonable value is no more than the lower cost-based value.

Other Patent Valuation Methods

The *relief-from-royalty method* is a blend of aspects of the income and market approaches. It assumes for analytical purposes that the user of a patented technology does not own the patent and seeks to determine the amount of a royalty it would have paid to obtain a license for its use based on market rates.

Value of a patent is calculated under the relief-from-royalty method at the present value of the hypothetical royalties (income approach), where the royalty rate is determined based on comparable marketplace licensing transactions (market approach).

The *return on assets employed method* is based on the assumption that the return earned by a business is an aggregate of the returns earned on each class of assets it employs. Essentially the analyst determines: 1) market rates of return for each class of assets other than the patent being valued; 2) multiplies those rates by the value of the corresponding asset class; and, 3) subtracts the sum from the company's total income. The remainder is the imputed return on the patent, which can be projected over the remaining life of the patent and adjusted for the appropriate discount rate to arrive at the derived present value of the patent.

Valuation professionals have developed and promoted *proprietary and semi-proprietary methods* based on their analysis of and experience with value patents. One such method is the Technology Factor Method (TFM), which was originally developed more than twenty years ago by Dow Chemical with the assistance of the consulting firm Arthur D. Little. The TFM is a formalistic method to implement an income approach based on weighted values on 10 utility attributes and 10 competitive attributes for the subject technology. By design TFM and other individualized valuation methodologies assume the significance of the dimensions of analysis they have modeled and, therefore, may or may not be appropriate under actual facts and circumstances reflected in a particular patent valuation analysis.

FAIR VALUE REPORTING—EVOLVING GAAP REQUIREMENTS

The Financial Accounting Standards Board has made substantial changes to Generally Accepted Accounting Principals (GAAP) with regard to intangible assets acquired through business combination. Statement of Financial Accounting Standard (SFAS) 141, *Business Combinations*, now requires that intangible assets be recognized apart from goodwill if they are separable or arises from contractual or other legal rights. A patent acquired in a business combination satisfies this definition and must be valued at "fair value" and recorded on the balance sheet. The value of the patent is determined using "fair value" which is an accounting based construct defined by SFAS 157, *Fair Value Measurement*. SFAS 142, *Goodwill and Other Intangible Assets*, requires that the recorded patent asset, as an intangible asset with a determinable useful life, is to be amortized. Additionally, during its useful life the patent must be tested for impairment (i.e. whether carrying amount for the asset group exceeds their current fair value) each year, and more frequently if circumstances warrant, under SFAS 144, *Accounting for the Impairment or Disposal of Long-Lived Assets*.

While certain so-called rules of thumb are sometimes offered by licensing and patent valuation practitioners as being indicative of the value of a patent, they are not valid or reliable substitutes for a careful and reasoned analysis of the facts and circumstances surrounding a patent and application of appropriate methods of valuation under one or a combination of the basic valuation approaches. An example is the *25 Percent Rule*.[4] This rule is based on the observation that several industrial-age patent licenses were observed to have a royalty rate that provided the patent owner with a royalty stream that equaled approximately 25% of the operating profits of the enterprise in which the licensed invention was used. Based upon this information, users of the "rule" conclude that a royalty rate based on an expected operating profit margin that provides the patent owner with 25% of the expected operating profits must generally be an equitable division of the economic profits between a licensor and licensee. In practice, experienced patent valuation analysts have observed that the actual percentage may vary significantly above or below 25%. In order to determine the applicable royalty rate under any particular facts and circumstances, the valuation professional must perform a more in depth analysis.

Valuation analysts can use "stochastic" or probabilistic financial techniques such as the *Monte Carlo Method* to value a patent. The Monte Carlo Method uses a computer to simulate various sources of uncertainty that may affect the patent's value and then to project the patent's value. The average projection can be determined and the volatility and other sensitivities can be observed from the resulting histogram of projected values. The Monte Carlo Method is not a valuation method, but simply a financial analysis technique. It must be applied to a valuation model based on one of the three basic approaches.

Sources of Value

A patent valuation analyst identifies the cash flows from a patent by examining the sources of patent value. In general terms, a patent derives its value through one or a combination of the following sources: (1) using the patented technology to increase sales of the patent-owner's products or to increase the profit margin on these sales or both; (2) licensing the patented technology to generate cash from use of the technology by others; (3) strategically restricting competitors from using the technology, or preserving an option value derived from the right to use a technology in the future that today has little or no value; or, (4) a variety of generic sources, including an active enforcement program that generates royalties with the aid of the legal system.

Just as there are several sources of patent value, there are several dimensions to patents that may be relevant to their value. Technical experts and legal experts will often describe patents in different terms, each stressing dimensions important to their view of the patent. For example, the technical person may speak of the "elegance" of the solution the patent provides, while the legal expert may comment on the "tightness" of the language used in the patent claims. Each of these viewpoints is important and can help to reveal the sources of a patent's value. However, for simplicity, we propose a two-dimensional framework to analyze the sources of patent value.

Analytical Framework

Our proposed framework evaluates the subject patents along vertical and a horizontal dimensions. The vertical dimension measures the patented technology's relative contribution to the profits generated by the sale of a product. This dimension is measured by the *Profit Contribution Ratio* (PCR), which is defined as the value added to the product by using the patent's benefits, divided by the total profit earned from the product. For clarity, the *product* is the ultimate good or service purchased by the consumer. Whenever the embodiment of a patent significantly differentiates a product from its competitors, this ratio will be high. For example, the market for disposable razors is highly competitive. Most of the disposable razors available have similar performance characteristics and sell at low price points. However, Gillette's MACH 3 razors contain patented technology that improves their performance and allows Gillette to charge a premium for its product. Based on casual observation, this premium is significant and implies PCR is high. Alternatively, some products contain patented technology that may be important but that does not add significantly to the profits from the sale of the product. If a product contains a patented feature that is one of many features and this feature is not particularly important to consumers, then the PCR will be low. This is true of many modern consumer electronics, which contain dozens of features, many of them patented. If the patented feature is not particularly important to consumers, then the patented feature likely adds little profit as a percentage of the total profit on the product and therefore the PCR ratio is low (see Exhibit 6.2).

The horizontal dimension describes the number of possible methods of accomplishing the functionality provided by the patented technology. The axis is labeled *Practicable Alternatives* (PA) and ranges from Many to Few. This dimension measures the "uniqueness" of the technology described in the patent. Some patents describe a feature that can only be accomplished through a small number of methods. For example, industrial abrasives are made by coating a medium with diamonds. A common problem is ensuring the diamonds are not dislodged from the medium. In general,

EXHIBIT 6.2 **SOURCES OF PATENT VALUE**

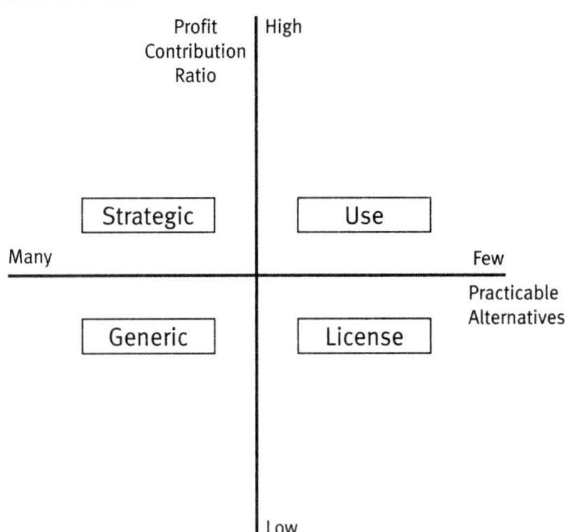

Source: Grant Thornton LLP.

there are only three methods to ensuring the diamonds remain attached to the medium: Form an electrical, chemical, or mechanical bond. If a patent covers one of these methods, that patent would fall to the right of this dimension on our scale. Alternatively, patents sometimes cover only one particular method of many possible methods to accomplish a particular goal. For example, increasing the time between battery recharges is an important goal to many consumer electronic manufacturers. There are dozens of patents that provide technology to accomplish that goal. While each technology is unique, no one technology provides the ideal general solution to maximizing the life of a battery. Therefore, these patents would fall on the left side of the PA scale. Using these two dimensions, we can explore the likely principal source of value for various types of patents.

Use of the Patented Technology

Patents that contribute a relatively large percentage of a product's profit and describe one of few methods of accomplishing the functionality of the patented invention (that is, they bear a High PCR and Few PA) would fall in the upper-right quadrant. An example would be patents that

EXHIBIT 6.3 **CASH FLOWS RELATED TO PATENT**

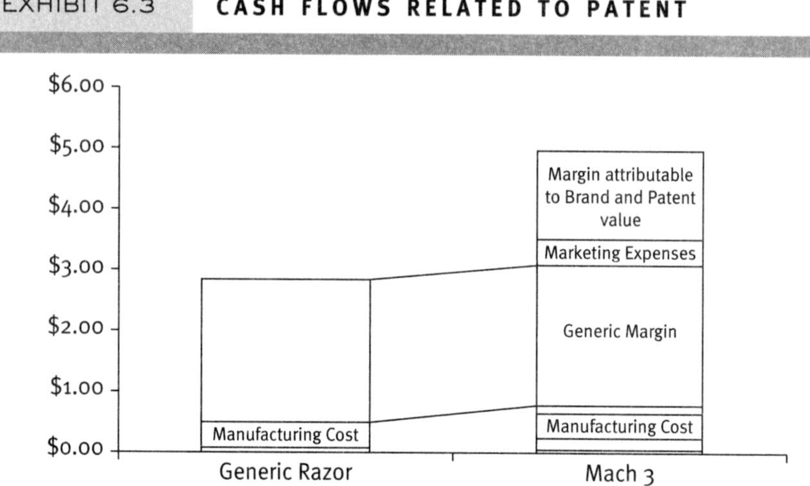

cover pharmaceuticals, such as Lipitor or Viagra. Patents in this quadrant are typically used by their owners in a tactical manner. These owners manufacture products covered by the patents and tend not to license their use (See Exhibit 6.3).

The patent valuation challenge is to separate the increase in sales volume or increase in resulting profit margin from the expected future use of the patented technology (see Exhibit 6.4). Once this increment is determined, the valuator can use the income approach to estimate the economic benefits from the patent to determine its value. For patented technology that is closely related to an end product, this process can be relatively straightforward. In the case of Lipitor, the patented technology is the product the doctor desires to prescribe. To estimate the value, one must estimate the number of prescriptions and the likely profit per pill, and account for the possible alternative treatments. While there may be numerous complications, the number of variables requiring estimation is relatively small and therefore, the valuation exercise is straightforward.

License Patent Rights

Patents that describe one of few ways to accomplish the functionality of the invention but contribute a relatively small amount of profit to the product (Low PCR and Few PA) fall into the lower-right quadrant.

EXHIBIT 6.4 **MANAGING IP RIGHTS FOR MAXIMUM RETURN**

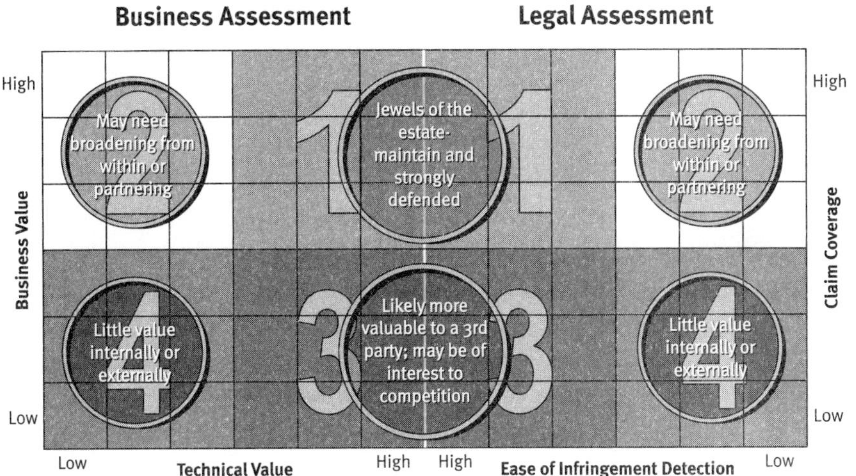

This chapter analyzes patent value by examining two dimensions, Practicable Alternatives and Profit Contribution Ratio. Alternative structures that have been proposed by various practitioners include Anaqua, which presents patents from a business and legal perspective in four values to help owners organize and maximize return on their patent portfolio. Anaqua provides software services for managing IP rights.

Source: Anaqua

These patents are often characterized as being only a small part of a "larger" product. For example, automobiles contain hundreds of features that are important to consumers. Most features contribute only a small fraction of profit of the automobile. A patent covering a particular type of turn signal indicator or particular type of tinted glass would fall in this quadrant. Patent owners typically license these patents even if they manufacture products coved by the patents because they can earn extra revenue without significantly affecting their competitive position. Similarly, since these patents add relatively little profit to a product, the ownership of the patent does not provide an economic justification to support the manufacture of the product, which implies that licensing is the most likely source of value from the patent.

Often, this source of patent value is the simplest to identify and value. If a patent has been widely licensed for a significant amount of time, then the valuation analyst only needs to project future royalties to determine its value. Firms such as Dolby Laboratories, Qualcomm, and Mosaid hold large portfolios of patents that have been extensively licensed.

The present value of the expected future royalties payments make up a large percentage of the value of these firms.

Valuing patents in this quadrant that are not licensed can be difficult because their value is often entwined with other, unpatented features. For example, a patented tread design could be an important feature of an automobile tire. However, there are many additional features beyond the tread design that factor into the customers' purchase decision. Features such as tire speed rating, existence of white walls, tire profile, expected tread life, and manufacturer reputation may all be considered by the customer. The challenge to the patent valuation expert is to separate out these effects and isolate the value provided solely by using the patented tread design. The patent valuation expert may be able to accomplish this goal by comparing the profits generated by tires that contain the patented tread design with the profits from similar tires that do not contain the patented tread design.

Strategically Restrict Competitors

Patents that contribute a relatively large percentage of the product's profits but have many alternatives (High PCR and Many PA) plot in the upper-left quadrant. While the patent owner may manufacture a product embodying the patented technology, the value of the patent often derives from more strategic sources. These patents may be used to restrict the actions of competitors by blocking access to certain technologies, or may be cross-licensed in pools to reduce conflict between major competitors.

If a patent owner uses a patent primarily to prevent others from marketing competing products or even researching alternatives to current products, he is employing a "blocking" strategy. Often, industry pioneers can employ this strategy because they have developed several generations of products already, and the early patents supporting those products discourage new entrants into the industry. The earlier patents create value by increasing the profit margins on the new generations of products which prevents new entrants from selling inferior prior generations at lower prices.

Alternatively, early industry entrants or those who have large numbers of patents may decide to cross-license the portfolio. Cross-licenses are agreements between companies that allow each to manufacture products covered by the others' patents. Often these agreements cover a company's entire portfolio of patents or all of the patents related to a division or subsidiary. These cross-licenses may benefit the patent owners by restricting entry into the marketplace. Many large companies have been accused of cross-licensing large pools of patents to discourage entry into the market for the products covered under the patents.

The value of patents used for strategic purposes is difficult to measure because you cannot easily determine the cash flows generated by the patents. That does not imply the cash flows are small. The cash flows could be substantial, but they are embedded in the profits from the sale of products covered by the cross licenses. Disentangling these profits is complicated by the fact that often no single patent can be identified as critical to the strategy.

Many semiconductor firms have extensive patent portfolios that are cross-licensed to competitors. Often this practice is described as providing "freedom to operate" because it reduces patent infringement actions between industry participants. Some have argued that these cross-licenses create value for the firms and the economy as a whole because they encourage innovation and avoid litigation over "old" technology. However, firms outside these cross-license relationships may be barred from entrance, thereby providing economic benefits to the parties to the cross-licenses. That blocking effect might mean the cross-licensed patents have significant value, but this value is extremely hard to determine.

Occasionally, one may gain insight into the value of patents held primarily for strategic purposes by examining transactions involving many patents. For example, in 2004 Broadcom announced the purchase of a portfolio of patents related to storage technology from Cirrus Logic, Inc.[5] Broadcom described the patents and patent applications as fundamental innovations in the magnetic and optical storage areas, including read channel and hard disk controller technologies. Broadcom paid $18 million for these patents. Since many companies manufacture and market magnetic and optical storage devices, it is unlikely that these patents are required to participate in this market. Therefore, the $18 million likely represents their strategic value as protection against potential infringement actions from competitors in the magnetic and optical storage device market. While it would be extremely difficult to identify the value of any one of these patents, the value of the portfolio may provide insight into the value of other portfolios of patents in the data storage industry.

Patent value may also result from the strategic preservation of rights to develop technologies in the future. A patent can be viewed as an option on future developments. That is, the owner has the potential to further develop the technology, but is not the obliged to do so if it is not expected to be profitable. A patent may cover a technology that is currently not marketable. The patent may not provide any tactical value or generate any licensing revenue today. However, the patent may still have value because the patent owner anticipates that a market for the patented technology will develop and he may be able to profit from this market.

There is widespread belief that the vast majority of patented technology is not embodied in products or services. Therefore this "unused" technology is either not valuable or it is "ahead of its time." Since significant resources have been expended to develop and patent the "unused" technology, it follows that patent owners must believe that many technologies are "ahead of their time" and their value will be realized in the future. To estimate the value of these patents today, there has been much work using advanced valuation techniques such as option-based methodologies and Monte Carlo analysis. Even with these advanced technologies, these patents are extremely hard to value because determining the cash flows associated with these future opportunities is arguably the most difficult source of value to quantify.

Patents in this quadrant have another interesting aspect. Sometimes a patent can be moved to the upper-right quadrant[6] through the establishment of standards. While there may be many methods of accomplishing the goal of the patented invention, once a standard method is established, there are few viable alternatives to the method. A patent that covers the industry standard method often moves to the right on our scale. Standard-setting organizations need to take specific actions to ensure that owners of these patents are willing to license these patents under reasonable terms rather than using the patents to prevent competitors from competing in the marketplace.

Other Sources

Finally, patents that provide only a small portion of the product's profit margin and are only one of many ways to accomplish the functionality of the invention (Low PCR and Many PA) fall in the lower-left quadrant. While these patents may be licensed, their small contribution to profits and the existence of multiple alternatives decreases the probability that someone would be interested in taking a license. These patents also generate little strategic or tactical value. However, you would be incorrect to conclude these patents are worthless.

Patents may provide value in a variety of other contexts. For example, there is evidence that large patent portfolios indicate an active research and development (R&D) program without regard to the value of the technology patented. It is possible that having a large patent portfolio increases corporate value because it signals the existence of a successful R&D program. This R&D program may generate technology that is included in current products, but the product cycle may be so short that the patents issue after the market has moved on to new technologies. Therefore the patent portfolio may have little market value, but still be highly valued as a signal of future corporate earning power.

Additionally, these patents may provide value through the legal system. Patent owners can receive compensation for infringements of their patent rights. Federal statute ensures that if a valid and enforceable patent is infringed, the patent owner will receive no less than a reasonable royalty for that infringement. Under certain circumstances, the patent owner may receive punitive damages and may be reimbursed for legal fees and costs. These payments for the infringement of the patent rights are cash flows related to the patent and a source of value.

As discussed in the opening paragraphs, estimating legal settlements is fraught with danger. The legal process is complex and notoriously difficult to predict. Yet many enterprising individuals and corporations have developed a business model around the gathering of patents to assert against participants in the marketplace. The value of patents involved in these actions is affected by the uncertainty of the payoff from litigation, the significant expense of litigating an infringement action, and the size of the potential royalty base. It remains to be seen if patent assertion litigation can sustain this business model over the long run.

Practical Application

Armed with this map, we can begin to understand some of the most complex issues in patent valuation. Consider the growing phenomenon of patent investors pouring substantial sums into the market to acquire patents from inventors in an effort to monetize them for a big return. How do these investors buy patents at a price below the expected present value of the royalty streams they often achieve by licensing them? In a word, it is because of the uncertainty.

Typically, the underlying patents sold by individual inventors or corporations to patent investors are non-core assets that fall in the lower-left quadrant. Low PCR and Many PA patents provide little incentive for alleged infringers or other potential licensees to spend money to determine: 1) the scope of the patented invention; 2) the legal enforceability of the patent; and, 3) the potential benefits of acquiring a license. Being economically rational, potential licensees do not spend any money exploring these three uncertainties and do not enter into negotiations to use the invention, or they assume their current activities do not infringe. A lone inventor often cannot exert a credible threat to a potential corporate licensee to justify his or her expense of substantial sums in resolving the uncertainty. As a result, the patent investor can arbitrage between the value of the patent to the investor and the value he or she can achieve in raising the stakes for the potential corporate licensee. In fact, the model works in part because the patent investor must be willing to buy many patents to find the one or two that represent substantial licensing returns. At times, the patent value realized by the patent investor closely approximates the value that would be negotiated between two manufacturers, one licensing to the other. However, the reality that the threat of a patent infringement suit and the cost associated with the defense of such actions is substantial can be leveraged by some patent investors into settlements that have little or no relationship to the patent value negotiated between manufacturers.

The map also helps us to understand why patent investors typically do not acquire patents that fall in the other quadrants. Unless both the PCR is Low and the PA is Many, other market participants have substantial incentive to resolve any uncertainty, and in doing so raise a patent's market value to the point were market arbitrage opportunities are squeezed out.

It is important to note that the use of the framework and its graphical illustration only indicates the most likely source of value for the various patents along the two identified dimensions. In certain circumstances, there may be other considerations that significantly alter the source of value for a particular patent. Additionally, this discussion does not relate to the actual value of the patents. For example, nothing discussed in this chapter indicates that patents in the upper-right quadrant are more valuable or have higher royalty rates than patents in the lower-left quadrant. This discussion is limited to the most likely source of the value, not the quantification of value. Nevertheless, there is significant analytical power in this simplified model that will enable you to identify and articulate significant sources of value for your patented invention.

ABOUT THE AUTHOR

James D. Woods, Ph.D., is a principal and the Economic Advisory Services practice leader for the Houston office of Grant Thornton LLP. Over the past ten years, Dr. Woods has assisted clients with a broad range of issues involving the valuation of various types of intellectual property. He has worked on projects with clients involved in numerous industries, including computer hardware and software, Internet transfer technologies such as TCP/IP and Voice Over IP (VoIP), microelectronics, and cellular telephones.

In addition to his practice at Grant Thornton he is an adjunct professor of finance for the University of Houston System, where he teaches business finance and financial statements analysis to undergraduate and graduate students. He is co-author of with Bruce Berman of "Patent Brands," which appeared in *From Ideas to Assets* (John Wiley & Sons, Inc., 2002). Dr. Woods holds a Ph.D. in finance from Texas A&M University, an M.B.A. from the University of Missouri at St. Louis, and a B.S.B.A. the University of Missouri. Grant Thornton LLP is the U.S. member firm of Grant Thornton International Ltd, one of the largest global accounting, tax, and advisory organizations. The firm has offices in more than 110 countries, including 51 in the U.S.

NOTES

1. I thank Nick D'Ambrosio for contributing the "Valuation Techniques" section of this chapter and for his and Crystal Leonard's editorial assistance.
2. Marc Tracy, "AT&T Wins Reversal of $156M Infringement Verdict," *Portfolio Media*, October 30, 2007; http://ip.law360.com
3. Mark A. Lemley and Carl Shapiro, "Probabilistic Patents," *Journal of Economic Perspectives*, Vol. 19, p. 75, 2005; http://ssrn.com/abstract=567883

4. Robert Goldscheider, Jason Jarosz, and Carla Mulhern, "Use of the 25 Percent Rule in Valuing IP," *Les Nouvelles*, December 2002.
5. "Broadcom Acquires Patent Portfolio from Cirrus Logic"; "Patents for Read Channel and Other Hard Disk Controller Technologies Further Strengthen Company's IP Position," *PRNewswire*, February 11, 2004.
6. The movement could also be to the lower right quadrant, but this is a separate topic. The important point for the discussion is that establishing a standard based on a particular patent tends to reduce PA.

CHAPTER 7

Measuring and Conveying IP Value in the Global Enterprise

BY JOE BEYERS

PERSPECTIVE How does a company know it has the IP rights it needs to succeed? How does it know it is receiving the proper return on them?

More innovative companies are accepting challenges to their IP strategy as an opportunity to strengthen their business model. Many businesses make patent licensing an intrinsic part of their revenue generation mix without determining whether strategic applications would ultimately have been more meaningful. The strong motivation to out-license is due in no small part to high profile patent cases and the huge damages awards reported in the media, as well as the high apparent profit margins associated with royalties. Indeed, it is easier to count licensing dollars (and euros and yen) than to understand the subtleties of how to best leverage patent assets. It takes a strong marriage of IP and senior management to survive challenges to a business' IP assumptions.

Vice President of Licensing at Hewlett-Packard, Joe Beyers, acknowledges that there is opportunity in out-licensing, but he also believes there is significant need for better management and performance measurement. "Given the risk inherent in such a [strategic IP] venture," says the former engineer and HP researcher, "it is critical that the board or executive team establish an appropriate set of performance metrics to ensure that a company's licensing activity provides true enterprise value and supports its business objectives."

(continued)

Beyers contends that performance measures that transcend simple cash generation are necessary for an effective corporate intellectual property licensing program. He presents a set of guidelines that both IP and businesses executives can share, and shareholders can follow.

For Beyers, IP return is only fractionally about licensing: "The second key metric [in addition to patent licensing] is what I call 'IP Value.' Quite often it is possible to obtain truly incremental profit for the company from IP in ways that do not directly involve the transfer of cash. This might be in the form of specific purchase discounts/rebates, elimination of current liabilities (such as royalty payments), or the gross margin on incremental product purchase commitments.

"While this can be controversial, it is important that performance credit be given to a licensing function for this type of financial benefit—particularly if it can be demonstrated that this value is tied to an IP transaction, is truly incremental, and has a profit impact in the current financial period. The critical factor for real value is the impact of the activity on the company's bottom-line profit rather than the form of this impact."

"In establishing goals for an IP licensing function," Beyers argues, "one needs to look not only at the revenue target, but also at the cost structure. While it may be widely believed that IP income is merely 'found' money and is nearly all profit. This definitely is not the case. In general, companies [that need IP] do not want to pay for IP, or if they do pay, they may not want to pay its actual value to the IP owner. Every IP licensing revenue dollar is a hard-fought battle that needs a significant amount of preparation, analysis, packaging, and negotiation."

Introduction

In today's fiercely competitive environment, a company must maximize the value it receives on its innovation investment. Typically this happens through the profits garnered on product sales or services revenue, but increasingly, companies are creating intellectual property licensing programs in an attempt to gain additional income beyond traditional revenue sources. Given the risk inherent in such a venture, it is critical that the board or executive team establish an appropriate set of performance metrics to ensure that a company's licensing activity provides true enterprise value and supports its business objectives.

This chapter outlines performance measures for a corporate intellectual property licensing program and presents a set of guidelines for what would constitute a successful program. Examples will show the true complexity of measuring the benefit of a patent licensing program and why a set of metrics, not just an analysis of cash flow or incremental profit, is required.

The perspectives described will be for a global enterprise with multiple innovative products sold in diverse locations. Some of the examples presented will be from my experiences as the head of Intellectual Property Licensing at Hewlett-Packard for five years, and others will be hypothetical models.

Strategic Intent of IP—A Changing Role

The first-level decision that a company's board or executive team faces is to determine the role of intellectual property in the company's business model. A service-oriented company will view the role of IP quite differently than a company that is investing large amounts in research and innovation. It is also important to realize that this role may change over time based on industry dynamics. Exhibit 7.1 shows an example of how this role has evolved in HP. The main focus by Bill Hewlett and David Packard was to develop and distribute innovative products that provided

EXHIBIT 7.1 **EVOLUTION OF HP'S IP STRATEGY**

Strategic Importance of IP	Timeframe	IP Actions by HP
IP creation to develop and ship products	50s & 60s	Main focus on shipping products
Use of IP to enable greater freedom of action	70s & 80s	Cross licenses with major companies
Use of IP to protect core product categories	90s	Enforcements of IP in selected products segments Rapid increase in patent filings
ADDED: Leverage of IP for Increased revenue/value	January, 2003	Launch of IP licensing function

significant, unique value to HP customers. The belief was that as long as the company kept providing this value, the company would be successful and others would not be able to innovate fast enough to catch up. Many innovations that were years ahead of the competition were not even patented.

The HP IP model shifted in the 70s and 80s. HP broadened into other product areas and soon realized that it needed to have IP licenses from other major companies to have operational freedom. At that time, limited focus was placed on enforcing HP's IP rights or licensing these assets to other companies. In 1975 I developed a patented invention and the claims of this patent might have read against many desktop multitasking operating systems. In a meeting in the mid 80s I proposed to Bill Hewlett and Dave Packard that HP could receive some significant value from this widely used patented invention. Their response was along the lines of, "No, we just file patents to ensure freedom of action for our products." Inventor Bill Hewlett was granted a patent in 1942 for HP's first product, the Model 200B oscillator.

This strategic model for HP changed again in the 90s. HP was starting to become challenged by "copycats" in several key product areas in which it held major investments. Printing technology was one such area. HP became more aggressive at defending its IP position in these few areas and also started a major ramp-up of patenting its inventions. This increase in the patenting process resulted in HP becoming one of the top recipients of U.S.-issued patents—HP has ranked between #3 and #5 in recent years.

For many companies, this focus on defense against copycats is the current strategic intent for their IP. At HP, this model changed significantly at a critical meeting of the HP board in January 2003. At that time, HP was a newly merged combination of four previous companies, all with a long history of innovation—HP (less Agilent), Compaq, Digital, and Tandem. With a research and development budget of $3.6 billion, and a strong innovation customer value proposition characterizing the HP products, the HP board decided to create a more focused program around protection and monetization of its IP assets. The majority of HP's IP was moved into a wholly-owned affiliate (Hewlett-Packard Development Company) to enable more top-level management of these assets, and the HP Intellectual Property Licensing function was created. In the five-year period that followed, the IP income for HP increased tenfold; HP's IP enforcement actions broadened; HP's IP has become the core of many new ventures; and the overall understanding of the value and importance of IP has materially increased throughout the company.

Structuring for Success—It Sounds Good But How Do You Get Everyone on Board?

A mandate from the board and the creation of an IP Licensing function are necessary steps in launching an effective IP licensing function within a large enterprise, but they are not the only actions required. For companies with little or no history in this process, the launch of this activity also requires a cultural transformation. IP now becomes a corporate asset, to be used to maximize overall enterprise value. Engineers, managers, and business unit leads can no longer think that they own their own IP and can independently manage and control it.

In HP, new review processes had to be established for business-related transactions that might encumber any form of the company's IP. In particular, a process was established (and also mandated by the board) in which every deal in the company that provided any form of an IP license or an agreement not to enforce an IP right had to be reviewed by the head of IP Licensing and that executive's legal counterpart. Over time, standard templates were created for classes of transactions so that the reviews focused more on exceptions or issues. In the past five years nearly 5,000 such transactions were reviewed and in nearly 50% of these deals the IP or business terms were significantly changed—to HP's benefit—as a direct result of this review process.

For a subset of the deals the head of IP Licensing also had to review these proposals with the Chief Technology and Strategy Officer, and for the first few years with the CEO—on roughly two-week cycles. There were also occasional reviews with the Technology Committee of the HP Board of Directors. These top-executive reviews helped to establish a common baseline agreement on HP's true strategic intent regarding IP, as well as on the licensing of this IP. This heavy top-level executive engagement greatly enabled broader cooperation across the company. Elements of these concepts were then put into a company-wide training class that has so far been attended by over 40,000 HP employees worldwide.

EXHIBIT 7.2 **THREE TYPES OF ENTERPRISE VALUE CREATED BY AN IP TRANSACTION**

Primary performance measure	Secondary performance measure	"Atta-boy" measure
IP Cash	**IP Value**	**IP Strategic Value**
Cash income that:	Other forms of value that:	Value that is likely to be beneficial to the company's operating profit but may be difficult:
a) Is tied directly to an IP transaction	a) Is tied directly to an IP transaction	
b) Is truly incremental	b) Is truly incremental	a) to accurately quantify or
c) Is "recognized" in the P&L	c) Is measurable	b) to prove that it was the sole/direct contributor
	d) Directly affects some aspect of the P&L	

Leveraging IP for Increased Value—But What Kind of Value?

Once a corporate executive team or board decides to drive an initiative to obtain additional value for its IP beyond product/service revenue, the next challenge is to determine the goals of the initiative and to measure its success or impact on the company. Exhibits 7.2 and 7.3 provide a model of a three-level set of metrics.

The first and probably the easiest to measure is the cash-income metric, which I call "IP Cash." This is the metric that one usually thinks of in an IP licensing function. This cash income is often from upfront IP payments, unit/revenue royalty payments, or ongoing milestone payments. In this model, other forms of cash payments should also be measured. These include equity cash payouts when equity in an entity had

EXHIBIT 7.3 **EXAMPLES OF ENTERPRISE VALUE CREATED BY THE IP LICENSING FUNCTION**

Primary performance measure	Secondary performance measure	"Atta-boy" measure
IP Cash	**IP Value**	**IP Strategic Value**
- Upfront cash payments - Royalty payments - Other cash payments, that may appear as a cost of sales or operating expense reduction	- Purchasing discounts/rebates - Elimination of current cash liabilities - Gross margin on incremental product purchases	- Reduction/elimination of litigation liabilities - Reduction/elimination of an assertion liability - Reduction/elimination of the potential cost of an IP License

originally been in the form of an IP payment, as well as other payments that might hit the cost of sales or operating expense lines instead of a normal royalty income line. The key criterion is that cash payments have a financial treatment that truly affects the company's bottom line in that particular financial period.

The second key metric is what I call "IP Value." Quite often it is possible to obtain truly incremental profit for the company from IP in ways that do not directly involve the transfer of cash. This might be in the form of specific purchase discounts/rebates, elimination of current liabilities (such as current royalty payments), or the gross margin on incremental product purchase commitments. While this can be controversial, it is important that performance credit be given to a licensing function for this type of financial benefit—particularly if it can be demonstrated that this value is tied to an IP transaction, is truly incremental, and has a profit impact in the current financial period. The critical factor for real value is the impact of the activity on the company's bottom-line profit, rather than what other forms this impact might take. In HP, we measure these first two metrics separately. More emphasis is placed on the IP Cash metric, yet the IP Value result can often be as large or larger than the IP Cash result.

The third type of metric, which I call "IP Strategic Value," is harder to measure. This involves the use of IP assets as an element of a broader negotiation or a negotiation that has a highly uncertain or very wide dynamic range of an outcome. In other words, the IP and the resources and processes behind it provide significant value to the company's bottom line, but there is too much uncertainty to pinpoint the exact amount. Rather than declare a value and credit it towards the performance measure of the licensing function, it is typically better to attribute general value to strategic performance and acknowledge its benefit broadly. Otherwise a firestorm of controversy might be created that could potentially undermine the integrity of the two other more quantifiable forms of value (IP Cash and IP Value).

An example of an IP Strategic Value deal might be the following: Your company is in litigation and you believe that it will likely lose the case and be subjected to a $100M payout. Your IP licensing team ramps up its assertion engine and finds or acquires IP to launch a strong counterattack. The result is a settlement in which your company pays only

$10M. One can argue that this IP action was worth $90M in savings to the company, but it is very difficult to truly predict the outcome of a jury trial, a set of appeals, and the size of the legal fees that would have really been spent to achieve a final adjudicated outcome.

IP Cash/Value—Who Gets the Benefit?

When the company's executive team/board has decided to initiate an IP licensing function and use the IP Cash and IP Value metrics to measure the function's performance, the next question is, "Who gets the 'Cash/Value'?" Some companies have created completely separate entities with independent profit and loss centers to drive this type of effort. In a global enterprise (and in most normal operating companies), that is a mistake. The model in HP is that the IP Cash flows to the "relevant" business unit—or in other words, the business or businesses that have the strongest tie(s) to the relevant IP. This structure is absolutely critical in securing strong business unit support for the IP licensing activities. A "pseudo-P&L" is still maintained for the licensing function to properly track its total profit impact (including all related costs) on the company, but the actual financial benefit flows directly to the business units' profit and loss statements. The gauging of licensing-related costs will be discussed later in this chapter.

While this financial flow model may be appropriate for a global enterprise such as HP, there are situations where the reverse may be more appropriate. In a global enterprise, it should be possible to have approximately 5–8% of the company's operating profit derive from IP licensing. At the other extreme, there are companies whose sole business model is IP licensing. Many other companies are more of a hybrid with a moderate product revenue stream and a relatively significant IP-licensing function. Once the IP-related profit reaches about 25% or more of the total, an independent and separate profit and loss function should be considered.

Revenue Recognition—So You Get the Cash, But Can You Count It?

One of the more frustrating elements of running an IP-licensing function is to close an IP-licensing transaction, receive a significant amount of cash for the transaction, and then not be able to recognize the cash as income (and credit against your performance measures) for years into the future. Elements of a specific IP transaction that may not have originally seemed to be core to a deal can potentially result in substantial delays in when the revenue for the transaction is recognized. In general, the head of an IP licensing function would usually prefer that the revenue for a transaction be recognized before retirement.

The final determination of the revenue recognition for a particular IP transaction is, of course, decided by a company's financial function, often working in collaboration with the company's auditors. I do not intend to offer any specific financial advice on this matter, but the following are some issues that should be considered for several different types of IP transactions. Any one of these six factors can have a major impact on when the IP-related profit benefit receives recognition, whether of the IP Cash or IP Value type.

1. Patent Licenses
   - Can past usage be separately valued and recognized?
   - The effect of a term vs. life of patent license
   - The effect of future captured patents or future wild cards
   - The effect of the first few licenses on a standards-based license program
2. Technology licenses
   - The recognition of NRE payments
   - The impact of service and warranty provisions
3. Contingency fees
   - Recognized as an operating expense or revenue reduction?
4. Blended deals
   - IP deals with customers of the company's other products or services
5. Patent acquisition costs
   - Expensed or amortized?
6. Accounting method
   - Cash received or accrual-based?

Understanding the timing of recognized benefit is very important to properly measure the value that an IP licensing activity brings to a company. While a set of goals and performance evaluation metrics needs to be the base for the current financial period, the future value created should also be a performance metric. The challenge is that for a particular

IP transaction, the licensing function may be only able to recognize—for example—$50K in the first year, but the deal may have an expected case income stream of $100M cumulative over the next five years. At HP we measure this via two separate goals. There is an IP Cash metric for the current fiscal year and there is also a metric for what I call the "tail." This tail is the expected case of the revenue to be generated over the first five years of a particular IP transaction (including the first year). Thus, for each IP transaction, we measure the actual results in the current year and the expected case projection in the first five years. These two numbers are measured against a current-year financial objective in total and against a total tail-value creation for all newly closed deals in a given year.

The net dynamic complexity of this situation can be demonstrated by studying Exhibit 7.4. This is a hypothetical example showing that in 2007, $100M of IP Cash revenue was recognized from deals that closed in the previous years and $20M was recognized for deals that closed in 2007. Question: Was this a good year for the operation or not? The goal for 2007 was $130M, so one can argue that the organization missed. On the other hand, the deals that closed in 2007 have a five-year expected case of $300M in revenue—far exceeding the target of $200M. Whether

EXHIBIT 7.4 **IP REVENUE RECOGNIZED OR FORECASTED BY YEAR DEAL CLOSED—HYPOTHETICAL EXAMPLE**

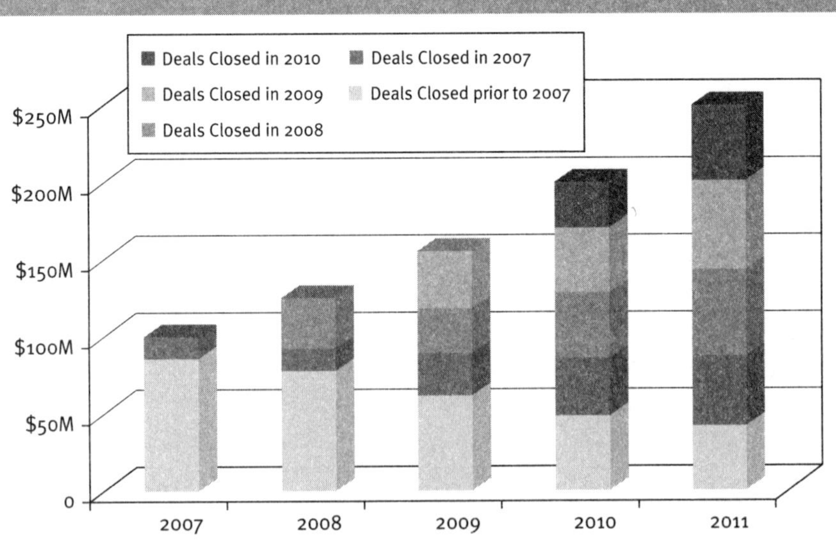

the executive team/board fires or promotes the manager of this function depends upon how the corporation trades off the short-term versus the long-term benefit of the IP revenue. Either way, it is vital that both types of financial metrics be established and tracked. It should also be noted that the size of the tail that is created is an early indicator of when and at what level the IP income for a licensing function that is in a ramp-up mode will ultimately level off. In this example, if the size of the tail created in a given year remains $300M for two or more years, it is probably a strong indicator that the licensing revenue will grow to this level and then level off. It is important to track this so that the cost structure of the licensing function does not grow too fast or reach too high of a level.

One additional point: I strongly believe that the financial goals for a particular fiscal year should be annual rather than quarterly. Of course the financial function wants strong quarterly smoothness and predictability. However, most IP-licensing activity is lumpy, dynamically changing, and highly uncertain. Sub-optimal results are obtained if a function has to scramble each quarter to meet a quarterly boundary. At HP, for example, we have over 150 active licensing projects. At least five to ten projects change status in some way each week. Each licensing project has a rhythm that, if artificially disturbed, can materially affect the value of the outcome.

Specific Business Models—What Are Reasonable Financial Goals?

In establishing goals for an IP-licensing function, one needs to look not only at the revenue target, but also at the cost structure. While it may be widely believed that IP income is merely "found" money and is nearly all profit, this is definitely not the case. In general, companies do not want to pay for IP, or if they do pay, they may not want to pay its actual value to the IP owner. Every IP licensing revenue dollar is a hard-fought battle that needs a significant amount of preparation, analysis, packaging, and negotiation. In addition, the different forms of IP licensing feature different investment and execution models. Exhibit 7.5 lists five such licensing models. Each one has a different cost model, revenue recognition timeframe, and degree of engagement aggressiveness (which often relates to the risk in doing or attempting the transaction). For a typical

EXHIBIT 7.5 **COST STRUCTURE OF THE IP LICENSING BUSINESS SEGMENTS**

	Business Segment	Ave Cost	Cost Drivers (top 3)	Revenue Recognition
Friendly	Technology Licensing	10–20%	Technology nurturing Technology analysis Business development	Long tail
Friendly	Brand Licensing	15–20%	Quality assurance Partner management Business measurement	Flat with some growth
Friendly	Patent Sales	5–20%	Sales agent fees Patent analysis and maintenance Business development	Upfront
Less Friendly	Standard Licensing	10–20%	Pool fees Patent analysis and maintenance Business development	Long tail
Less Friendly	IP Assertions	25–35%	Litigation costs Legal claim charting Counter assertion analysis	Lumpy
	Blended average cost	**20% of IP revenue**		

global enterprise driving all five of these models, one should expect about a 20% overall net expense envelope for the realized IP income. A higher cost structure might result if one only did patent assertions, and a lower one if only patent sales are executed.

A hypothetical financial model for an IP-licensing function in a typical global enterprise could be the following: The company has $20B in revenue, $2.4B in operating profit, $1B in research and development, and $200M in IP income (cash plus value). Securing $200M in IP income requires $40M in annual expenses—about half expended in the corporate IP licensing function and the other half a to cover business unit and litigation costs. The operating profit from the IP-licensing function is $160M—6.7% of the company's total profit. My belief is that global enterprises that are considering the potential to start an IP licensing function should consider this type of financial model as a benchmark set of objectives. Of course, these levels cannot be reached in the first year of the creation of such a function. There is a ramp-up time for the resources and infrastructure for such a function that could take two to three years. In addition, a complex IP transaction typically has an 18–24-month "time to money" life cycle. Ultimately, achievement of this type of financial model within five years of inception should be viewed as a very successful IP licensing venture.

TRADEOFFS—SETTING THE GOALS AND MEASURES OF SUCCESS

The old adage, "Be careful what you ask for as you just might get it," is very applicable in setting goals for a corporate licensing program. The true measure of the success or failure of such a function is not just whether the financial metrics are achieved, but also the methods or actions used in achieving these objectives. A licensing program that realizes $XM in licensing income can negatively impact the future operating profit of the company by many times this number if prudent steps are not taken in the licensing actions. Such a scenario could emerge if, for example, critical IP is licensed to a competitor, resulting in the company losing its competitive advantage in a major product line. Another example would be a case in which a brand license action is taken that damages the image or value of the brand.

In addition to establishing a set of metrics for a corporate licensing program, the board or executive team also needs to establish a set of governance processes to better ensure that the total enterprise value is optimized in the IP-licensing actions, not just the value of the IP income. The governance process needs to provide for an appropriate set of "checks and balances," but not be so cumbersome as to significantly slow the effective execution of the licensing program.

A critical element of an effective governance process is to define the critical IP stakeholders—functions that can be materially impacted by an IP licensing action. There are three general categories of such stakeholders. The first consists of the major business units of a company. A particular business unit (BU) becomes a stakeholder in a proposed licensing transaction if the transaction:

- Affects the IP created by or utilized by the BU
- Affects a major supplier or customer of the BU
- Affects a major partner of the BU
- Affects a major competitor of the BU
- Creates a potential IP counter assertion risk for the BU

The key business unit individuals that get most engaged in these discussions are usually the chief technologist, the business general manager, and the IP or patent attorney that supports the BU. Quite often, the chief technologist is the primary driver of the IP strategic issues for the BU.

A second stakeholder is the corporate marketing function, which usually is accountable for the integrity of the brand or brands of a company. They are a critical stakeholder in any transaction that involves the licensing of a brand of the company.

The third stakeholder category is the broader legal function. Most IP-licensing projects involve a triad of resources—business (licensing), technical, and legal. The legal resources that are directly part of a licensing project play a critical role in the project strategy and execution process. In some projects other functions within the legal organization become additional critical stakeholders. For example, the litigation section plays a key role in a patent assertion action. They may need to assess the analysis that was performed of the potential counter assertion risk to the company, or to assess the relative strength of the assertion case should the project ultimately lead to litigation. Patent sales is another area that involves a broader legal engagement. In that scenario, a cross-company analysis of licensing encumbrances on patents may be necessary for a patent sale.

The following table summarizes the key decision stakeholders for the five major types of IP licensing actions:

IP License Type	*Key Stakeholders*
1. Patent or technology License	Relevant BUs
2. Patent assertion	Relevant BUs, Legal function
3. Standards licensing	Relevant BUs, Legal function
4. Brand licensing	Relevant BUs, Corporate Marketing
5. Patent sales	Relevant BUs, Legal function

Another critical element of an effective governance process is the method for resolving disagreements between the IP-licensing function and the relevant stakeholders on the direction or desirability of an IP-licensing transaction. There often can be differing views on whether the transaction is in the best interest of the company—even though all parties are evaluating the opportunity based on truly maximizing the company's total enterprise value. These divergent views are usually due to differences in understanding, access to information, experiences, differences in projections of future trends or potential actions that other companies might take, or differences in the individual's or the organization's aversion to risk. Having the financial benefit of an IP transaction flow to the relevant BU as discussed in Section IV above definitely improves the likelihood of alignment with these stakeholders. Nevertheless, disagreements still are likely to occur. It is extremely important that a well-defined disagreement resolution process exist to address these issues quickly and effectively.

There are three important steps in the issue resolution process. In Step #1, a discussion is held between the stakeholders and the head of the IP-licensing function. My experience has been that in the vast majority of cases (estimated to be over 90%), the improved understanding by the relevant stakeholders and the IP-licensing function has resulted in agreement on a course of action. This resolution has ranged from agreeing to the original proposal, to an agreement to not proceed, to an agreement on a new approach. If agreement is not reached in this discussion, then Step #2 is a discussion with the stakeholders, the head of IP licensing, and the company's Chief Technology and Strategy Officer. If the disagreement arose from the legal function stakeholder, the company's General Counsel is also involved. In the five years of the existence of the HP IP-licensing function, all disagreements have been resolved by this step of the process. If such an agreement is not reached, Step #3 is a review by the CEO.

The result of this governance process is that there is clarity on the decision-making process and a shared understanding of the relative benefits and risks of an IP transaction.

Summary

A successful intellectual property licensing program is vital to the success of innovation-based companies such as HP. Licensing a company's IP can provide significant value and thus enable a greater return on the company's innovation investment. Execution must be consistent with the company's overall strategic objectives and have the discipline to make the proper tradeoffs to maximize the total enterprise value, not just maximize the cash stream for licensing the company's IP. The company's board and executive staff also need to carefully define a set of performance metrics and approval processes to drive the right focus and speed of execution, while assuring the right holistic behavior and actions. In addition, the company must have the foresight and patience to realize that this return can be unpredictable in both size and timing.

Implementing a corporate IP-licensing program with the right balance of objectives is no easy task. However, done effectively, it can be extremely rewarding. I often tell my staff that, when faced with difficult tradeoffs in the execution of HP's IP-licensing program, "Well, if it was easy, they could just hire trained monkeys to do the work."

ABOUT THE AUTHOR

Joe Beyers is the Vice President of Intellectual Property Licensing at the Hewlett-Packard Company. He is responsible for patent licensing, technology licensing, brand licensing, standards-based licensing, and patent sales and acquisitions for HP, as well as for being a key driver of IP strategy for the company.

In his 33 years with HP, Mr. Beyers has held a number of positions, starting as an engineer on operating system design and then as the lead inventor of the world's first 32-bit computer chip. He then led M&A and technology partnership activities for HP, followed by a lead role in corporate strategy. He was also previously headed of a number of HP worldwide software businesses. Mr. Beyers holds an MS in Electrical Engineering from the University of Illinois (1975) and a BS in Computer Engineering (1974); he received the Distinguished Alumni Award from the University of Illinois in 2007. His chapter, "Managing Innovation Assets as Business Assets," appeared in *Making Innovation Pay* (John Wiley & Sons, Inc., 2005).

CHAPTER 8

Strategic Patents and Return On Investment

BY WILLY SHIH

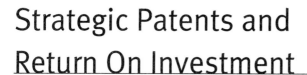

PERSPECTIVE Two decades of record-setting patent litigation damages awards, some in the billions of dollars, have captured the attention of everyone from Wall Street to the executive suite. Patent revenues are something managers and shareholders can relate to; intangible assets are not. With 90% or better profit margins, most managers agree that patent royalties go right to the bottom line and their impact can be discernable on even the balance sheet of a large company like IBM.

Harvard Business School professor and former technology company executive Willy Shih believes sees a dangerous pattern is emerging. This narrow view of how best to monetize IP assets can be dangerously shortsighted. "While patents can be turned into cash," says Shih who served in senior executive and development roles at Kodak, Silicon Graphics, Thomson and IBM, "greater and more enduring value often can be realized by making patents play a role in a firm's business strategy."

"Protecting a franchise by excluding others can generate extraordinary value," he continues. "Outside of patent licensing firms, few firms who are in the business of developing and selling goods and services in the information technology or semiconductor industries sue IBM for patent infringement because it is highly likely that IBM will have something in its portfolio to throw back at them. IBM's far-reaching portfolio positions

(continued)

the company with a favorable balance of power that forces competitors to negotiate cross licenses."

Shih says that despite the obvious accounting benefits it is frequently a mistake to put royalty income targets in the budget.

"Executives point out that giving the licensing team 'accountability' is important. This presumes that licensing professionals are otherwise unmotivated to deliver results. But it is too easy to adjust the budgeted numbers upwards late in a quarter, especially when it appears that the firm might otherwise miss that quarter. This puts the licensing team in the position of having to settle for a discount in order to bring a settlement in sooner."

Responsible senior executives and boards of directors, Shih points out, need to take the time to understand and consider the full range of strategic IP options, which frequently are worth more to an innovative company than the incremental cash from licensing.

With Patents, Cash is Not Necessarily King

Recent high-profile patent litigation awards have focused CEOs and investors on the value of a firm's patent portfolio. Fed by the media, many executives believe that a patent portfolio can be unlocked to provide a golden stream of royalties and incremental income.

This is a narrow view that can be extremely shortsighted—even dangerous. While patents can be turned into cash, greater and more enduring value often can be realized by deploying the patents in the firm's business strategy. This chapter will take a look at several ways a company with a significant patent portfolio might leverage intellectual property assets. It will start by looking at the intangible attributes of patents and then examine several examples of how patents can be applied, as well as some examples of the drivers of large differences in valuations. Finally, we will examine some strategies for maximizing value.

Valuing a Patent Versus Valuing a Technology

Patents provide an exclusive right of limited duration over a new and nonobvious invention, conveying to the inventor a right to exclude others from making, selling, offering to sell, or importing the claimed invention. This grant is intended to encourage innovation by giving inventors an exclusive period of benefit, in exchange for the early public disclosure of that invention so that later inventors can build upon that knowledge, either during the period of exclusivity provided they provide proper compensation, or after the end of the period of exclusivity.

But patent grants do not convey the right to make something. They grant the right to exclude others from using the patented invention. While this exclusionary right can be quite valuable, it is also intangible, making its valuation highly circumstance-dependent.

Patents tend to have a high fixed cost of acquisition, represented by research and development investments associated with developing the invention, and a negligible incremental cost not subject to the diminishing returns characterized by physical assets. Because intangibles are difficult to trade, and since active markets for intangibles are thin or do not generally exist, patents cannot be reliably valued.[1,2]

While there have been some efforts to systematically value patents,[3] in practice their value is set through infrequent but relatively conspicuous commercial transactions or through the outcome of litigation.[4] Though marketability is not a condition for asset recognition, the value of a firm's patents generally are not recognized as assets in the firm's financial statements. Research and development is usually recognized as a period cost and is expensed, and patents are then carried at a zero or nominal value unless they are acquired externally as part of an acquisition (FASB 141 and 142). Recent innovations in Internet-based technology exchanges and the developing market in patents have started to stimulate thinking and debate on the issue, but today there are few reliable, market-based ways to establish the value of a patent as a standalone piece of property. And what markets exist are still characterized by a lack of transparency.

Categorizing Patent Valuation

Assessing the value of patent rights is further complicated by the highly skewed distribution of observable values, with some patents worth a substantial amount, but most worth only a little. Many researchers have noted the wide range of values for a patent,[5,6,7,8,9] yet they persist in trying to build economic models for their valuation based on firm size or market structure, or they try to correlate them to research investment or use patents as a short-run indicator of R&D output. Examination of a sampling of valuable patents suggests some measures:

- A patent's *scope* in delineating and delimiting a franchise.[10] To the extent that a patent or portfolio of patents can exclude others from a profitable business franchise, those patents have a substantial accretive value. Excludability is quite dependent on field of endeavor.
- The extent to which a patent or cluster of patents can be subject to *substitution* alternatives. Composition of matter patents can possess a very sharp delineation, as chemical structure variation can have a dramatic impact on physical or chemical properties of a substance. The substitution of as little as one atom in a molecule can radically alter properties, as in the case of pharmaceuticals. Similarly in many high-tech industries, where products incorporate a wide range of technologies that are built on large cumulative bases of knowledge, patents that are non-foundational tend to be individually worth less, but substantial value can be created by careful portfolio construction.
- The degree to which a patent is foundational to later inventions, but is not itself built upon many others. An indication of where a patent might fall in such a hierarchy is the number of backward and forward citations. Backward citations point to prior inventions that it might be built upon, and forward citations indicate the extent to which it is built upon by others.

It is a combination of these circumstances that drive the valuation, but the wide range of fields and their differing scopes of coverage leads to a broad range. Let's look at some examples of how firms create substantial value for their strategies by examining some specific circumstances and characterizing the drivers of valuation. Then we will examine other examples of how firms use their portfolios, and the steps they take to maximize the effectiveness of those portfolios.

Protecting a Franchise by Excluding Others: Broad Scope, Sharp Delineation

Protecting a franchise by excluding others can generate extraordinary value. In pharmaceuticals, one patent (or a relatively small number of patents) can directly protect a large field of use. This is because a patent can describe a single chemical compound or class of compounds and its application to a specific therapy—"any new and useful process, machine, manufacture, or composition of matter, or any new and useful improvement thereof."[11] This broad scope characteristic is most observable in pharmaceuticals, though it is also evident in the field of catalysis and some classes of specialty materials.

Protecting a Franchise by Excluding Others: Broad Scope, High Cumulativeness, First-Mover Advantage

While pharmaceutical patents generally have attractive properties because of their broad scope and sharp delineation in usage, other technologies such as electronic communications or information technology have a somewhat different set of circumstances. Products in these fields often depend on a great deal of *cumulative* innovation. A personal computer embodies thousands of inventions in everything from microprocessor architecture and silicon process technology, to the mechanical and electromagnetic features of disk drives or the implementation of information displays and the devices that package or power the product. How does one value patents under these circumstances? The range empirically seems to go from very strong to very weak.

Frontier inventions, such as IBM's patent on the "Perforated Record Card" (punch card) and a sorting machine for these cards, can be foundational to a firm's early business.[12] When a patentee is able to file a broad scope claim to an entirely new field, those patents can embody tremendous value because they convey a significant first-mover advantage.[13] The early tabulating card patents were so valuable that IBM chose to lease its equipment only, and was able to accumulate rich profits. Texas Instruments successfully translated frontier work in semiconductor integrated circuits into an immensely valuable patent portfolio. While IBM was not the first mover in electronic computing, it's early aggressive investments in R&D, coupled with commercialization of first-mover products across the core computing and peripheral sectors produced foundational inventions like direct memory access (DMA), the dynamic random access memory cell, and rotating disk-based magnetic storage.

As these technology-intensive fields grew, R&D investments fueled explosions in innovations and patents. Patents on incremental improvements could come from many sources, and most products would necessarily employ many innovations. During much of the infant years of the computer industry, IBM was bound by its 1954 consent decree with the Department of Justice to "grant to each person making written application therefore an unrestricted, nonexclusive license to make, have made, use, and vend tabulating cards, tabulating card machinery, tabulating machines or systems, or electronic data processing machines or systems under, and for the full unexpired term of, any, some, or all IBM existing and future patents."[14] Other computer companies would negotiate cross-licenses with IBM, so patent valuation was manifested as freedom of action and access to competitors' technologies. It was difficult to exclude IBM from entering just about any technology field; for instance, its DMA patent was used by just about any product that used a computer.

An alternate driver of valuation became prominent in the early 1990s. This was the disruptive power of a patent that could address some narrow slice of the cumulative pyramid of inventions within a product. An inventor who held such a patent asserting a "right to exclude" could monetize that patent without necessarily having to engage in a product business. A landmark example was *Eolas Technologies Inc. v. Microsoft Corp.* in which a patent licensing firm used a patent from the University of California at Berkeley to attack a narrow feature in Microsoft's Internet Explorer Web browser and won $565 million at trial.[15] While this right to exclude has always been accepted as a fundamental notion under patent law, it was the collision with the dependence on cumulative innovation that attracted attention. It is also likely the root cause of the perception among many executives that isolated patents have value that is easily monetized.

The Importance of Time: Patent Life and the Development of Substitutes

Firms who pioneer new areas and also possess a strong patenting ethic can develop profitable franchises by aggressively "picket fencing" a field with a thicket of patents. The 3M Company was a first mover in the light management films used to produce uniform backlighting in liquid crystal displays (LCDs). John Martens' U.S. Patent 4,576,850 for "Shaped Plastic Articles Having Replicated Microstructure Surfaces" assigned to the 3M Company was one of the frontier patents in the field of plastic light management films that would distribute light uniformly to the back of an LCD matrix. A mapping of the backward and forward citations for this patent demonstrates the pivotal role it plays in the field (see Exhibit 8.1). Filed in 1978 in the early days of development of back-lit LCDs, it cites eight prior patents, mostly in materials. But the '850 patent is cited by 272 patents (forward citations), including 6,621,973 "Light guide with protective outer sleeve," and 7,220,026 "Optical film having a structured surface with offset prismatic structures." The '973 patent cites 54 patents, and the '026 cites 43 patents, in both cases including key 3M patents on reflective film and retroreflective articles. Exhibit 8.1 illustrates the web of interlocking patents that 3M filed over the course of the early development of LCD backlights. Further examination of forward

EXHIBIT 8.1 **BACKWARD AND FORWARD CITATIONS OF 3M '850 PATENT**

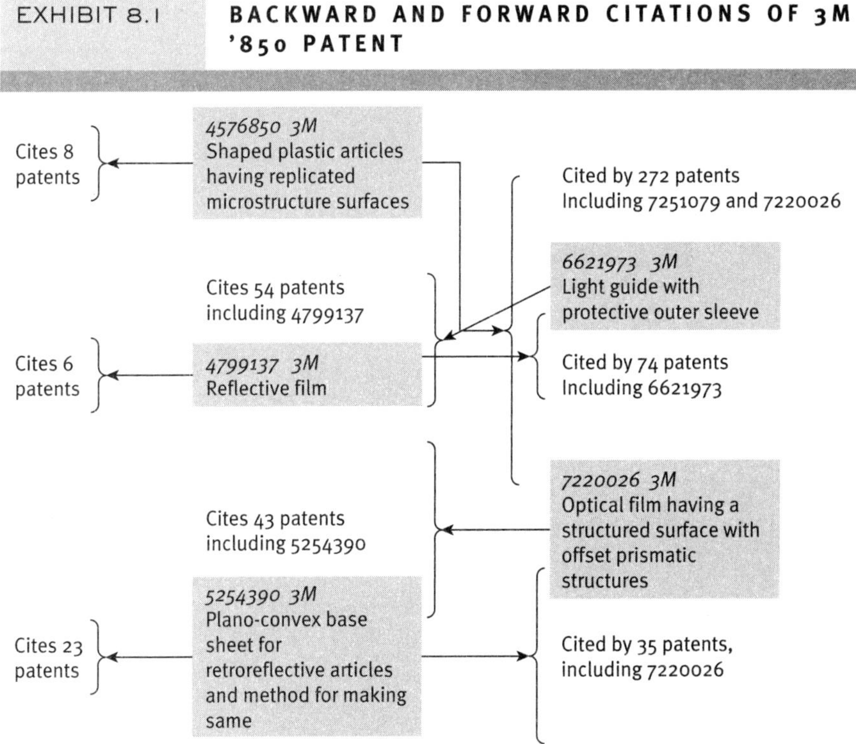

citations reveals that these 3M patents are in the web of backward citations for many other companies. GE has numerous patents in the field because of the interests of GE Plastics in applications of polycarbonate, but invariably they all trace backward to 3M patents.

What does one learn by studying the 3M patent tree? 3M was not the only inventor in the category of patterned plastic films, but through a deliberate process of patenting foundational concepts, and aggressively building an interlocking web that delimits application to a narrower area, they succeeded in effectively forestalling competition.

Arguably the foundational '850 patent is worth a lot, but the real value is expressed with the interlocking web. 3M's Display and Graphics segment accounted for typically 16–17% of overall company revenues for the period 2003–2006, but a substantially higher proportion of overall company profits (see Exhibit 8.2). Net income for the segment was almost a third of revenues, and Display and Graphics includes things besides just light management films. During this interval, the LCD panel business (manufacture of LCD display subsystems) experienced rapid growth, driven by the sales of notebook computers, flat panel displays, and flat panel televisions. But there were very few substitutes for 3M's light management films, and short supply ensured strong pricing. The hyper-competition

EXHIBIT 8.2 **3M COMPANY: DISPLAY AND GRAPHICS SEGMENT AS COMPONENT OF TOTAL 3M COMPANY**

(Dollars in Millions)	**2002**	**2003**	**2004**	**2005**	**2006**
Display and Graphics Segment					
Revenue	2,228.00	2,962.00	3,406.00	3,558.00	3,765.00
Net Income	534.00	885.00	1,131.00	1,159.00	1,062.00
3M Company Total					
Revenue	16332.00	18,232.00	20,011.00	21,167.00	22,923.00
Net Income	3,046.00	3,713.00	4,578.00	5,009.00	5,696.00
Display and Graphics % of Total 3M					
Revenue	14%	16%	17%	17%	16%
Net Income	18%	24%	25%	23%	19%

among panel manufacturers ensured cutthroat pricing on finished panels. The search for cost savings and profit among panel manufacturers in turn drove a search for substitutes, which started to appear in 2006. These patents added considerable value to simple polycarbonate plastic for a long time. Heavy investment in patenting can build significant barriers to entry, or delay the onset of competition.

Strategic Use of Patent Portfolios

Some valuable applications of a firm's IP portfolio include enabling access to strategically important fields, warding off attacks from competitors, and imposing structural cost differentials.

Since a patent is a right to exclude and not a right to use, having patents in a field does not give a firm the freedom of action to practice in that field. This is a painful realization for many young firms trying to enter active fields such as nanomaterials, where there has been a lot of patenting by others. It is also a challenge for new entrants in mature technologies, where incumbents have large patent bases. Freedom of action is not always readily obtained. Developing, purchasing, or otherwise obtaining *some* portfolio, even with limitations, can help a firm to gain access to a field that is strategically important to its business.

An example of the value of freedom to practice comes from the inkjet printer industry. IBM's immense patent portfolio enabled it to receive royalty-free cross licenses from Hewlett-Packard (HP) and Canon, Inc. (and others). HP and Canon had both laboriously built comprehensive inkjet portfolios over the previous decade. In 1990, when IBM spun out its Office Products Group as Lexmark International, the new company inherited those agreements.[16] The printer ink business had been immensely profitable for HP and Canon and they clearly would have preferred not to license their portfolios and let another player into the field. One former HP executive claimed bitterly that the value of the cross license was worth billions of dollars in lost profits to HP. Lexmark could not have existed without the cross, so how much were the patents worth?

Unfettered access to a field can be valuable, especially as it enables the growth of a firm into adjacent and complementary markets with its business model or distribution system.

Attacking a Competitor or Imposing a Structural Cost Differential

Though it was perceived primarily as a photographic film company, the Eastman Kodak Company actually had an early interest in digital cameras. Its Research Labs produced its first model in 1976. Kodak's pioneering R&D investments led to many frontier patents, as part of a portfolio of close to one thousand patents spanning a wide swath of the technology. Kodak researchers invented core technologies such as the Bayer pattern color filter array, a technology that enabled the use of a single sensor for full color capture in still and video cameras. As the consumer digital camera market took off around the year 2000, it became evident that the market would become highly fragmented and dominated by East Asian manufacturers. Kodak could try to stop the market with its patent position. That was not really practical nor would the marketplace view that as a constructive use of those assets. By choosing instead to license its patents, Kodak could ride the crest of a rising technology wave, and impose a structural cost on its competitors in what was an intensely competitive and mostly loss-making business. Though license income was not disclosed publicly, that income stream helped finance many initiatives within Kodak.[17]

Many firms prefer to pay a one-time fee for a paid-up license to a patent to avoid this dilemma. Prospective licensees usually are able to secure such a deal from a patent owner, because an immediate cash payment that would boost earnings in the current quarter is quite attractive and paid-up deals are easier for both parties to negotiate. Smart patent owners should consider whether a running royalty is more valuable.

Warding Off Attacks

Outside of patent-licensing firms, few firms who are in the business of developing and selling goods and services in the information technology or semiconductor industries sue IBM for patent infringement, because it is highly likely that IBM will have something in its portfolio to throw back at them. IBM's far-reaching portfolio positions the company with a favorable balance of power that forces competitors to negotiate cross licenses.

Compare this to Microsoft's position when it was a young company and had not developed a substantial portfolio. In the early 1990s Microsoft became embroiled with Stac Electronics over the inclusion of a data compression feature that it called DoubleSpace in its DOS 6.0 operating system. Stac sued because Microsoft had done due diligence on the code when it had previously discussed licensing Stac's technology. A California jury awarded $120 million in compensatory damages. Microsoft eventually settled, but not before it pulled DoubleSpace from its product. As a wealthy company without an extensive portfolio that a company like Stac might need a cross-license to, Microsoft became a "target."

By the late 1990s Microsoft realized the importance of investing in portfolio building. It launched initiatives aimed not only at filing patents, but at building up its sophistication in licensing and managing incoming litigation. The patent filing process has a relatively long incubation time, however, and it was not until 2006 that the company began to appear in the upper ranks of patent filers.

Is R&D Solely for the Purpose of Generating Patents a Sustainable Business Model?

Can inventions be separated from the business of commercializing products? This is the premise employed by more and more firms who find commercialization and go-to-market difficult or too risky.[18]

There are reasons a pure R&D plus patent licensing model is difficult to sustain:

- Many of the best patents result from commercialization work. It is during the reduction to practice that many obstacles to practical implementation are encountered, and the resulting solutions are the source of many inventions. Even UOP (now a division of Honeywell), a legendary developer and licensor of catalysts and process technology for the petroleum refining, gas processing, and petrochemical industries, maintains a large engineering staff to help licensees implement its patented technology.
- The invention–filing–enforcement lifecycle tends not to have a time horizon that is matched to that of investors, who are incented to maximize short-term revenues. Patent awards are generally outside of the horizon of most investors today, and enforcement is even farther out.

- Frontier patents with high valuations usually come from basic research in new technologies. Practical commercialization tends to be outside the horizon of most investors. In the technology sector, foundation patents in new fields may not be realized in mass market products for ten years or more. It can take four years or more to get a patent filed and awarded, and then the invention must be used in products. Enforcement depends on usage in products or services, and it can take quite a few years for a large enough market to develop to make enforcement worthwhile.
- The likelihood of conceiving the kinds of broad scope, sharp delineation inventions with a low threat of substitution described earlier is very difficult in fields that have a lot of attention and competing research. Getting this type of a portfolio necessitates working at a much earlier stage of development, before the field gets crowded. That is more and more difficult these days.

Thinking Strategically about Patents

How should executives think about fashioning and maintaining their patent portfolio? Focus on the scope and content of the firm's portfolio, and be prepared to defend it.

Some think size is all that matters. Some Asian companies have accumulated large portfolios. Hitachi, Samsung, Canon, and others are high on the annual list of top filers at the USPTO, and some are also aggressive purchasers when patents come on to the market (see Exhibit 8.3). While strength in numbers is helpful, the quality of patents is more important. Motivated competitors can attack weak patents with prior art, obviousness arguments, or litigation. Quantity can mitigate the size of balancing payments, since few firms want to crawl through patents one by one when negotiating renewals. The knowledge that a particular firm has a strong portfolio can also ward off attacks if that firm signals accordingly.

Keep the Portfolio Current with Business Needs

Filing and maintaining patents is an expensive burden. Keeping the portfolio forward-looking and anticipatory of future strategic directions helps to focus this spending. Successful cross licenses also come up for periodic renewal,

EXHIBIT 8.3 **TOP 20 PRIVATE SECTOR PATENT RECIPIENTS FOR 2006**

Rank	Firm	Patents Granted
1	International Business Machines Corp.	3,621
2	Hitachi, Ltd.	2,581
3	Samsung Electronics Co., Ltd.	2,451
4	Canon K.K	2,438
5	Matsushita Electric Industrial Co., Ltd.	2,360
6	Hewlett-Packard Development Company, L.P	2,111
7	Intel Corp.	1,959
8	Sony Corp.	1,906
9	Toshiba Corp.	1,820
10	Micron Technology, Inc.	1,673
11	Siemens A.G.	1,622
12	Fujitsu Ltd.	1,487
13	Microsoft Corp.	1,473
14	General Electric Co.	1,414
15	Koninklijke Philips Electronics N.V.	1,355
16	Seiko Epson Corp.	1,200
17	Infineon Technologies AG	914
18	Fuji Photo Film Co., Ltd.	906
19	Texas Instruments, Inc.	883
20	Sun Microsystems, Inc.	849

Source: Intellectual Property Owners Association, "Top 300 Organizations Granted U.S. Patents in 2006."

and maintaining ongoing strength in licensed portfolios is a way to preserve income streams, or avoid a shift in the "balance of trade" where past royalty payers become recipients instead. Many Asian firms that have licensed Western technology in the past are intently focused on shifting this balance of payments, anticipating that when the license comes up for renewal, the rate will decline and eventually the direction of royalty flow will reverse.

Maximize Coverage of Key Detectable Art

There is little point in patenting inventions that are not detectable. This is often the case in process technology, though increasingly it is coming into play in semiconductors, where the complexity of a device is high and the cost of reverse-engineering to demonstrate infringement is out of reach for even the most sophisticated litigants. More and more firms protect such inventions as trade secrets, or recognize that time-to-market is the more important competitive advantage.

Supplement with Strategic Purchases

It is almost impossible for a firm to develop all of the ideas around its new technologies. It is challenging to get a sufficiently broad idea flow into the funnel, and it is even harder to make the right call on every possible investment decision. So there is no shame in acquiring patents, especially to buttress a position, expand the scope, or better delineate around a technology.

The cumulative nature of most new technologies, as we saw in some of the examples above, suggests that there is an accretive effect if one strategically acquires patents: the whole can very well be worth more than the sum of the parts. The same kind of methodical interlinking that we saw in 3M's light management film portfolio is a good model for building through acquisition. The examination of forward and backward citations, the identifying of key links that might be in the hands of a party that might not value it as highly—these are all good strategies for building strength through acquisitions.

Incorporate Patents into Standards

In the technology sector, network effects increasingly drive winner-take-most economics. Technologies like the GSM or CDMA mobile telephony standards, the MPEG video compression standard, or the VHS videotape standard demonstrated that increased network size provided positive feedback to members of that network, further enhancing the rate of adoption of those networks. Network effects are common in the information technology, communications, and consumer electronics markets.

Networks are facilitated by compliance with standards, as standards tend to reduce consumer lock-in and uncertainty. Many firms have recognized that incorporating their intellectual property into standards is a good way to secure a long-term advantage as well as an income stream. Most standards bodies now require patent holders to commit to the licensing of all comers at reasonable and non-discriminatory (RAND) rates. Though there have been some documented abuses, this has been a successful route for many firms to enjoy license streams as well as first-mover advantages in many technology products. The MPEG-LA license pool on essential patents for the MPEG video compression standard is an outstanding example of effective patent use. The pool enables the industry by providing one-stop shopping for users of the technology (thereby facilitating industry growth) and providing a rich stream of royalties to the holders of essential IP included in the pool.

Be Willing to Litigate

Litigation is the ultimate test of a patent. The process subjects the patent to intense scrutiny, with opposing parties motivated to establish for the record how the claims are constructed and to test the patent's validity. When a patent owner prevails in litigation, that patent becomes a matter of the law, and it is actually strengthened. The holder can then demand royalties from unlicensed parties, and will usually seek a higher rate than it sought prior to litigation. If it sets a running royalty rate on the patent, that rate becomes the de facto standard. When Kodak litigated a set of patents with Sun Microsystems and prevailed in a jury verdict, it sent a message to other potential licensees.[19]

If however the litigation does not go to completion or the patent holder loses, the patent is often weakened. Prior art is usually carefully scrutinized, and depositions and trial testimony become part of the record that can be used in later litigation.

There are also intermediate points between these extremes. AT&T Lucent Technologies' reissue patent 32,580 (a reissue of U.S. Patent 4,472,832) described a foundation patent in digital speech coding. Lucent chose to litigate this patent against Microsoft Corporation, asking for $250 million in royalties.[20] When AT&T settled before the end of the trial phase, it received a significant payment. Had it gone all the way to a jury verdict and prevailed, it likely would have won considerably more. But it had to balance the risk associated with losing at the jury verdict against taking a settlement during the trial. It mitigated the risk by agreeing to a high-low settlement: a high amount if it prevailed, and a low amount if it lost.

Patent licensing firms ("patent trolls")[21] exploit market inefficiency and risk asymmetry in the litigation process. Because the cost associated with litigation is high, defendants often find that rational economics dictate early settlement. The specialist licensing firms often employ contingent legal fee arrangements so their risk is minimized. Thus while successful licensing firms will claim that their patents are of high quality because they have been exposed to litigation, it only takes one defendant to demonstrate otherwise. *Ampex Corporation v. Eastman Kodak Co.* is a demonstration of the perils of this approach. Ampex had prevailed against Sony Corporation, but Kodak adopted an aggressive counterattack and significantly devalued Ampex's sole assets in a hard-fought battle in Delaware court.[22]

Experience has shown that the willingness to litigate a portfolio is an important signal to potential licensees that the portfolio is strong and worthy of licensing.[23] Willingness to proceed is a necessary part of realizing maximum value in licensing or cross-licensing.

Short-Term Cost Benefit Trade-Off: Avoiding "Drug Addiction"

When a patent portfolio has been used to generate cash license income, that income is generally recognized within the current accounting period. Since R&D investments usually have been expensed and the portion of that investment that is traceable to the patents in question is unclear, many executives view license income as "found money." As the firm becomes successful licensing other targets, the cash stream starts to become significant. If this pattern starts to look regular or predictable, executives ask questions like, "Can you forecast it for next quarter or next year?"

The next step down the slippery slope is putting royalty income targets in the budget. Executives point out that giving the licensing team "accountability" is important. This presumes that licensing professionals are otherwise unmotivated to deliver results. But it is too easy to adjust the budgeted numbers upwards late in a quarter, especially when it appears that the firm might otherwise miss that quarter. This puts the licensing team in the position of having to settle for a discount in order to bring a settlement in sooner. Some would argue that the net present value of the money sooner is better than a higher payment negotiated later. Potential licensee targets recognize these economics as well, and quite a few have come to realize that the best time to settle a patent dispute is at the end of a fiscal quarter or year, particularly when the opponent is a Western company.[24] The author calls this "the road to (patent) drug addiction." A short-term perspective can lead to the wrong cost-benefit trade-offs, but it is the source of acrimonious debate in "addicted" companies.

The wide range of circumstance governing the valuations for patents, and the intangible nature of many of the benefits they convey suggest that patent licensing is not a simple mechanical process with a high degree of predictability. While many IP licensing professionals would like their bosses to believe that patent licensing is more art than science, the steady stream of income that many portfolios have been able to produce gives rise to the belief in many CEOs and CFOs that license income is indeed predictable and bankable. In fact, what they see is the statistics of a portfolio of transactions, and many of the features of good diversified portfolio construction apply here as well.

Where does one draw the line? Striking a balance between aggressive targets and giving the licensing team flexibility is important. Increasing discipline around infringement analysis and documentation, and litigation preparedness help. The goal should be to maximize the benefit to be derived, both from a cash perspective and a strategic perspective. This is the place for an educated judgment by senior management. Good licensing agents generally have a feel for how quickly income can be developed, as well as what trade-offs might be made to accelerate a payment. Too much pressure to deliver a predictable stream of license income can constrain licensees, and damage future potential.

How Does a Firm Know If Its Patent Strategy Is Successful?

In this complex, multifaceted field, success is sometimes fleeting and often hard to gauge. Some good indicators of IP success are:

- The firm's core business has the freedom to operate in key future directions where it sees its business evolving.
- The firm's employees recognize the value that a strong patent portfolio can bring, and contribute by appropriate patenting of their ideas.

- Financial value is realized either through strong strategic business positions buttressed by a strong IP position, or by monetary benefits conveyed through licensing or application of leverage.

A broad understanding of the different uses of a patent portfolio and of the processes associated with maximizing its value can strengthen the strategic position of a firm, and give it options it might not have otherwise considered. Responsible senior executives and boards of directors need to take the time to understand all of their strategic IP options in order to act upon them in a prudent and timely manner.

ABOUT THE AUTHOR

Willy C. Shih is a Senior Lecturer at the Harvard Business School, and is part of the school's Technology and Operations Management unit. Prior to joining HBS, Dr. Shih spent 18 years in the computer industry, principally at IBM, followed by stints at Digital Equipment Corporation and Silicon Graphics Computer Systems. He then spent eight years in consumer electronics, leading the establishment of Kodak's consumer digital business, and launching its digital still camera licensing program. This was followed by a position at Thomson leading Corporate Research and IP licensing.

Dr. Shih is an experienced practitioner in the field of intellectual property, having structured numerous IP licensing programs, with extensive work in license negotiations and litigation. He has two S.B. degrees from the Massachusetts Institute of Technology, and a Ph.D. from the University of California at Berkeley. He serves on the board of directors of Atheros Communications, Inc., Santa Clara, CA, Flextronics International, San Jose, CA, and is the Non-Executive Chairman of QD Vision, Inc., Watertown, MA.

NOTES

1. Baruch Lev, *Intangibles: Management, Measurement, and Reporting* (Washington: Brookings Institution Press, 2001).
2. F. Gu and B. Lev, "Markets in Intangibles: Patent Licensing," Parker Center for Investment Research Working Paper, 2001.

3. See for example, Robert Pitkethly, "The Valuation of Patents: A Review of Patent Valuation Methods With Consideration of Option-Based Methods and the Potential for Further Research," Judge Institute Working Paper WP 21/97, Cambridge CB2 1AG (1997); or James Bessen, "The Value of U.S. Patents by Owner and Patent Characteristics," Boston University School of Law, Working Paper Series, Law and Economics, Working Paper No. 06–46.
4. See for example, Ocean Tomo's auction, http://www.oceantomo.com/auctions.html
5. F.M. Scherer, "Firm Size, Market Structure, Opportunity, and the Output of Patented Inventions," *The American Economic Review* 55, No. 5. (1965): 1097–1125.
6. M. Schankerman and A. Pakes, "Estimates of the Value of Patent Rights in European Countries During the Post-1950 Period," *The Economic Journal* 96, No. 384. (December 1986): 1052–1076.
7. Zvi Griliches, "Patent Statistics as Economic Indicators: A Survey," *Journal of Economic Literature*, 28, No. 4. (December 1990): 1661–1707.
8. D. Harhoff, F. M. Scherer, and K. Vopel, "Citations, Family Size, Opposition, and the Value of Patent Rights," *Research Policy* 32 (2003): 1343–1363.
9. E. Schwartz, "Patents and R&D as Real Options," *Economic Notes by Banca Monte dei Paschi di Siena SpA* 33, No. 1. (2004): 23–54.
10. J. Lerner, "The Importance of Patent Scope: An Empirical Analysis," *RAND Journal of Economics* 25, No. 2, (Summer, 1994).
11. Section 101 of Title 35 U.S.C., http://frwebgate.access.gpo.gov/cgi-bin/getdoc.cgi?dbname=browse_usc&docid= Cite:+35USC101.
12. A. W. Mills, "Perforated Record Card," U.S. Patent 1,928,209, assigned to International Business Machines Corporation (February 7, 1930), and G. Lowkrantz, "Sorting Machine," U.S. Patent 1,982,216, assigned to International Business Machines Corporation (April 12, 1933).
13. Richard J. Gilbert and David M. G. Newbery, "Preemptive Patenting and the Persistence of Monopoly," *The American Economic Review* 72, No. 3. (June 1982): 514–526.
14. Section XI of *United States of America v. International Business Machines Corporation*, S.D.N.Y. 72–344 (1964).
15. *Eolas Technologies Inc. v. Microsoft Corp.*, N.D. Ill., No. 99 C 626, 8/11/03.
16. The license agreements permitted a change of control in the form that IBM used. This spin-off highlighted the importance of having proper change of control language vis-à-vis intellectual property in any cross-license agreement. The author speculates that the cross-licenses dated from a time when this was less of an issue.
17. See for example Kodak's Form 8-K for January 31, 2007, in which it states, "Gross profit margins were 26.4% in the current quarter, up from 23.0% in the prior year quarter. This was driven by operational improvements across the company's business units, most notably *Kodak Picture* kiosks, the *Kodak Gallery*, and the favorable impact of the previously noted licensing arrangements."

18. Nathan Myrhvold founded Intellectual Ventures on the assumption that patent ownership could be separated from product commercialization, just as IBM's 1969 unbundling separated hardware from software.
19. *Eastman Kodak v. Sun Microsystems, Inc.,* No. 02-CV-6074T, (W.D.N.Y. September 7, 2004).
20. W. Shih and K. Lustig, "AT&T v. Microsoft (A): IP Litigation Strategy," Harvard Business School, Case 9-608-080 (2007).
21. This perjorative term was coined by Peter Detkin when he was vice president and assistant general counsel in charge of patents, litigation, and licensing at Intel. Detkin subsequently joined Intellectual Ventures.
22. *Ampex Corporation v. Eastman Kodak Corp*, et al, No. 1:2004cv01373 (D. Del. October 21, 2004).
23. This statement applies to firms that are in the business of producing products and services. Specialist licensing firms are frequent users of litigation because their risk reward ratio is so different. They have so much more to gain and they use fear of litigation to extract settlements.
24. Watch for SEC filings at year end that indicate material transactions coming from licensing income to recognize this pattern.

CHAPTER 9

Patent Litigation: The Changing Economics of Risk and Return

BY RONALD J. SCHUTZ

PERSPECTIVE Patent litigation may be harder to win and more costly to engage in, but there still are opportunities for the right patents and patent holders to license. According to one of the nation's leading patent litigators, Ronald Schutz, winning a patent infringement case today is about objectives and risk management—it is as much a business decision as a legal one.

"While court decisions and some antipatent sentiment have made litigation riskier, more costly, and arduous than just five years ago," says Schutz, who with his firm is responsible for more than $2.5 billion in patent damages awards and settlements for clients, "opportunities for patient, well-capitalized patent owners still exist." Schutz contends that the economics of patent litigation have changed and that both plaintiffs and defendants need to look at the economics of a case, available data on trends, and less obvious legal merits—analyses that are not always performed.

"The definition of a 'win,' or what constitutes success, will depend on who the patent owner is and what the patent owner's objectives are. Practicing patent owners who are suing a competitor may have objectives ranging from putting their competitor out of business through an injunction to obtaining a cross-license to their competitor's patent portfolio. Nonpracticing patent owners who are also suing are probably only interested in money."

Alleged infringers need to understand what the endgame might look like for them and this can depend on who the patent owner is. "No

(continued)

alleged infringer should embark on a 'take no prisoners' litigation defense strategy without first conducting the same type of analysis that the patent owner should have conducted prior to filing suit." Research In Motion (RIM) comes to mind here. It could have settled a suit in 2002 for $50 million, but instead chose to play hardball. The result was a $612 million settlement and a lot of professional fees.

Among the overlooked facts presented in Schutz's chapter:

- The first strategic decision is the most important, (i.e., where to file suit). Filing suit in a favorable jurisdiction can substantially increase the odds of prevailing. But it is important to note that even favorable jurisdictions can have judges who don't like patent cases.
- Most cases settle.
- If a case doesn't settle at the summary judgment stage, the accused infringer is more likely than not to win.
- If the patent owner survives summary judgment, he is likely to win at trial.
- If the case proceeds to appeal, the accused infringer is likely to win.

The Only Constant is Change

There have been a lot of changes in patent litigation in just the past few years. While court decisions and some antipatent sentiment have made litigation riskier, more costly, and arduous than just five years ago, opportunities for patient, well-capitalized patent owners still exist. The threat of an injunction and paying damages are still formidable. The key, today, is risk analysis that encompasses the business, as well as the legal merits of a case. Because the landscape for patent litigation is not the same today as it was just a few years ago, it is important to take a fresh look at the economics of patent litigation and the risks associated with it. The bottom line is that for most patent holders, the risk of not being successful has increased and the potential returns have decreased. Conversely, for most alleged infringers the risk of an adverse outcome has decreased.

The PricewaterhouseCoopers *2007 Patent and Trademark Damages Study* concurs:

> Reduced filings of business method patent actions, recent Supreme Court rulings, the increased cost of litigation, and reduced damage

> awards have all conspired to put pressure on plaintiffs regarding their return on investment from IP lawsuits. Nevertheless, as long as companies continue to face fierce global competition, changing business environments, and a heightened desire to be first to market with products or processes, litigation to establish or preserve a market position and serve as a barrier to entry will continue to be a critical corporate strategy. Damages awarded in these matters are both a deterrent to potential infringers and a compensation for economic benefits lost due to the infringement.[1]

Executives faced with making decisions relating to intellectual property rights, and patent rights in particular, need a framework and data to guide their decisions. That framework will be provided in this chapter and includes a look at how the landscape of patent litigation has changed and what the effects of those changes have been.

The Rules of the Game Have Changed

The significant changes in the landscape of patent litigation have occurred primarily in the Supreme Court. Just recently, it was rare for the Supreme Court to decide a patent case. In the last few years, however, the Court has decided a handful of cases that have had a significant impact on patent litigation. The impact of these decisions has affected all players differently as will be pointed out later in this chapter. And the full impact of these decisions may not be known for several years. Two of these cases are specifically worth noting because of their impact on the risk/reward analysis.

The first significant change in the rules came with the Supreme Court's decision in *eBay v. MercExchange LLC*, 547 U.S, 126 S.Ct. 1837 (May 15, 2006) where the court made it much more difficult for a patent holder to obtain an injunction after winning at trial. Prior to this decision, courts routinely issued injunctions against companies found to have infringed a patent. This often put enormous pressure on defendants to settle. In fact, without threat of an impending injunction, it is doubtful that RIM would have paid NTP $625 million to settle the patent infringement case brought against the BlackBerry. In the MercExchange case, the Court made it very difficult for a prevailing plaintiff in a patent infringement case to obtain an injunction unless the plaintiff was a competitor of the defendant and could show irreparable harm absent an injunction. The effect of this decision is that licensing companies, such as NTP, no longer automatically have an injunction in their litigation arsenal.

Another significant change in the rules came through *KSR Int'l. v. Teleflex, Inc.*, 550 U.S., 127 S.Ct. 1727, 1734 (April 30, 2007). In KSR, the Supreme Court diluted the prevailing test for obviousness in favor of an arguably less stringent, more subjective standard. Prior to KSR it was rare for a trial court to find that a patent was invalid on the basis that the invention was obvious. The impact of KSR will be felt more in the short-term than in the long-term. Prior to KSR, patent holders did little in the course of litigation to defend against an obviousness attack on their patents because such an attack seldom carried the day. Now, patent holders will spend more time preparing to address this defense. In addition, as the Patent Office begins examining patent applications under the KSR standard, it will be issuing fewer but stronger patents. Patents issued by the PTO that have been granted based on the KSR standard could well prove to be extremely formidable in court. But it will take a few years before this scenario comes to pass. In the meantime, there will be a lot of litigation involving patents issued before the KSR decision.

In addition to decisions by Supreme Court, the court that decides patent case appeals from trial courts, the Federal Circuit, has also issued several significant decisions that make life more difficult for patent holders. A detailed discussion of these cases is beyond the scope of this chapter, but the decisions include cases that limit the scope of patent protection and make it more difficult to prove willful infringement.

The Rules May Change More

For the past several years, Congress has been considering various so called "patent reform" bills. The software industry has been the loudest voice for change while the pharmaceutical industry has been urging caution. Individual inventors and universities have also been urging caution. Given the amount of money spent on lobbying for passage of a bill, it is likely that some type of "patent reform" legislation will be enacted in the near future.

Some provisions of the proposed bills that will impact patent litigation include the following:

- Apportionment of damages
- Increasing the standard for finding willful infringement
- Establishing an administrative post grant review process for issued patents
- Restricting the locations where patent suits can be filed
- Elimination of the best mode requirement

If any "patent reform" legislation is passed, it is most likely going to make enforcing patents more difficult. Nothing in any of the proposed legislation is designed to make it easier or less expensive for patent owners to enforce their rights.

Risk/Reward Analysis

Any patent owner considering patent litigation needs to understand both the potential pitfalls and potential rewards. Further, the definition of a "win," or what constitutes success, will depend on who the patent owner is and what the patent owner's objectives are. Practicing patent owners who are suing a competitor may have objectives ranging from putting their competitor out of business through an injunction to obtaining a cross-license to their competitor's patent portfolio. Owners who are not practicing the patent being asserted are probably only interested in money.

Likewise, alleged infringers need to understand what the endgame might look like for them and this can depend on who the patent owner is. If the patent owner is a competitor, there is the risk of an injunction. If the patent owner is a licensing company, then there is very little likelihood of an injunction. This distinction alone may dramatically alter how an alleged infringer approaches the litigation.

Patent Litigation Is More Expensive

One common challenge affecting both plaintiffs and defendants is that patent litigation is expensive. Every two years the American Intellectual Property Law Association (AIPLA) issues a report on, among other things, the cost of patent litigation. The most recent report, issued in 2007, states that the cost of a case where more than $25 million is at risk at the third quartile is on average $7 million. The median cost is $5 million. Both of these figures are up substantially from six years ago and are likely to continue rising.

Why is patent litigation so expensive? Several reasons. The lawyers handling these cases often have very high billable rates. Senior partners at large East and West Coast firms charge $850–1000 per hour for patent litigation. Experts are also expensive, especially economic or damage experts. They too often charge rates equally as high, and sometimes exceeding, the senior partners on the case. And most cases often require several experts (damages, infringement, and inequitable conduct). The proliferation of electronic documents and the discovery of those documents has substantially increased litigation costs. Also, many cases require that discovery be conducted in foreign countries, which necessitates a lot of travel and the hiring of translators for documents and interpreters for depositions.

Risk/Reward from the Patent Owner's Perspective

Patent cases often hit the news, and reports of large verdicts and injunctive relief may tempt patentees to jump hastily into patent litigation without properly considering all of the costs. No patentee should initiate what is almost always a complex, hard-fought, long, and expensive litigation, without first carefully assessing the risks and rewards. In other words, the patentee should carefully identify the company's business objectives and determine whether it makes economic sense to file a patent infringement lawsuit. To arrive at this decision, the patent owner needs to consider:

- What is the best result? Is it an injunction to maintain exclusivity in the market, or past damages and a license agreement?
- How is the infringement affecting business? How does it affect licensing opportunities and/or royalty rates? Is the patent owner losing profits? Are products losing "shelf space" to the infringer or other competitors?
- If there is more than one potential infringer, who should the patent owner sue first? A patent owner should consider the strongest and weakest infringers and whether to sue more than one infringer at a time. A win against a weaker infringer may pave

the way against a stronger opponent. However, a larger infringer may learn from the mistakes of the earlier sued infringer. Another consideration is that if a patent owner is going to spend a dollar, it might be better spent pursuing a larger (and probably stronger) infringer because, if successful, there will likely be a higher return on the invested dollar. And if successful against a large strong infringer, all of the other infringers will probably come to the bargaining table very quickly.

- What is the potential damages recovery? Is it worth the cost and risk of litigation? The patent owner should realistically calculate the amount of money damages at stake, the longevity of the relevant market, and whether infringers can easily design around the patented technology.
- How strong is the patent? Can infringers easily design around the patented technology? Is the relevant field replete with prior art? A long, complex file history means that counsel may have to spend a substantial amount of time adequately explaining the file history to successfully deflect accusations of prosecution history disclaimer or estoppel. In addition, if the relevant field contains a large amount of prior art that can be used against the claims, counsel will need to spend more time and money to defend against contentions of invalidity or inequitable conduct.
- How strong is the infringement case?
- How long will litigation last and how intrusive will litigation be to the patent owner's business? Trial counsel will need to work with the inventors, in-house counsel, management personnel, and administrators to explain documents and act as witnesses and/or corporate decision makers. Opposing counsel may depose a number of employees. Third parties connected to the patent owner's business, such as customers, suppliers, manufacturers, and other business partners, could also be subject to subpoenas and depositions.
- Who will and should be involved? It is critically important for litigants to be aware that patent litigation generally requires the cooperation and extensive involvement of company employees and executives. Due consideration should be given to former employees—particularly inventors—who may be important witnesses.
- Will they cooperate? Are any of the critical witnesses disgruntled?

- Will the potential defendant(s) retaliate? A patent owner should keep in mind that a defendant may own an extensive patent portfolio. Litigation may prompt a defendant to retaliate with a suit alleging infringement of its own patent(s). Then, instead of looking at a return on the investment of litigation expenses, the patent owner is looking at spending money in an attempt to avoid an infringement finding and damages.

One way that some patent owners have changed the risk/reward analysis is to engage a law firm on a contingent fee basis to enforce their patents. In considering this option, it is important to understand that there are three relevant viewpoints: the patent holder, the law firm representing the patent holder, and the defendant.

When the patent holder retains a law firm to represent it on a contingent fee, it reduces its financial risk by shifting some or all of that risk to the law firm. As in any type of investing, however, reduced risk usually equals a reduced reward. The typical contingent fee arrangement entitles the law firm to a fee of 33–40% of any recovery. In some circumstances, there may be a sliding scale containing both higher and lower percentages than these depending on the stage of the case when the recovery occurs.

From the law firm's perspective, it is usually acting as a merchant banker (i.e., investing its own time and money). As such, the law firm will want a return on its investment that takes into account several factors including risk, the time value of money, and lost opportunity costs. In most cases a minimum return is 3:1. This means that to recoup a $5 million investment in time and costs, the law firm will need to be paid $15 million. Under a 40% contingency fee, this will require a recovery of $37.5 million.

If the defendant knows that the plaintiff's lawyers are handling the case on a contingency fee, it may change the way the case is handled and/or the approach to settlement. If the law firm handling the case has a reputation for successfully handling contingent fee patent cases and is well capitalized, the defendants will know that a scorched earth defense policy will not necessarily yield a better result. A scorched earth defense policy may be the right approach, however, if the defendant's firm does not appear to have the resources necessary to fight a long drawn out battle.

Risk/Reward from the Alleged Infringer's Perspective

No alleged infringer should embark on a "take no prisoners" litigation defense strategy without first conducting the same type of analysis that the patent owner should conduct prior to filing suit. In other words, the alleged infringer should also carefully identify its business objectives and determine whether it makes economic sense to fight or to consider a settlement. To arrive at this decision, the alleged infringer needs to consider:

- What are the worst- and best-case scenarios? Is it an injunction or only past damages and a future license agreement?
- How important is the alleged infringing product to the business?
- What is the potential damages recovery? Is it worth the cost and risk of litigation?
- Can the patent be easily designed-around?
- How strong is the patent? Is the relevant field replete with prior art?
- Does the patent owner have the financial wherewithal to aggressively pursue the case?
- What impact will a settlement have on future litigation against the company? Will the company be seen as an easy target for future plaintiffs if it settles early?
- How long will litigation last and how intrusive will litigation be to the business? Trial counsel will need to work with in-house counsel, management personnel, and administrators to explain documents and act as witnesses and/or corporate decision makers. Opposing counsel may depose a number of employees. Third parties connected to the business, such as customers, suppliers, manufacturers, and other business partners, could also be subject subpoenas and depositions.
- Who will and should be involved? Just as with the patent holder's considerations, it is critically important for litigants to be aware that patent litigation generally requires the cooperation and extensive involvement of company employees and executives. Due consideration should be given to former employees who may be important witnesses. Will they cooperate? Are any of the critical witnesses disgruntled?
- Do you have the potential to retaliate by asserting your own patents or other causes of action?

- The high reversal rate by the Federal Circuit.
- The more favorable landscape as a result of recent Supreme Court decisions.

Other Factors That All Parties Need to Consider

Jury Bias. In the assessment stage, counsel should not overlook an evaluation of possible jury partiality. Some jurors tend to be biased against large companies. For example, a 1998 national survey established that jurors felt "cynical and mistrustful of large corporations and their executives."[2] Skilled trial lawyers, who represent small corporations or individuals, can take advantage of these partialities to persuade jurors to side with "the little guy." Alternatively, pure licensing companies might not receive the benefit of this partiality, because some jurors might be biased against the fact that they neither manufacture the claimed apparatus nor practice the claimed methods.

Public Scrutiny. One often-overlooked consequence of initiating patent litigation (or even becoming an unwilling participant as a defendant), is the attention that patent suits now almost routinely receive in the press. While this consideration is rarely a reason not to file suit, counsel should direct management's attention (as well as the attention of the company's financial analysts) to this issue to ensure that any newsworthy aspects of the case are appropriately dealt with in the media or shareholder communications.

Impact on Stock Price. Depending on a number of factors, an adverse ruling in a patent case can impact a company's stock price. Sometimes the mere filing of a patent suit can have this effect. A recent notable example of this is the significant hit that Vonage's stock took shortly after going public when it was sued by Verizon. And in some circumstances an adverse ruling can result in a company going out of business.

Forum. Where a patent suit is filed can have a significant impact on the potential outcome. The firm LegalMetric reports: "For districts with a significant number of judgments in patent cases, the district with the highest win rate in favor of patentees is the Eastern District of Texas (44%). The district with the lowest win rate is the Southern District of Ohio (6%)."

Technology Involved. LegalMetric also reports that "the contested win rate (excludes consent and default judgments) for telecommunications cases is 33% while the contested win rate in software patent cases is only 18%. (The average contested win rate for all technologies is 25%.)"

A Report From the Trenches

Any analysis of the risks and rewards of patent litigation must be made in view of real-world data. This data should prove extremely useful to decision makers.

There are 94 judicial districts in the United States. As pointed out earlier, how patent owners and alleged infringers fare can vary significantly depending on the district in which the case is filed. The ten busiest districts as of the end of fiscal 2007 were the following (with total number of 2007 patent filings and percentage of total filings in parenthesis):[3]

- Eastern District of Texas (352; 12.7%)
- Central District of California (308; 1111%)
- Northern District of California (181; 6.5%)
- District of New Jersey (174; 6.3%)
- District of Delaware (147; 5.3%)
- Northern District of Illinois (128; 4.6%)
- Southern District of New York (104; 3.7%)
- Southern District of Florida (78; 2.8%)
- Northern District of Georgia (66; 2.4%)
- District of Massachusetts (57; 2.1%)

As a general rule: The busier the district the more favorable it is to patent owners. This is borne out of data compiled by LegalMetric which reports that the most favorable districts are Eastern District of Texas; Middle District of Florida; District of Delaware; Western District of Wisconsin; and the Eastern District of New York. None of the busiest districts are listed by LegalMetric as the least favorable districts (i.e., Southern District of Ohio, Southern District of California, Eastern District of Pennsylvania, Western District of Washington, and the District of Maryland.)

Professor Paul Janicke of the University of Houston Law Center has conducted several studies of patent litigation and published an article entitled "Patent Jury Verdicts: Myths and Realities" in *Intellectual Property Today*. Among his findings in analyzing patent case dispositions in 2006:

- 86% of patent cases are neither tried nor adjudicated in any other way, but settled.
- 7% of cases were decided by summary judgment with the majority in favor of the accused infringer.
- 2.2% were disposed of by jury trial.
- 0.9 % were disposed of by bench trial.

Professor Janicke also recently conducted a study of patent infringement verdicts for an organization called The Innovation Alliance entitled, "Moving Beyond the Rhetoric: Jury Damage Verdicts in Patent Infringement Cases 2005–2007." Professor Janicke looked at the results of 93 patent infringement trials from 2005 to 2007. He concluded that there is "no pattern of runaway jury verdicts in patent cases." He also confirms "that trial judges routinely review those verdicts and set aside awards that are not supported by the evidence."

As one would expect, the top ten awards include some huge verdicts, the largest being $1.5 billion. But that award was set aside by the trial judge, as were 3 of the other top 10 awards. The second largest award was $306,900,000 which was also set aside by the trial judge. There were 30 verdicts in excess of $10,000,000.

Professor Janicke's specific findings also show the following:

- In 22 of the 93 cases, the jury found no damages.
- In 13 of the 93 cases, the jury found damages of $500,000 or less.
- In 47 of the 93 cases, the jury found damages of $2,000,000 or more.

Of the 47 cases where the jury found damages of $2,000,000 or more:

- In 9 of the cases, the award was either set aside by the trial judge or the appellate court.
- In 3 of the cases, the trial judge found that the damages were not supported by the evidence.
- In 4 of the cases, the trial judge increased the damage award based on a finding of willful infringement.
- 21 of the cases are still under review by either the trial court of the appellate court.

The PricewaterhouseCoopers 2007 Patent and Trademark Damages Study presents some additional useful data that is largely consistent with the data presented by Professor Janicke:

The disparity in plaintiff win rates among jurisdictions is substantial, varying from 12 to 63%.

- The median award in 2005 was $6 million.
- The median award for jury trials is greater than for bench trials.
- Since 2000, 65% of patent damage awards have been based on reasonable royalties.

As we know from reviewing Professor Janicke's analysis of patent jury verdicts from 2005 to 2007, a case is not necessarily over after disposition in the trial court. The next stop is the appellate court. Probably the most recent and comprehensive analysis of what happens on appeal was presented in an article, again by Professor Janicke, with help from LeLan Ren.[4] This article examines cases that reach the Court of Appeals for the Federal Circuit and is based on data for 2002–2004. The article defines a win as a situation where at least one claim is ultimately found to be infringed and not invalid. Patent owners won 24.4% of the cases analyzed.

There are some obvious conclusions that can be drawn from this data.

- The first strategic decision is the most important, (i.e., where to file suit). Filing suit in a favorable jurisdiction can substantially increase the odds of prevailing. But it is important to note that even favorable jurisdictions can have judges who don't like patent cases.
- Most cases settle.
- If a case doesn't settle at the summary judgment stage, the accused infringer is more likely than not to win.
- If the patent owner survives summary judgment, he is likely to win at trial.
- If the case proceeds to appeal, the accused infringer is likely to win.

Conclusion

This data is likely to be sobering for patent holders and encouraging for accused infringers. But patent owners still win and sometimes they will win large verdicts. What few if any recent articles about patent infringement risk take into account, and they cannot, is the strength of the case at the start. Even though the environment has gotten tougher for patent holders, good cases will still be won.

ABOUT THE AUTHOR

Ronald J. Schutz is chairman of the Intellectual Property Litigation Group at the national law firm of Robins, Kaplan, Miller & Ciresi L.L.P. (Minneapolis, MN office). Robins, Kaplan was named by *The American Lawyer* in 2003 as IP Litigation Department of the Year. Mr. Schutz has tried several patent infringement cases to verdict, and his personal patent awards and settlements total over $500 million (his firm's totals $2.5 billion). His trial victories include *Fonar Corporation v. General Electric* (a patent infringement case in which a federal jury in New York awarded Mr. Schutz's client, Fonar Corporation, $110.5 million). The *National Law Journal* listed this case as one of the largest jury verdicts of any type in 1995. The case was affirmed on appeal in the amount of $103 million, and was cited by *IP Worldwide* as the largest patent jury verdict ever upheld on appeal at that time. Fonar Corporation v. General Electric Co., 107 F.3d 1543 (Fed. Cir.), cert. denied, 118 S.Ct. 266 (1997). The final award with interest was $128 million.

Mr. Schutz received his B.S.M.E. degree from Marquette University and is an honors graduate of the University of Minnesota Law School. After law school, he completed his undergraduate ROTC scholarship obligation by serving four years in the Army Judge Advocate General's Corps, where he tried approximately 20 felony jury trials. Mr. Schutz was named by the National Law Journal in 2008 to their annual list of the nation's Top 10 Winning Litigatons.

NOTES

1. This is a direct quote from the PricewaterhouseCoopers *2007 Patent and Trademark Damages Study*.
2. *See* Peter Aronson et al., *Jurors: A Biased, Independent Lot*, Nat'l L.J., Nov. 2, 1998, at A1.
3. "East Texas Now Busiest Patent Litigation Venue," *National Law Journal* (2007).
4. "Who Wins Patent Infringement Cases?" *American Intellectual Property Law Association Quarterly Journal*, Vol. 34, p. 1 (2006).

CHAPTER 10

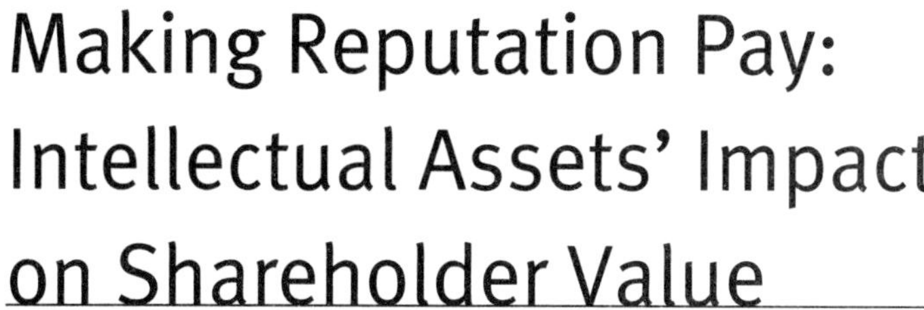

Making Reputation Pay: Intellectual Assets' Impact on Shareholder Value

BY JONATHAN LOW

> *Postindustrial enterprises run on intangible assets, such as information, research, development, brand equity, capacity for innovation and human resources. Yet none of these intangible assets appear on a balance sheet. That is another way of saying that, according to today's accounting practices, the worth of a brand name has no value.*
>
> —Walter Wriston, CEO, Citibank, 1969–1984

PERSPECTIVE A company whose reputation for quality or innovation precedes it is worth more than one that is less clearly understood. This is also is true for a business's intellectual property assets, which are heavily influenced by reputation.

Jonathan Low, a management consultant who focuses on how reputation impacts brand and other IP assets, says that in an acutely competitive environment where knowledge is capital, perceptions matter a great deal. Low contends that most public companies are at risk because they do not have accurate, detailed knowledge about the components of their reputation. "The sustainability of an organization," he says, "its very

(continued)

license to operate—may depend on how financial, reputational, and human capital markets value the impact of such investments."

Companies like Intel, IBM, and Microsoft have long benefited from the perceived impact of their innovation. Intel Inside is a deft mix of patent and brand value where the perceived sum is greater than the components.

The perception of greater value helps create a virtuous circle, says Low, where patents and other forms of IP help create competitive advantage, which in return throws off higher than average profits. This helps fund strong research, for which patents are a proxy measurement, assisting in the recruitment of great minds who in turn create still more value. In addition, given the need for global strength, such companies are better positioned to win others to their web of alliances.

"The cost basis [for IP assets] may be low in accounting terms but the return may be above average—or as economists refer to them, 'offering excess rents'—because the market has expanded to include potential bidders whose outlook is 'strategic' rather than strictly financial."

Quantifying brand and other IP values, and communicating them to the right audiences, has become a powerful resource in a global environment where brand name products and technology cross borders at lightning speed. IBM's sale of its ThinkPad division to China's Lenovo was an IP asset as well as a business transfer that was made more viable by positive global perceptions of a brand and the patent value associated with it.

The Reemergence of Reputation

Prior to the adoption of conventional accounting methods in the late 19th century, a person's reputation—the ultimate intangible—was the basic building block of business acceptance. Ironically, in the hyperconnected, technologically dominated global economy of the early this century, reputation is once again a crucial determinant of success. There are several reasons for this: the volatility of information makes it easier to build, ruin, and sometimes rehabilitate a reputation (e.g., Robert Nardelli of GE, Home Depot, and Chrysler) so that organizations are less able to manage it; the global nature of business, with its geographical, linguistic, and cultural differences, makes reputation a relatively uncomplicated base on which to build a commercial relationship; and the service-oriented economies of virtually all post-industrial nations demand that value be generated from intangibles like reputation rather than the performance or cost of tangible assets like property, plant, and equipment.

Intangibles such as reputation, research and development, communications, brand, and IP may account for 50 to 80% of corporate market value in an increasingly service-based economy. Institutional investors have reported in surveys that more than 35% of their portfolio allocation decisions are based on intangibles. A *Forbes* magazine report on the 25 most valuable corporate brands, which included such companies as Procter & Gamble, Coca-Cola, Microsoft, and GE, demonstrated that some corporate brand values are greater than the parent company's market value. Related research has established causal relationships between inputs such as IP and outcomes such as sales growth, market share, and stock price performance. Extensions of this research have further demonstrated the impact that communications about these intangibles has on financial and operational results.

The implications of this methodological approach are significant. The demands of global markets, with their emphasis on comparability of data, standards, and greater transparency are requiring institutions in the private, public, and not-for-profit sectors to provide more data about their allocations of people and capital. The markets are further demanding that the efficacy of these investments be demonstrated. In this acutely competitive environment where knowledge is capital, perceptions matter. And *perceptions of reputation* are particularly vulnerable to manipulation. That most public companies do not have accurate, detailed knowledge about the components of their reputation is a significant risk. The sustainability of an organization—its very license to operate—may depend on how financial, reputational, and human capital markets value the impact of such investments.

In the IP context, patent importance generally refers to the number of times that a patent is referenced in other patent applications. One can argue that patent importance is therefore a measure of patent reputation. In addition, however, the prominence of a corporate reputation also influences patent importance because patent *trolls* and others will invariably search for patents filed by corporations with prominent reputations.

The supposition is that those patents may have greater value. There are two industries in which this is particularly prevalent; technology and pharmaceuticals. In the tech context, Intel, IBM, and Microsoft have long benefited from the perceived value of their patent portfolios. Google now enjoys that same advantage.

The perception of greater value helps to create a virtuous circle; patents and other forms of IP help create competitive advantage that throws off higher than average profits. This helps fund strong research, for which patents are a proxy measurement, assisting in the recruitment of great minds who consequently create still more value. In addition, given the need for global strength, such companies are better positioned to win others to their web of alliances. Sony learned from the Betamax video debacle in which its highly respected technology was defeated as the global standard by JVC's VHS format. Many critics considered Beta the superior solution, but JVC created the winning commercial alliance. Sony rebounded, recently prevailing with its Blu-ray technology over Toshiba's DVD-HD format. In this instance, the combination of superior patented technology, combined with a viable business strategy, won the global competition.

In pharma, the value of corporate performance is often tied to the strength of the patented research pipeline. However, challenges from developing nations and the relentless demand for less expensive solutions has led to a wholesale restructuring of the industry. Creation of Contract Research Organizations (CROs), alliances with or acquisitions of biotechnology firms, and related strategic business decisions have all sought to capture the value of research patents while spreading costs over a wider array of potential funding sources. The major pharmaceutical companies, commonly referred to as "Big Pharma," have seen their role shift to that of consolidator, marketer, and packager as research shifts to the most efficient level. However, *reputation* for superior research—and a history of life-saving patents, helped Merck weather a series of legal challenges as well as recover its former preeminent position as a source of valuable patented research. Conversely, the loss of patent protection for many of its major drugs, combined with a failure to replace them with drugs of similar economic value (and the concomitant impact on its stock price) led to the early retirement of Pfizer's CEO and the company's restructuring.

Intellectual Property as a Global Differentiator

While the technical valuation process will be discussed further in this chapter, of greater importance is the recognition by managers and investors that IP and other intangibles have a value that can be monetized. The elements of the reputation that form the basis for that valuation must first be established.

To gain entry into the global value chain, a business must convince customers, suppliers, investors, and lenders of its reliability. To attain that status, companies must identify and communicate information about their intellectual property: their processes, procedures, standards, and governance; their ability to innovate; the quality of the training their employees receive (and frequently the rigor of the background checks to which potential employees are subjected before hiring); as well as the quality of their products based on recognized international standards. In 2007, China suffered a serious blow to its reputation as a global supplier based on safety issues related to the lead content of toys, the pollution of foodstuffs from dog food to farmed fish, illegal toxic additives to pharmaceutical ingredients, degradation of the environment, and abusive working conditions. While it would be premature to announce that China is no longer the global manufacturing platform of choice, this consistent stream of ugly revelations has led corporations to recalculate the cost advantages of basing in China versus regions closer to home in which standards and the absence of bad news may reduce the cost of regulatory scrutiny, legal ramifications, and the reputational cost to the company itself.

The harsh reality of global sourcing requires that no company wastes time or resources due to the continuing pressure from lower cost suppliers in other geographic locations. In particular, no company can underestimate the potential impact of an asset like IP in which it has invested or in which value may be accruing in spite of the fact that it may not meet GAAP standard criteria. Intangibles like patents and other IP must be recognized and managed as business assets even if they do not yet qualify as financial ones. In fact, it is not clear that the so-called GAAP standard is even particularly meaningful anymore; companies continue to search for beneficial ways in which to disclose their information. As of late 2007, over 400 public companies produce supplements to their annual reports on such issues as sustainability, child labor, product quality, and other matters. Growing global wealth, especially in developing nations, combined with technological advances, leads to decrease in the opportunity for sustainable competitive advantage because competitors, lenders, shareholders, suppliers, and customers all have access to more information. With that power, they can make better judgments about what actions are in their own best interest. To achieve even first-mover advantage for a short period of time, effective utilization of every corporate asset becomes a significant competitive differentiator. That means that training, process improvements, knowledge support, and other functional applications of intellectual capital are critical to global success.

Intangibly Denominated Objectives

The challenge for managers and investors who accept this precept—or those who may remain skeptical—is the lack of comparable quantitative measures by which to evaluate success or failure in attaining intangibly denominated objectives. From a financial, regulatory, and managerial perspective, the component participants in the global economy have been unable—or unwilling—to define values that impact organizations' abilities to allocate capital, to make adequately informed internal investment decisions, or to communicate value to the capital markets. This kind of valuation analysis is not going to become a governmental function (though governments may eventually mandate it). That means it will be up to each organization to develop its own priorities, procedures, and measures for brand value, reputation impact, and other intangible determinants of positive or negative economic activity. Of the approximately 400 U.S. companies currently producing supplements to their annual reports about various elements of their intangible value chain. Examples include Nike, Timberland, GE, and Eli Lilly.

The reasons for the lack of interest or will in the public policy arena are numerous. First, there has been a lack of perceived need. The assumption has been prevalent that Tobin's Q or goodwill are adequate explanations for the impact of intangibles on economic value. While these are useful concepts from the standpoint of economic theory, they are no longer acceptable in a universe in which 50–90% of a public company's market value is attributable to intangibles.

Secondly, there is considerable unease about who stands to gain or lose from the codification of intangibles; significant segments of the economy in which assets such as software and other manifestations of intellectual property could arguable be treated as costs or investments. The tax and related financial impacts of those decisions vary depending on whether one is a creator, investor, lender, or buyer. The accounting industry, the venture capital industry, and the software development industry can all passionately and articulately argue several sides of this question depending on their book of investments, client profiles, or personal philosophical position. Suffice it so say, finding common ground is difficult when enormous amounts of money are at stake.

Thirdly, governments and their attendant regulatory bodies disagree about how to treat such data depending on ideology and resource base. Human capital–oriented European countries may have a much more sympathetic view of intangibles than U.S. or Middle Eastern countries whose markets are focused primarily on tangible short-term returns. Current U.S. policy is driven by a combination of concerns about potential tax consequences (if you acknowledge it, someone may want to tax it) and an overarching predisposition against any sort of government participation in the policy formulation process. However, the growing acceptance of International Accounting Standards suggests that the cost of maintaining separate sets of books, combined with the instantaneous flow of information, make it increasingly likely that U.S. corporations will begin to measure and manage intangibles simply because they determine that it is in their competitive best interest to do so.

Refining Techniques for Quantifying Reputation

Government bodies like the European Commission, the U.S. Securities and Exchange Commission, and the Financial Accounting Standards Board are not going to take any action until they see more private sector support for this sort of quantification. This suggests that measures and metrics are best developed, refined, and perfected as useful business management tools before advancing them to the public policy arena.

Because disclosure is an element of the general rubric of communications, this aspect of the issue returns one to the basic question of reputation and brand: how does any sort of communication, whether voluntary or mandatory, benefit or harm the reputation or brand of an enterprise such that, in the private sector, revenues and profits either increase or decrease?

Reputation and brand, by themselves, are intriguing and much-discussed assets. However, in most countries they have little or no balance sheet or income statement recognition, let alone agreed-upon financial value. Globalization has enhanced the ability of organizations to monetize the value of these assets. The potential return is considerable because corporations have usually invested substantially in these assets over long periods of time and may have already expensed or written off those investments.

The cost basis may be low in accounting terms but the return may be above average—or as economists refer to them, "offering excess rents"—because the market has expanded to include potential bidders whose outlook is "strategic" rather than strictly financial. For instance, when Ford announced it was putting its Jaguar and Range Rover marques up for sale in 2007, one of the surprisingly strong bidders to emerge was Tata Group of India. Tata saw the opportunity to acquire premier brands connoting an aristocratic legacy of luxury and, to a lesser extent, quality. The growing middle class in Asia might one day aspire to own such brands, but more importantly, Tata's push to develop and sell an affordable $2,500 automobile for the masses could be boosted by the acquisition of Jaguar and Range Rover because ownership of such brands would lend credibility to its efforts to establish itself as the purveyor of quality cars to the huge, emerging Asian middle class. That such a purchase represented both a reversal of fortune for an ageing imperial master and provided, in the "buy versus make" context, a means of leapfrogging Japanese and Korean competitors to say nothing of European and American, was an added benefit.

In the economy of the first decade of the 21st Century, private equity firms and other financial buyers traditionally cut costs, covered their debt obligations, pulled out their equity, and then attempted to sell relatively quickly (three to five years). Strategic buyers are positioning themselves for a secular shift in economic conditions that they believe can provide them with a dominant competitive position for years to come. The risk of acquiring brand and reputation, therefore, is worth more to strategic bidders because the return they envisage is also greater.

This global context also enhances brand and reputation because such ownership provides a form of first mover advantage. Cultural barriers decline and traditional buying habits change as wealth increases in emerging markets. Transition periods can be fleeting and identifying those moments can be frustrating for overcommitted executives. Iconic brands and exemplary reputations help companies "translate" their offerings for new customers because the values inherent in them provide a short-hand interpretation of what they have to offer. This becomes the IP equivalent of a picture being worth a thousand words.

Keeping Brand Promises

It should be remembered, however, that reputation and brand require continued, frequently expensive, upkeep. It is also essential that the promise connoted by the brand and reputation be inextricably tied to actual performance. Failure to maintain that connection will result in an exponential loss of value because of the exposure, embarrassment, and obvious incongruity between promise and delivery.

British Petroleum (BP) is perhaps the most notable big company example of this value loss. BP recognized in the late 1990s that one of the crucial strategic advantages in its industry was to be seen as a good partner to less developed nations that it would need to explore or replenish its reserves. It also correctly perceived that so-called "green" or environmentally friendly positioning would begin to play increasingly well with consumers. Sales and profits in the consumer sector of the energy industry were being driven not only by sales of the core product but by sales of convenience foods and drinks, as well as by various financial products, including the interest income from company credit cards.

In 2000, BP's adapted new logos, coloring, signage, and advertising, all designed to reinforce the notion that BP stood for "beyond petroleum" and was environmentally friendly. This contributed to positive business media coverage and, consequently, enhanced stock price performance and sales growth. The company's CEO, John Brown, was acknowledged as an iconic business leader and in fairly short order was honored by the Queen of England, becoming "Sir" and then "Lord" John Brown.

This accumulation of good will lasted for several years. However, the company's performance began to fail to match its image. Explosions at a company refinery in Texas City, Texas, resulted in fifteen deaths and over one hundred injuries. A few years later, a leak in BP's pipelines on the North Slope of Alaska resulted in a substantial oil spills. All incidents resulted in charges of negligence. The damage to the company's brand and reputation were substantial. As a final exclamation point to the declining image, Lord Brown announced his retirement before the reputational damage could be repaired. Unfortunately, allegations about his personal life found their way into the press and sadly contributed to a further weakening of both Lord Brown's and the company's once iconic images.

A commonplace of modern management theory holds that good reputations and brands take a long time to build but a short time to damage. A corollary to that is that repairing the damage takes longer—and may be more expensive—than creating the original image. From an IP standpoint, the issue is that these assets must be managed carefully, especially since we do not fully understand their strengths and weaknesses. Too many businesses believe they "know" their brands and what those brands mean to the outside world. However, it is just such facile assumptions about brand that lead to poorly designed and executed strategies.

New Measurement Rigor

It is precisely because there is a growing need to better identify, measure, and manage valuable assets like brand and reputation that new methodologies have emerged to assist in that process of professionalization. There are limited amounts of comparable data and many skeptics who question the validity of the process, let alone the data themselves. However, brand and reputation have simply become too valuable—and the consequences of mismanaging them too costly—to permit anything less than the employment of a rigorous quantifiable approach to incorporating information about them into a comprehensive strategy.

Rigor is essential because IP generally and brand or reputation in particular make money for companies in several ways: First, they make a company more effective at what it does; in the brand and reputation case, for instance, identifying and "closing" with the most appropriate market for its goods or services. Second, they can be sold as IP as in selling a brand (i.e., the net present value of its projected stream of earnings).

Third, they can be sold as a service such as providing consulting advice to other companies. Procter & Gamble, Caterpillar, Dow, Walmart and other corporations are examples of companies that have converted their internal expertise into externally generated revenue. Fourth, they can enhance the long-term value of the enterprise both in terms of equity value and in terms of transactional value if all or part of the company is to be sold to another entity.

Most U.S. and European companies already capture data on 70% of their intellectual capital. Typically, this information resides not in corporate management information systems, but in operating unit databases. Frequently, the biggest challenge is *not* measuring the value or impact of these intangibles but in getting the people in disparate business units to share that knowledge with each other.

The most common reasons corporations cite for measuring IP generally, and brand or reputation specifically are to measure the impact of brand, reputation, or other intellectual capital drivers on financial outcomes like sales or price/earnings ratio; to determine a range of values for financing purposes such as securing a loan based on the value of an intangible; to assess a value for transactional purposes if one is selling or acquiring an IP asset through licensing, acquisition or, passively, through merger.

The problem that executives in this situation face is that the information they get from their own companies on these assets is usually inadequate. In a study conducted several years ago by the author and his former colleagues at Cap Gemini Ernst & Young, financial executives at Global 500 companies were asked to tell the researchers:

1. The most important drivers of value for their businesses, and
2. How useful was the information they were receiving from their own companies with regard to addressing that question.

There was a sizable gap between the importance of the information needed and the adequacy of the information provided. The research demonstrated that if one could close the gap between the importance of the information and the quality of the information, there were significant statistical correlations with financial performance measures such as return on equity, stock price performance, and compound annual sales growth.

The measurement and management of brand and reputation have suffered particularly from the absence of credible and comparable data. Even in the Internet era, where corporations are increasingly shifting advertising budgets from traditional media like television, newspapers, and magazines to the Web and consumer generated media, it is still commonplace in the communications profession to simply list the number of stories a corporation received over some period of time as a sign of success.

Inevitably, this will change. Companies and their service providers recognize that they must more effectively measure the impact of their communications strategies. Advertising, public relations, and promotions are all being reevaluated in light of these developments.

As an example, Predictiv/CCW, the author's firm employs a statistical approach to measuring the impact of brand, reputation, and corporate communications on financial results such as sales growth, volume growth, market share, price/earnings ratio, and stock price movement. This method quantifies the causal relationship between communications about a company's products, services, or other attributes and the resulting financial implications of change to any of those factors.

Input data are derived from original sources such as media analyses provided to companies by outside vendors who specialize in tracking such variables as reach, frequency, and tone; proxy surveys of a company's customers, competitors, suppliers, and/or financiers. With survey data, rankings on a range of 1 to 10 of drivers such as communications about price, image, functionality, familiarity, and favorability are typically assembled. Once this information has been gathered, the results are aggregated and tabulated to a scaled score with a range of 0 to 100 for each driver (see Exhibit 10.1).

Simple linear regression is used to determine the correlation between each driver once each driver has received a verified score. A predictive or causal model is then created to determine the statistical relationships between the drivers, including how the drivers are linked causally to each other and how they are linked causally with respect to other performance measures. These analyses can be focused on a particular topic or public relations/communications message. Further evaluation can assess how those messages impact increases and decreases in financial outcomes like sales growth or p/e ratio, and can also assist in quantifying the components of brand, reputation, and other intangibles (see Exhibit 10.2).

EXHIBIT 10.1 **LINKAGE TO PERFORMANCE CALCULATED BY CAUSAL MODELS CONNECTING DRIVERS AND OUTCOMES**

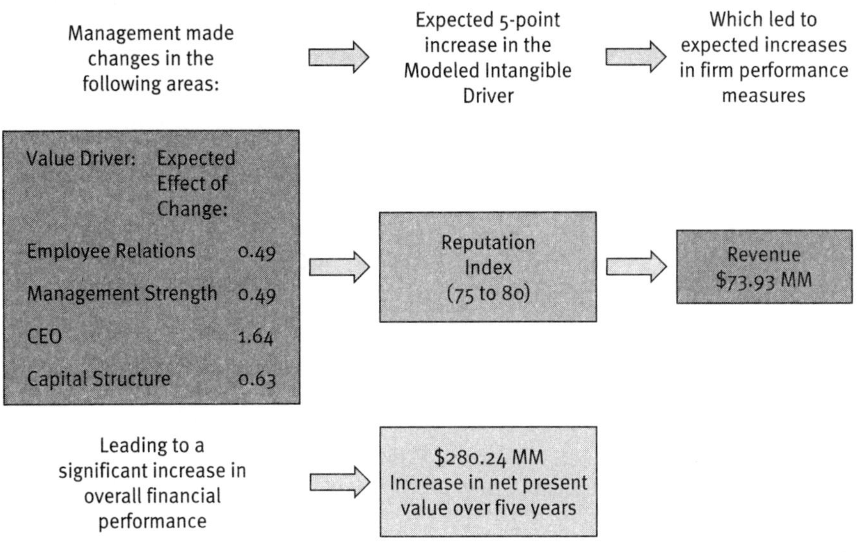

EXHIBIT 10.2 **PERCENT OF THIS COMPANY'S MARKET VALUE COULD BE ATTRIBUTED TO THESE THEMES**

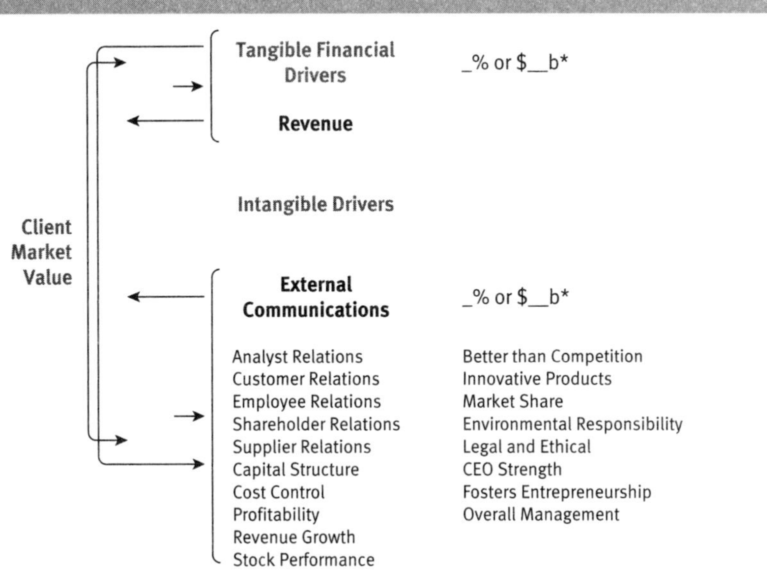

Use of longitudinal or time-series data in these analyses, spanning quarters or years, permit corporate executives to examine trends over the long-term rather than relying on one-time "snapshots" that may be instructive but are inadequate for the purposes of longer-term strategic planning.

Making Informed Decisions

This type of analysis gives executives the tools to make informed decisions about the quantifiable impact a particular change in, for instance, the influence a CEO's reputation has on brand, can affect other financial outcomes. It can also mitigate damage caused by unavoidable or unforeseeable changes such as product recalls or environmental mishaps. In such cases, an increase in company communications about other more positive but equally weighted brand or reputation drivers can offset the negative impact, creating, in effect, a communications arbitrage.

When confronted with the need to conduct more static, transactional types of analyses, specific values can be determined for the components of corporate brand or reputation. *Forbes* magazine asked the author and his colleagues at Predictiv to rank the top 25 U.S. corporate brands. One intriguing outcome of this project was not that values could be assigned to these brands (it has been done before) but specific drivers of brand value could also be identified and statistically validated. While in this case the four most significant drivers of corporate brand were reputation, management, human capital, and innovation, of potentially greater significance within the larger IP context is that for 11 of the top 25, brand value equaled or exceeded market value.

This finding provides further support for the contention that in most respects, brand and reputation are no longer intangible in the traditional sense. Increased levels of sophisticated analysis employed by large global corporations have created the basis for that development (see Exhibit 10.3). The ability of those companies to adapt to their need for better internal measures is the truly revolutionary development because 100 years of conventional marketing wisdom had to be overcome to do so.

Brand and reputation can now be defined in context. To whom does the company want the brand or reputation to matter most? What

EXHIBIT 10.3 **CERTAIN MESSAGES HAVE A PERSISTENT IMPACT ON STOCK PRICE THAT CAN BE MEASURED THROUGH IMPACT ON SHARE TRADING**

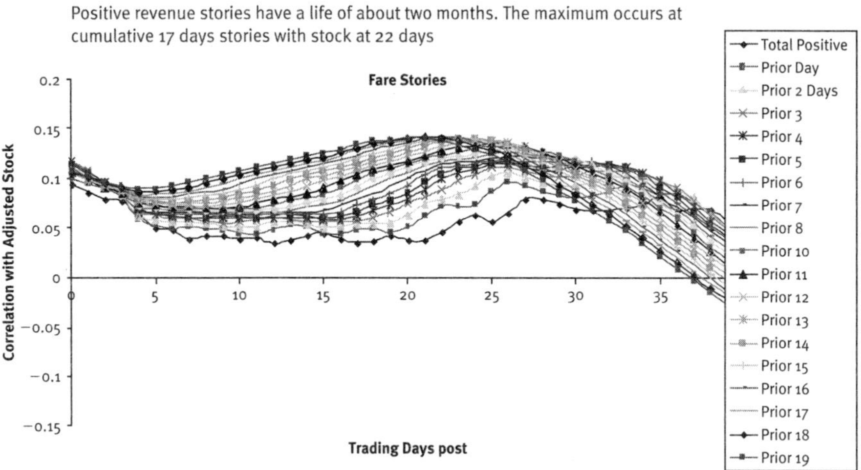

Source: Copyright © Predictiv LLP, 2007. Permission is granted by Mr. Low.

behavior does the company want that asset to drive? What sort of measurable outcome does the company expect?

The measurement process allows companies to begin defining the how, what, and why of managing brand value or reputation. The Predictiv/CCW methodology and others like it take a combination of publicly available and proprietary information provided by client companies to compare the company's performance against both internal hurdle rates and competitors' benchmarks to achieve critical data for strategy planning and execution.

Today's markets, driven by large infusions of private equity, government-sponsored investment vehicles, and the profusion of information available through a variety of barely controlled channels demands that sort of rigor. Anything less is unacceptably subjective. The markets insist on quantitative linkages and explanations of performance. The ability of managements to provide these markets with credible, quantifiable bases for their decisions about brand, equity, and other intangibles will serve the interests of all market participants.

ABOUT THE AUTHOR

Jonathan Low is a Partner in Predictiv, a consulting firm specializing in the valuation of intangibles such as intellectual capital, brand, reputation, leadership, and alliances. Predictiv partners with Omicom/Fleishman-Hillard in Communications Consultants Worldwide (CCW), which provides consulting services on the impact of communications on financial outcomes. Mr. Low has directed four major research reports on the role of intangibles in the global economy (Measures that Matter, Success Factors in the IPO Transformation Process, Decisions that Matter, and The Value Creation Index). He is the coauthor of *Invisible Advantage*, a book published by Perseus Press in 2002, was coeditor of *Enterprise Value in the Knowledge Economy*, copublished in 1997 by the OECD and Ernst & Young, and was a contributor to *Business Power: Creating New Wealth from IP Assets*, published by John Wiley & Sons, Inc., in 2007. His work has appeared in the *Wall Street Journal*, the *New York Times*, *Forbes*, *Business Week* and other publications.

Mr. Low has presented his findings to the U.S. Securities and Exchange Commission, the European Commission, the OECD, and the Federal Reserve Bank of New York. He has worked with corporate clients of all sizes in North America and Europe. He served as Deputy Assistant Secretary for Work and Technology Policy at the U.S. Department of Labor from 1993–1996. In that position, he served on the SEC's Steering Committee on the Future of Accounting and Financial Reporting and represented the United States at the inaugural OECD Conference on Corporate Governance. Subsequently, Jon served as co-chair for Strategic and Organizational Issues of The Brookings Institution's Task Force on Understanding Intangible Sources of Value. Mr. Low is a graduate of Dartmouth College and Yale University's School of Management.

PART 3

IP Transactions

CHAPTER 11

IP Asset Sales, Still A Work in Progress

BY JAMES E. MALACKOWSKI[1]

PERSPECTIVE Until the 1980s, the value most patent owners realized from their assets was almost exclusively strategic. Intellectual property managers regarded patent value as defensive or exclusionary. The goal of patents was not profit generation, but revenue preservation. Led by Texas Instruments and IBM, and inspired by the newly formed Court of Appeals for the Federal Circuit (the highest IP court) and the recently enacted Bayh–Dole amendment, many patent holders in the early 1980s embraced patents for direct revenue generation. No one figured that the disputes over invention rights would get so bloody.

In recent years, new options for monetization have emerged that reflect a more profound understanding of patent leverage and business development. Among these is the buying and selling of patents to facilitate business goals.

"The IP market is transitioning away from licensing as the only means of [value] transfer, to patent sale and title transfer, and what that shift entails," says James Malackowski, a patent valuation expert whose company, Ocean Tomo, pioneered the public patent auction. "The motivations for this transition are not new: fear, greed, and the comfort of being second (or not being first) so that new markets and strategies can be better utilized. This movement to IP sale can also be attributed to a growing appreciation for portfolio management theory as applied to

(continued)

intangible assets. We have entered a new era that may aptly be called the 'rise of the active portfolio manager.' Development of an IP estate, in particular a patent estate, is no longer the job for a simple rights collector who monitors the latest discovery in the lab and prosecutes those that appear to be inventive."

Malackowski believes that a strong case could be made that, until recently, most corporations have been remiss about maximizing the return on their IP assets. This is especially true with patents and copyrights that are viewed primarily as defensive tools. "Patents were considered a default output of research and development," he asserts. Better analytics have given IP managers a clearer understanding of what is and is not in their and other portfolios, and which rights they need to do business. As a result, active fine-tuning of portfolios is no longer viewed as a weakness but a core competency.

Accountants experienced in tangible assets and antiquated (GAAP) accounting rules have not helped the situation. Malackowski notes that GAAP generally record the investment to innovate as an expense on financial income statements and that patents are not capitalized like tangible assets. New accounting rules requiring the value of patented innovation to be recorded as an asset on the balance sheet or written down would arguably have accelerated more active IA management and generated more invention.

In the past, patent ownership was transferred in select instances. The process included only a handful of potential buyers with results often far below the true market value of the portfolio. Today, a more transparent and efficient market is emerging, which is generating a higher number of IP purchases and sales. There also is greater candor, internally, at least, about the need to "exchange" patents and other IP assets to achieve necessary leverage. Many believe, Malackowski among them, that this will benefit businesses worldwide, as well as innovators, shareholders and economies.

From Technology Transfer to Title Transfer

Most major IP owners, traditional operating companies, share a strategic mandate to monetize their intangible assets. While for some this goal has been in place for 20 years, progress has been sporadic, regardless of the resources committed. Successful and measurable monetization of intangible assets is not linear. Rather, it remains a work in progress moving forward in a step function with a flurry of new activity every decade or so. The IP community has reached a new plateau built on the outright sale and title transfer of IP. Companies today are buying and selling patents with enthusiasm. Budgets have been established specifically to acquire patents and new marketplaces are being formed and endorsed. Ten years ago such a concept was unthinkable.

This chapter will examine why the IP market is transitioning away from licensing as the only means of transfer to patent sale and title transfer, and what that shift entails. The motivations for this transition are not new: fear, greed, and the comfort of being second (or not being first) so that new markets and strategies can be better utilized. This movement to IP sale can also be attributed to a growing appreciation for portfolio management theory as applied to intangible assets. We have entered a new era that may aptly be called the "rise of the active portfolio manager." Development of an IP estate, in particular a patent estate, is no longer the job for a simple rights collector who monitors the latest discovery in the lab and prosecutes those that appear to be inventive. Applying business school approaches designed for such investors as hedge funds, IP estates are increasingly today the product of portfolio theory. Such methodology relies upon three principles:

- Limit internal prosecution to innovation that can be most cost effective and deployed rapidly internally
- Acquire those assets that are more efficiently developed by others
- Sell or otherwise eliminate IP not relevant to current management strategies, reallocating those resources and rebalancing the portfolio.

Prior to this most recent market evolution, a strong case could be made that corporations were failing to maximize the return on their IP assets. This was especially true with patents and copyrights. Viewed as primarily defensive tools, patents were considered a default output of research and development. The accountants have not helped the situation as their principles generally record the investment to innovate as an expense on financial income statements—patents are not capitalized. New accounting rules requiring the value of patented innovation to be recorded as an asset on the balance sheet would surely have accelerated more active management of IP assets. Cold, hard cash value was rarely extracted from IP assets; noncore patents were occasionally (cross) licensed, but rarely exploited through sale. In the select instances that patents were transferred, the process included only a handful of potential buyers with results often far below the true market value of the portfolio.

A new global IP marketplace, characterized by increased efficiency and continual evolution, has brought higher returns into clearer focus. New markets and new attitudes have come quickly. Many of the recognized IP visionaries, editors, and bloggers barely finished their forecast of doom for such transactions before they began to embrace the new view as something here to stay. As IP assets garner more recognition as financial assets, corporations are more comfortable to apply modern management principles. As stated above, IP owners are beginning to behave more as portfolio managers than patent collectors or caretakers. Greater management attention begets greater strategic appreciation. Forward looking corporations have begun to realize that the control and effective management of IP rights is pertinent to securing a role on the global stage. With the emergence of competitive markets and participants, patent holders are reconsidering the best method to maximize the value of their IP. Corporations that historically "maintained inventory" or licensed patents are more frequently looking towards what once was seen as a last resort—patent sale or acquisition.

The catalysts driving the movement towards patent sales over licensing include an increased awareness by shareholders of intellectual property and a demand for more effective management of these newly discovered financial assets, a momentum in the marketplace resulting from growing infringement damages awards, and the fear of new market participants and competitors.

A Tradition of Patent Licensing

Since the first patent was issued, patent owners have negotiated the transfer of specific rights to their invention to acceptable licensees. Allowing the patent holder to retain significant rights to the asset, licensing has appealed to those desiring to "have their cake and eat it too," or use the technology in their own products, and also recover their investment in the technology by sharing with others. Licensing transactions are often confidential and shrouded in secrecy. In most cases, their terms are never publicly reported unless a party to the agreement is publicly traded and obligated—based on materiality—to report the activity to the SEC. The licensing process is typically long and complex, with corporate counsel or attorneys often involved on both sides. Typically, the determination of the appropriate economic terms has been as much an art as a science. Those active in licensing typically perform analyses to "triangulate" on an appropriate royalty rate, evaluating the potential profits to be earned by the licensed products or services, rates earned by comparable technologies in the market, and the costs incurred to develop the technology. Estimates, such as the "25% Rule," are used as common guidelines.

While often tedious and bureaucratic, some corporations have experienced significant success in the field of IP licensing. In the 1980s, for example, Texas Instruments instituted a broad patent licensing campaign that generated millions of dollars in licensing revenues for the corporation. For many, Texas Instrument's program confirmed that licensing was a viable means for extracting significant value from patents.[2] These efforts represent a significant step forward. Others were soon to follow. By 2006, global licensing revenues across all firms exceeded $150 billion, growing at 25–35% each year. Today, some of Wall Street's strongest performers, including corporations such as IBM and Qualcomm, boast successful patent licensing programs. Such success in technology transfer can also be seen at Stanford University and the University of Wisconsin's Alumni Research Foundation (WARF),[3] among others. IBM alone reported collecting more than $1.5 billion in licensing revenues in 2005. On the flipside, Microsoft reports having paid more than $1.4 billion in royalties for select key technologies during that same year. Marshall Phelps, the architect of Microsoft's current strategy, boasts loudly and rightfully of this investment in innovation. His work serves as a role model for others to follow and reinforces the third leg of the portfolio management—buy from others that which is most cost effective.

Emergence of New IP Marketplaces

With the then newfound success of licensing, and the long entrenched fear that most patents would be used for potential defensive purposes, the sale of a patent was historically an unpopular method for capitalizing on the value of an IP estate. Other than in situations of insolvency or bankruptcy, the sale or auction of a patent was rarely seen before the year 2000. Individuals and corporations were apprehensive to both sides of the transaction. Times have changed. The first decade of the new millennium is witness to a tall leap in IP markets. Patent sale transactions are becoming accepted. In recent years, such transactions have become arguably commonplace with several notable sales commanding the attention of main stream media. For example, in December 2004, the United States Bankruptcy Court mandated the liquidation of 39 Web patents and patent applications of a bankrupt software and Web services company, Commerce One. Employing an auction structure, the patent portfolio was offered for sale. JGR Acquisition, later identified as Novell, purchased the portfolio for $16.6 million, $15.5 million above the stalking-horse bid for the assets. Later in September 2005, Openshark, with the assistance of an intermediary, sold a patent portfolio no longer core to the strategy of the firm, achieving a price 60% higher than what was offered before engaging a broker.[4] Other recent significant sales include the following transactions:

- Lupin sold certain patent applications and other related intellectual property to Laboratories Servier for $26.7 million (2007).
- NeoMagic sold certain patents to Faust Communications for $3.5 million (2005).
- Mobility Electronics sold a portfolio of 46 patents and applications for $13 million (2005).
- Hologic acquired IP from Fisher Imaging for $32 million (2005).
- Sun Microsystems purchased intellectual property rights from Procom Technology for $50 million (2005).
- Cirrus Logic sold select U.S. and foreign patents to Broadcom for $18 million (2004).
- RIM's purchase of GPS patents from a yet undisclosed seller for $170 million (2007).

New marketplaces have emerged to accommodate this increase in transaction activity—online listings, multilot live auctions, and intellectual property exchanges—having each been recently established. As with conventional equity and derivative markets, the IP transactional industry is being molded and driven by the existence of each new market's ability to amplify the liquidity of IP. Such liquidity is primarily driven by

EXHIBIT 11.1 **COMMON CHARACTERISTICS OF CURRENT IP MARKETS**

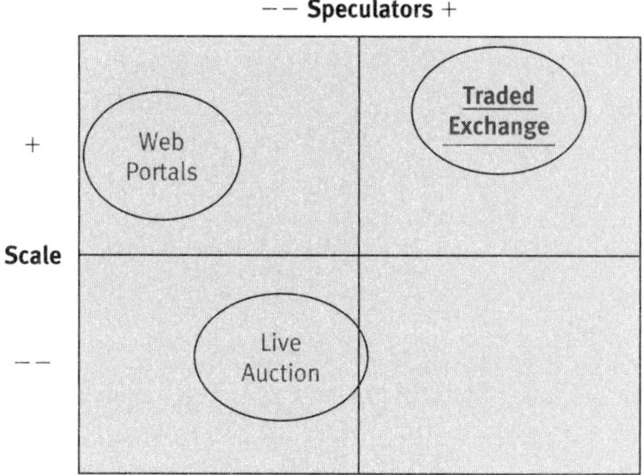

scalability of the new markets and the existence of speculators. Good old fashioned greed has entered the new economy. Dare we say "trolls are good?" As any trader knows, a strong market is not made with operating buyers and sellers alone. It is the investors and speculators that drive liquidity and provide for the definition of a new asset. Analysis of this dynamic is shown in Exhibit 11.1, depicting the placement of these new marketplaces with respect to the core parameters of success.

Although earliest in development, this analysis speaks highly of the potential of a traded exchange for IP (e.g., www.IPXI.com). Such intangible market forces are likely even larger and more rapid to develop than what has been seen at the Chicago Climate Exchange with its asset carbon credits. Each of these new transactional arenas is discussed further later in this chapter.

Online Listing Services

Contemporary online listing services seek to increase the awareness of IP available for sale while simultaneously reducing transaction costs. Here, too, we see a work in progress. In the late 1990s there were as many as sixty online marketplaces for intellectual property. During that same period, there were also similar sites for dog food and groceries, all of which now RIP. In fact, of the original sixty-plus online IP forums, less than five survived the dotcom bust. Survivors such as Yet2.com and Utek.com have made a noteworthy impact on the market. More recently, additional players have joined the IP online marketplace, including The iBridge Network from the Kauffman Innovation Network and The Dean's List. Some individual corporations have their own portals for selling or licensing their noncore patents, (e.g. Ford Global Technologies hosts all of Ford Motors' patents currently available for sale or license). On occasion, patents are even listed for sale on the popular market listing portals eBay and Craigslist, although with expected limited success (see Exhibit 11.2).

Online IP marketplaces, even those that have historically been successful, are faced with continuing challenges. Because all online marketplace platforms carry only a very small number of technologies, compared to the universe of technologies that are available, search is a crucial step in the process. If the buyer cannot easily find the IP asset that they are looking for, they are unlikely to return to that marketplace. The taxonomy of the IP assets and categorization is what creates liquidity—yet the taxonomy utilized by one market participant could vary greatly from the next. There are many jewels among the clutter, but it can be extremely hard to decipher the gems from the junk, even with the assistance of know-it-all Google. Compounding the complexity, almost all descriptions of technologies are written in technical jargon, which can be especially hard to

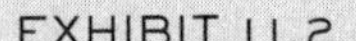
EXHIBIT 11.2 THE FOCUS OF LEADING ONLINE IP MARKETS

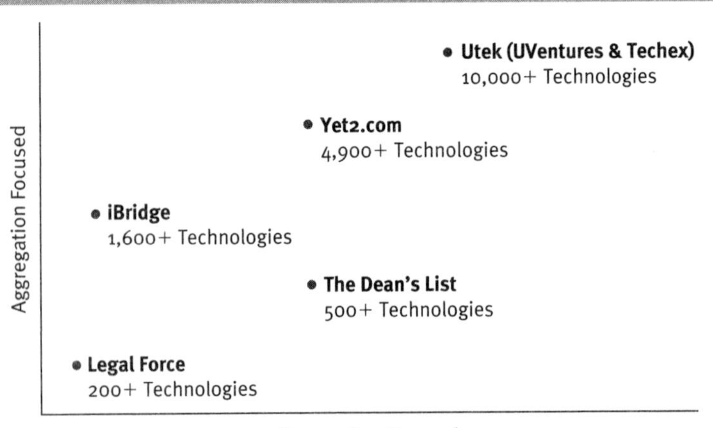

follow for those without a relevant scientific background. More recently, a non-profit consortium, Open-IP.org, has been created to address this issue and consolidate the basic patent offer for sale to a central repository providing for critical mass at all member portals. Although too early to forecast the success of this effort, its backers and founder are commended for the effort. On a brighter side, today there are already seven million U.S. issued patents and many raw inventions available for transaction. For now, the space is broad enough for challengers, both old and new, to compete for eBay-King-of-IP status. Friendly rivalry between portal providers will force competitors to provide outstanding services in the attainment of increased transaction rates and market leader position.

Live Multi-Lot Auctions

The concept of a multi-lot, live auction for IP was born with the intent to introduce to the marketplace a forum for facilitating the exchange of intellectual property with a critical mass of buyers. An auction format uniquely brings a sense of urgency and closure to IP transactions, creates a center for IP liquidity, and effectuates transparency for a market in which none has historically existed. For the active portfolio manager, the auction brings a needed solution.

In contrast to the more traditional approaches for monetizing IP, the live public auction format provides various benefits from the perspective of both a seller and a buyer. The auction format does not allow for discussions to go stale and stagnant. From the perspective of a seller, the auction is the first forum for transacting IP in which the burden of purchasing is shifted to the buyer. The auction structure mandates a seller to offer a group of predetermined deal terms and conditions, including a minimum price (i.e., the auction "reserve" price). Live IP auctions provide greater public exposure to a seller's IP and afford sellers the benefit of a true "market clearing sale." For buyers of IP, the live public auction provides market transparency and pricing. Such conditions assure that the buyer will pay the true market price for the IP assets it seeks to acquire.

In April 2006, the first live public IP auction was held in a ballroom in San Francisco's The Ritz-Carlton, featuring a total of 78 patent lots for sale. Receiving as much skepticism and cynicism as enthusiasm and publicity, patent sales exceeding about $3 million were achieved with sales of

26 lots on the auction floor, an average of $116,000 per lot. Although the per lot sale success rate reached only 33%, these sales provided successful transactions for more than 50% of the participating sellers. In the weeks following the live auction event, an additional five lots transacted for a total of $5,420,000, bringing the value of the total patent sales for this first auction to more than $8.4 million. Independent of the final totals, the auction was fascinating to watch as more than 400 senior IP professionals and thought leaders sat quietly in near perfect rows for more than two hours. Former PTO Commissioners, Fortune 100 portfolio managers, and IP thought leaders sat in their chairs and took notes, lots of notes—all witnessing what the market would bear for someone else's patents. April 2006 was the first true price discovery for an industry.

In the two years that have passed since the first-of-its-kind live multi-lot public auction for IP was introduced, evidence of growing marketplace acceptance of the live auction as a viable (albeit interim) platform for monetizing IP is apparent. During this progress period, six more IP auctions in the U.S. and Europe, hammered in a new era for IP transactions. To date, the total sales of patent assets on the auction floor (i.e., exclusive of post-auction transactions and transactions of nonpatent IP assets) have exceeded $80 million, with an average seller success rate (cumulative overall auctions) for on-floor transactions 40%. Marketplace acceptance continues to improve as evidenced by the continually increasing support of and participation in the process by a growing number of large corporations, as well as small companies and independent inventors, as compared with two years ago.

The IP Exchange

Moving to the upper-right quadrant on our chart of market scale and speculation (Exhibit 11.2) is an initiative to launch the Intellectual Property Exchange International ("the IP Exchange") to offer a full range of IP-based or derivative financial products priced and traded on one platform. Not surprisingly, the IP Exchange originated in Chicago, home to the financial futures industry and a city full of traders accustomed to new products. It is interesting to consider the evolution of the commodities and stock exchanges as a parallel or precursor to the evolution of the IP marketplace. The evolution of the stock markets, from the curb-side brokers to the formal stock exchanges took over one hundred years and continues to develop today. The stock market was not generally accessible to the average individual investor fifty years ago. In the 1960s, all transactions took place at the physical stock exchange between the hours of operation. With the advent of Electronic Communications Networks (ECN), individual investors can now buy or sell stocks for as low as $5 per trade through TDAmeritrade, ETrade, or numerous other platforms. Such efficiency was not previously possible as orders could not be matched electronically. Today all NASDAQ, NYSE, and bulletin board stocks trade in real time. As the establishment of regulated exchanges provided the essential means to trade units of corn and stock, the IP Exchange will broaden the market of active participants in the IP space, provide new means to monetize IP, and enhance the transparency of pricing. These exchanges will undoubtedly and dramatically increase the efficiency of IP transactions.

IP Assets: Tomorrow's Currency

A paradox exists between the resources spent on research and development (R&D) and acknowledgement of those efforts. While a majority of a company's value is likely captured within its intellectual assets, R&D and resulting IP is captured only as an expense on the financial income statements, not as an asset on the balance sheet. Research and development dollars are not recoverable and such budgets are in general declining. Look no further than Pfizer to see widespread cuts in R&D (with concurrent greater reliance on a few blockbuster drugs). Fast followers not to be ignored, Pfizer's actions were quickly imitated by several other major pharmaceutical companies.[5,6] Major IP owners on a regular basis abandon a significant portion of their patent portfolio. The decision is driven by the fact that these "noncore" patents are not utilizable by the company and hence "worthless." This model is now changing as patents are now recognized to be often underutilized (see Exhibit 11.3). There could be significant amount of value left in the patents that are currently being abandoned, trolls and patent brokers recognize that fact and try to capitalize on this unused value.

EXHIBIT 11.3 **UNDERUTILIZATION OF IP ASSETS**

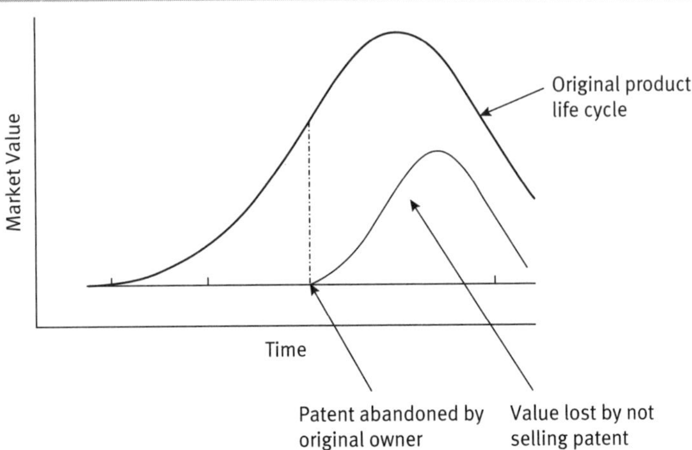

This simple illustration (Exhibit 11.3), repeated on countless whiteboards in executive conference rooms, demonstrates active portfolio management theory. Sell what you don't need. R&D sunk costs can be recovered, not by abandoning the patents, but by thinking creatively how to utilize those technologies either in the current field of use by companies in similar space or by selling it to companies in complementary industries. Shareholders have not compelled corporations to recover this sunk cost, but in a tight economy, this could become the norm rather than the exception. The fear of transferring IP into the hands of other competitors or third parties who may enforce against customers has constrained corporations from selling their IP assets. This situational paralysis is likely to be overcome by an even greater fear of shareholder accountability. Perhaps we will see the first true business case where two wrongs make a right.

A shrinking R&D budget and a frozen collection of patent assets negatively affects everyone. Shareholder value as well as the competitiveness of the U.S. economy is depressed. Innovation is recognized as the key driver of the economy and accordingly, logic dictates that the value of relevant IP assets should be on the rise. In the near future, hubs of innovation such as universities and research institutions will realize a more prominent place in the market because of the IP they routinely generate. The value of the most coveted IP should benefit from the new markets discussed above. The increase in number and value of patent transactions has been driven in part by an increased awareness of intellectual property and its value by shareholders, as previously discussed. Alerted by significant drops and boosts in stock market value of publicly traded companies after issuance of court decisions pertaining to patent spats or allowance of key intellectual properties, shareholders and analysts are investing more time and concern in these intangible assets that for years have been ineffectively and inefficiently discussed.

In accordance with archaic metrics, companies have been principally valued by their tangible assets. As the readers of this book likely know but worth restating, in 1975 less than 20% of a company's valuation was derived from intangible assets; the remaining 80% tangible "lock, stock, and barrel." Over the last several decades, the market has experienced an economic inversion with now approximately 80% of the S&P® 500 market capitalization accounted for by intangible assets.[7] The primary value driver behind this new economy is not property, plant, and equipment; but rather intellectual assets. While shareholders may be aware of IP held by the corporation, in many instances there may be no mention of any type of IP within an annual report other than references made in connection to research and development expenses. But wait, don't these assets now account for a majority of the company's value? Where is the SEC or AICPA when you need them?

Market Momentum

The change in progress towards patent and IP sale is also being driven by the general market increase in both royalty rates and IP damages amounts. While the average negotiated royalty rates across all industries increased from 5.1% in the 1980s to 6.2% in 1990s, rates increased further to an average of 6.8% in 2006.[8] Seminal inventions in the areas of software and medical products have fetched rates of up to 77% and 50%, respectively. Likewise, rates resulting from litigation have followed suit—in *Monsanto Company v. McFarling* (2007) the CAFC affirmed a reasonable royalty equal to 140% of the product's purchase price to compensate the plaintiff for the defendants' infringement. Damages figures too have reached extraordinary levels with multiple settlements to the tune of one billion dollars plus being reported—$1.35 billion in *Michelson v. Medtronic* (2005) and $1.25 billion in *Sun Microsystems v. Microsoft* (2004).[9]

The magnitude of these billion-dollar-plus examples encouraged both lawyers and licensing executives to take a more active role to both protect and litigate IP assets. They pointed to high-profile examples within an industry and thought: "Well, if that small company (or individual) can get x million, we should at least be able to get 2x." This thinking spurred yet more offensive litigation, but also a build-up of a war-chest of assets to arm themselves. The billion-dollar damages awards led other corporations to reconsider their business strategy as it relates to IP, oftentimes to discover that not only is the value of their IP not being maximized, but also the method they may be currently employing has no potential for doing so, opening up the possibility of asset sale and/or purchase, further expanding the marketplace. Perhaps nowhere else is there a clearer representation of the synergistic and related impact of fear, greed, and the desire to be second (or at least not first).

New Market Participants

As the market looks to increase their IP activity and new marketplaces are established, new participants appear. With advanced tools and advancement into the Internet age, marketplace participants are able to trade much more cost effectively and efficiently. Internet-accessible platforms have been established to enhance the process and ease of conducting patent sale transactions through increased availability of relevant documents. Even ten years back, the USPTO did not have all U.S. patents in its searchable database. Since 2001, the USPTO has advanced by providing all patent file wrapper information in digital format and readily accessible to anyone. Likewise, mega-innovator Google launched Google Patent Search in late 2006, allowing retrieval of patents and wrappers using a user-friendly format. Today, all major M&A transactions are still performed using legal help, as they should be, but documents related to the transaction are often viewed in online data rooms hosted by ShareVault or Intralinks. The ability to perform most due diligence associated with the transaction instantaneously has undoubtedly added some fuel to the patent sales process. Prior to this newfound access to information, it was often not cost beneficial to invest in discovering and preparing for sale those assets that were not considered core to operations.

New resources have emerged that are helping to facilitate transactions. Historically, the analysis of patents and patent portfolios was performed predominantly by law firms. With the advent of advanced analytics, information is more widely available at a lower cost. Such resources, themselves a work in progress, lower a significant barrier to patent transactions. Today, patent analysis can be performed quickly and efficiently internally, or though small brokers using a variety of software tools. Legal opinions discussing the freedom to operate and claim coverage are still most often performed by law firms, but claims analysis, patent quality determination, encumbrances, and title analysis can now also be substantially performed in an automated fashion by attorneys and non-attorneys alike. Other readily available advanced analytics include identification of high value patents by assignee and by technology and identification of likely buyers based on sophisticated relevancy algorithms well beyond simple citation or word-based links. It is now common to search for the needle in entire haystacks at a time using a large and powerful magnet.

With the advent and ease of the advanced informational and analytical tools, new principal players (i.e., those willing to put up cash) are joining the IP marketplace, increasing the liquidity of the market and generating fear among traditional IP-owning operating companies. New market players, Patent Licensing and Enforcement Companies ("P-LECs," the politically correct name for "trolls"), are often associated with the attack on traditional operating companies (think NTP which received $612 million from RIM). P-LECS have devised a business strategy. While some acknowledge the efforts of P-LECs have been a catalyst to benchmark the valuation and therefore subsequent promotion and protection of corporate IP rights, they are not well understood or liked by the majority of the market or legislators. Although not a P-LEC itself, Ocean Tomo does believe that it would benefit everyone to have a better understanding of the business rationale behind the model. A discussion of the current market participants may assist in the understanding of this business strategy.

In general, the market may be segmented into the following players, each with a unique advantage and perspective:

CURRENT IP MARKET PARTICIPANTS
A Review of Business Model Advantages

Business Model	*Unique Advantage*
Private Inventor (PI)	Entrepreneurs wager
Contingent Counsel Partnership (CCP)	Perceived and real access to enforcement resources
Private/Public Dedicated Business (DB)	Market or exit multiple leverage
Technology Pools (TPools)	Community operability
Corporate Pools (CPools)	Subsidized freedom to operate
Special Purpose Investment Vehicles (SPI)	Flexibility and market arbitrage

Within the IP marketplace, each of the above paradigms already exists. We have studied the business models of these common players to understand their relative competitive position. As shown in Exhibit 11.4, IP owners can be assessed along two dimensions: their degree of connectivity to the inventive process and whether or not the participant is acting in a predominantly offensive or defensive position. For instance, Private Inventors (PI) and Contingent Counsel Partnerships (CCP) play largely offensive roles in the marketplace. They are not interested in a cross-license and have no defensive concerns. Augmenting the resources of the inventor, CCP's bring both perceived and real access to enforcement resources. Other models, including those of a Private or Public Dedicated Business (DB) and Special Purpose Investment (SPI) vehicle, play offensive roles, but have less of a connection to the inventive process. The economic models of Technology Pools (TPools) and Corporate Pools (CPools), however, operate more defensively. Still, here too we have seen recent migration into the offensive territory where such pools seek to recoup their investment in technology or even provide a return to their stakeholders.

Perhaps what is most interesting about Exhibit 11.4 is the readers' view on placement of the traditional operating company business model. Our experience suggests placement in the center of the chart, overlapping all four quadrants with a strong bias to the inventive process and a defensive strategy. With the general placement of traditional IP owner/operators at

EXHIBIT 11.4 **CURRENT IP MARKETS ARTICIPANTS: AN ANALYSIS OF COMMON BUSINESS MODELS**

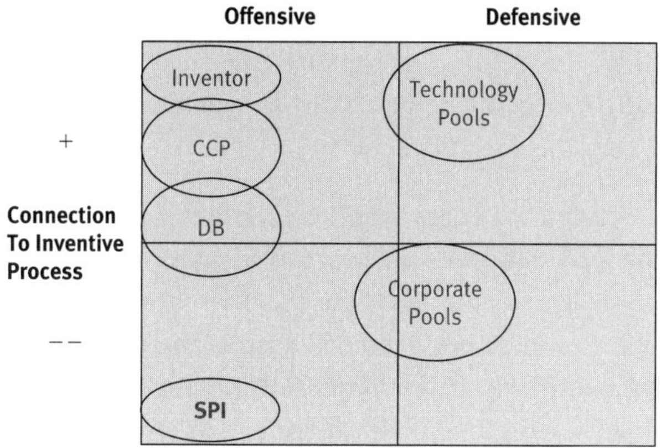

the center grid, P-LECs emerge as a threat. The farther any given P-LEC business model is from the center (i.e., from a traditional operating business model), the greater the fear that such an entity will become a competitive or economic burden. Perhaps most feared of all (rationally or not) as a result of their scale is Intellectual Ventures. Intellectual Ventures (IV) is an intellectual property developer, investor, and licensor. They are also one of the more successful and well-known hybrid P-LECs actively amassing—and creating—technologies. Founded in 2000 by former Microsoft chief technologist Nathan Myhrvold, the firm was well funded initially (to the tune of $300 million) by investors and operating companies including Microsoft, Nokia, and Sony.[10] More recently, Intellectual Ventures has announced plans to raise as much as $1 billion or more to develop and acquire patents in Asia. Intellectual Ventures has the backing and support of some of the industry's most patent-heavy firms. Their reach has been extensive but their full business strategy has yet to unfold. Many in the industry are watching to see when and how the firm will launch any patent infringement enforcement efforts.[11] To date, two observations regarding IV are clear: They have facilitated the growing recognition of IP value and they have brought a new level of professionalism and business expertise to the industry. Intellectual Ventures has been active at IP trade events and is a common participant at legislative hearings. Myhrvold's comments stem from a belief that the U.S. is dependent on innovation for its economic growth and that the value of patents should be protected.

Markets abruptly introduced to new and well funded competitive business models expectedly fear the unfamiliar and uncertain. The debate surrounding P-LECs and their appropriate role in future marketplaces will continue though in many respects the fear of the patent troll is grossly exaggerated. Reasons for this include:

- P-LECs currently benefit from market inefficiency. They are able to purchase patents at relatively low and attractive prices only because it is costly for sellers to otherwise clear the market price. This is a temporary condition, and new developments such as the public auction floor are likely to greatly impede the progress P-LECs currently enjoy.
- Most P-LECs are investment driven and therefore rational and predictive. These newer professionally managed entities are often far easier to work with than the stereotypical individual inventor. Too often, the individual inventor becomes emotionally invested in his discoveries. Complimentary financial investment often brings a strain to the entire situation.
- The P-LEC business model is a fragile one. In addition to the cost of patent acquisition, their strategy requires extraordinary investment in legal fees and other costs. These investments are constantly at risk of falling to zero based on a number of extraneous events and authorities out of the control of the P-LEC itself.
- Several P-LECs are now themselves public companies, providing other market participants the opportunity to hedge the general risk of a growing troll threat. If P-LECs are a significant business expense, their success should be reflected in increased share pricing. Perhaps purchasing futures on a basket of P-LEC stocks will someday be viewed much like a currency hedge.
- Recently, the Supreme Court has acted in ways that severely limit the bargaining position of P-LECs. This is most notable in the eBay decision and the KSR decision that effectively limited the risk of permanent injunctions and eliminating many fringe patents, respectively.[12]

Those with angst over the feared patent troll should take comfort in that there simply are few such firms. Naming ten P-LECs is a challenge; naming twenty is almost impossible.

Conclusion

In recognizing the value in intellectual assets, operating companies are reinventing themselves from patent collector to active portfolio manager. Companies no longer simply gather good inventions that happen to come out of R&D, but seek the right IP—whether created in-house or bought from others. Portfolio managers wisely manage their assets and progressive operators now make what they can create best, buy what is cheaper to outsource, and sell what is not needed. Portfolio managers are also realizing that every R&D project should have a second stage-gate decision of continuing to build, and patent no longer as a priority for internal use but rather for the sole purpose to sell in the emerging market. The potential positive impact of harvesting the invention rights of what appear to be errant R&D dollars is enormous, and one that shareholders will likely expect companies, and their management to nurture.

Although the IP marketplace remains a work in progress, portfolio managers are beginning to assess the quality of the intellectual assets that they hold and their relationship to the business strategy; if the patents are not strong but do not read on the right products (theirs and others), they have little business value. Worse still, patents can give a false sense of security, the so-called "illusion of exclusion." Even strong patents have their limitations if not exploited efficiently. A basic understanding of IP value, widely held, serves as a strong foundation for continued progress.

About the Author

James E. Malackowski is President and Chief Executive Officer of Ocean Tomo, LLC, an integrated Intellectual Capital Merchant Banc that provides valuation, investment, and risk management services. Mr. Malackowski is internationally recognized in the field of IP management, as well as a noted expert in business valuation and IP strategy. He is a member of the IP Hall of Fame Academy and was recognized in 2007 as one of the fifty most influential people in intellectual property. Prior to forming Ocean Tomo, he served as a finance and investment advisor working with one of the nation's oldest investment banks. Mr. Malackowski spent 15 years as a management consultant and forensic accountant focused

(continued)

on intangible assets. In this capacity, he served numerous roles, growing the practice to the nation's largest before its sale.

He is a member of the President's Council for the Chicago Museum of Science and Industry and a current Director of Invent Now, Inc., a subsidiary of the National Inventors Hall of Fame, where Mr. Malackowski previously served as Trustee. He is a past president of The Licensing Executives Society USA and Canada, Inc., and a former director of the International Intellectual Property Institute. On more than thirty occasions, Mr. Malackowski, a Registered Certified Public Accountant, has served as an expert in Federal Court on questions relating to intellectual property economics, including business valuation. As an inventor, he has nine issued U.S. patents. He is an Adjunct Instructor at the University of Notre Dame Mendoza College of Business where he was a Summa Cum Laude graduate.

Notes

1. President and Chief Executive Officer, Ocean Tomo, LLC. The views expressed herein reflect that of the author and not necessarily those of Ocean Tomo or its affiliates. The author wishes to thank Dipanjan Nag and Susan Aylward for their substantial assistance in the preparation of this Chapter.
2. Daniel Sorid, "Patent Payoffs Fuel Rush of New Start-Ups." November 4, 2004. http://forbes.com/business/newswire/2004/04/11/rtr1328534.html
3. WARF—Wisconsin Alumni Research Foundation is the Technology Transfer arm of University of Wisconsin. WARF is attributed the success of licensing Vitamin D analogs, one of the most successful university licenses.
4. "Openshark Chooses IPotential Patent Brokerage Services for Sale of Wireless Technology Patents; IPBS's Value Added Services Result in a 60-Percent Higher Price Than Original Offer." http://findarticles.com/p/articles/mi_m0EIN/is_2005_Sept_13/ai_n15388432
5. Theresa Agovino, "Pfizer to Cut 10,000 Jobs, Close Plants." *Washington Post*, January 22, 2007. http://www.washingtonpost.com/wp-dyn/content/article/2007/01/22/AR2007012200577.html
6. The Star-Ledger Continuous News Desk. "Drugmaker Wyeth Plans 5,000 Job Cuts." *Star-Ledger*, January 25, 2008, http://www.nj.com/news/index.ssf/2008/01/drugmaker_wyeth_plans_10000_jo.html
7. Ocean Tomo Research. See www.OceanTomoIndexes.com
8. Alan Ratliff, "The In-House Counsel Institute Damages," Paper presented at the annual AIPLA Meeting. Washington, D.C., October 18-20, 2007.

9. Marius Meland, "IP Litigation Yielded $3.4B in 2006: Survey." *IPLaw360.* December 29, 2006.
   FTI Consulting. "Intellectual Property Statistics." www.fticonsulting.com/media/3491/Intellectual_Property_Statistics.pdf
10. Kenneth Cukier, "Voracious Venture." *The Economist,* 22 Oct 2005.
11. Rebecca Buckman, "Patent Firm Lays Global Plans." *Wall Street Journal.* November 12, 2007.
12. *eBay Inc. and Half.com, v. MercExchange, L.L.C.,* 547 U.S. 388 (2006).
    KSR International Co. v. Teleflex Inc., 550 U.S., 127 S.Ct.1727 (2007).

CHAPTER 12

The Evolving Role of IP in M&A: From Deal-Breaker to Deal-Maker[1]

BY RON LAURIE

PERSPECTIVE Over the past several years, patents have come to be recognized by the financial community not just as a bundle of legal rights, but as an independent commercial asset class, like real estate and corporate securities. Innovative new models for monetizing patents have emerged based on the creative adaptation of existing models used with more traditional asset classes such as asset-backed securities and more traditional strategic models.

"This shift in perception about the uses and the value of patents," says Ron Laurie, an IP investment banker and former patent attorney who focuses on transactions, "has spawned a proliferation of market makers, intermediaries, and service providers, including patent aggregators, enforcers, investors, financiers, brokers, exchanges, and auction houses.

"New business models are emerging every day. More recently, institutional investors, in the form of private equity firms and hedge funds, have come to see investing in patents, or in patent litigation, or trading public company shares based on patent-related information, as a natural expansion of their existing business."

Laurie contends that the shift in perception regarding IP assets has until now had little, if any, impact, on corporate mergers and acquisitions. The reasons are both structural and environmental, and derive in

(continued)

large part from the problem of corporate valuation, especially when it involves intangible assets. IP was traditionally viewed in M&A transactions as a possible "deal-breaker," effectively an afterthought that IP lawyers attended to. When it came to consummating a transaction, these professionals were much more likely to regard all news as bad news. Today, IP in M&A is starting to be seen as an important deal facilitator that the bankers, private equity capital providers, and others need to understand from the start.

Not Just a Bundle of Rights

It's no secret that there has been a fundamental shift in the way that business and financial communities view intellectual property, especially patents. Patents have been seen historically as exclusionary legal rights, which give their owner the ability to exclude competitors from particular markets (via injunction); to tax competitors for the privilege of participating in those markets (via license fees); or to force them to "design-around" the protected subject matter. Over the past five years or so, however, patents have come to be recognized not just as a bundle of legal rights, but an independent commercial asset class, like real estate and corporate securities. Innovative new models for monetizing patents have emerged based on the creative adaptation of existing models used with more traditional asset classes.

This shift in perception about the uses and economic value of patents has spawned a proliferation of market-makers, intermediaries, and service providers, including patent aggregators, enforcers, investors, financiers, brokers, exchanges, and auction houses, and new business models are emerging every day.[2] More recently, institutional investors, in the form of private equity firms and hedge funds, have come to see investing in patents, or in patent litigation,[3] or trading public company shares based on patent-related information,[4] as a natural expansion of their existing business.

There is one area of business activity, however, in which this shift in perception has had little, if any, effect—the world of corporate M&A (mergers and acquisitions). There are a variety of reasons for this, some of which are structural and derive from the intrinsic nature of intangible assets and others of which result from environmental factors relating to the way that the management of the M&A process has evolved. By far, the most significant impediment has been the inherent difficulty in valuing intangible assets, and in particular the intellectual property component of corporate value. This chapter will examine some of these challenges, and suggest possible ways to more effectively integrate IP into the value calculus in mainstream M&A activity.

First Generation M&A Mindset: IP as a Deal-Breaker

For decades, the role of IP analysis in M&A transactions has been limited to the identification and allocation of IP-related risk. Foremost among these is actual or prospective third-party infringement litigation that presents the threat of substantial monetary damages exposure, or worse yet an injunction that shuts down a product line or an entire business. Other IP-related risk factors include the potential loss of a critical inbound license upon sale or change of control of the target company, clear title defects such as jointly owned IP, or third-party ownership claims based on the absence of critical employee or consultant invention assignment agreements, and compulsory licensing obligations arising from participation in industry standards organizations. The risk identification process is referred to as "IP due diligence," and risk allocation is achieved through a combination of contractual provisions including representations and warranties, (with attached knowledge qualifiers and materiality thresholds), closing conditions, indemnification, escrow of some portion of the purchase price, and other risk shifting mechanisms.

In this model, the primary mission of the acquirer's IP diligence team is ultimately to advise the company if they find any risk factor that is so significant that the acquirer should consider aborting a deal that has already been agreed upon, both as to overall structure (e.g., reverse triangular merger, forward merger, asset sale, stock sale, etc.) and, more importantly, in terms of valuation, (i.e., purchase price). Thus, the focus is almost entirely on IP risk and not on IP value, and the role of the IP analysis is solely that of a potential "deal-breaker." (It is a relatively rare occurrence where the discovery of a previously unknown IP-related risk causes the parties to revisit, and adjust, the deal price.) In this context, IP diligence should be contrasted with technology diligence, where substantial resources are devoted to analyzing the expected synergies and efficiencies in combining the technologies and associated markets of the target company with those of the acquirer, and those synergies or efficiencies are then translated into, or at least validate, the deal price.

As mentioned above, the reasons for this lack of attention to IP in deal pricing fall into two categories: structural and environmental. The most important structural factor is the perceived inability on the part of the companies involved in the transaction, and their investment bankers and accountants, to accurately calculate (or even estimate) the IP component of the target's corporate value. Most of the traditional metrics used to value companies simply don't apply to intellectual property assets.[5] These valuation methodologies come from two sources: valuation of tangible assets such real property or industrial equipment, and valuation of businesses.

Tangible asset valuation methods, such as the cost, income, and market approaches have been "ported" to IP assets with little success. The cost of developing a noninfringing substitute for patented technology may have little relevance to the true value of the patents in question. The net present value of the predicted future income stream(s) attributable to the patents in question (aka discounted or risk-adjusted cash flow) may be entirely speculative, especially in the absence of past earnings attributable to those patents. With regard to the market approach, patents tend to be unique and largely nonsubstitutable, and therefore a "comparables" analysis, while often providing some useful data points on value, cannot be relied upon to the same degree as with real property, industrial equipment, antiques, fine art, or classic cars because the inherent uniqueness of patents makes the notion of a comparable patent, or patent portfolio, elusive at best. The inherent difficulty of using comparables to value IP is compounded by the fact that historical transaction (price) data for patent sales, as opposed to licenses, is very hard to come by because purchasers view their IP buying strategies as highly confidential. This will be discussed further later in the chapter.

As to existing methods of valuing companies, the traditional accounting performance metrics such as EBITDA, free cash flow, debt/equity ratios, and, in the case of public companies, market cap and price/earnings multiples, are inherently retrospective. That is, they are based largely on historical performance, and on the fundamental assumption that past performance is a reasonably good indicator of future success. Thus, from an accounting perspective, the value of tangible assets and of going-concern businesses, and the predicted future income streams that they will generate, is based on looking in the rear-view mirror. Alternatively, the intrinsic value of intellectual property assets depends, for the most part, on future events. This is especially true for the most valuable of all IP assets, patents covering breakthrough or disruptive technologies with no history of commercialization and financial return, but which turn out to cover "the next big thing."

Another difficulty in valuing patents is that their true value is heavily dependent on the existing patent portfolio and competitive position of the acquirer, and the use to which it intends to put the acquired patents, (e.g., strategic [increased market share via exclusion of competitors or market expansion by using IP rights as contributions to joint ventures or alliances], financial [top line revenue enhancement via licensing or cost reduction via cross-licensing], or defensive [settling or pre-empting patent attacks by litigious competitors].) This contextual aspect of intangibles valuation involves the concept of "value in use."

There are also a variety of environmental impediments to integrating IP value analysis into corporate M&A transactions. Some of these result from the valuation challenges discussed above, while others are inherent in the M&A process itself, and from the organizational status of the IP function within most large technology companies.

If an M&A transaction can be analogized to a symphony, then the investment bankers on each side of the deal are the orchestra conductors. The "i-bankers" play a central role in coordinating among, and integrating the contributions of, the various subadvisors such as lawyers and accountants. The lawyers are in turn led by the corporate lawyers who initially structure and then "paper" the deal with the assistance of various legal specialists such as antitrust, tax, environmental, employment, and of course, intellectual property lawyers. The i-bankers, and thus the parties to the transaction, typically do not focus on IP during the early stages of M&A activity, such as target selection and deal pricing. There are several reasons for this. (It should be noted that while most large i-banks have one or more IP lawyers on staff, these IP specialists rarely become involved in the M&A process, and instead are tasked with protecting any potentially patentable techniques, methodologies, business models, or financial "products" developed by the i-bank.)

One reason that investment bankers avoid focusing on IP value in deal pricing has already been mentioned: the difficulty in valuing IP. Most of the investment bankers' compensation for M&A advisory work is paid in the form of a success fee that is contingent on closing the transaction. Thus, if at all possible, i-bankers will avoid introducing any unnecessary closing risk into a deal in the form of economic issues as to which the parties may not be able to agree. Stated more directly, the last thing an i-banker wants to see is a potential deal-killer. Because IP valuation is an art rather than a science, and in many cases, buyer and seller will have a significant difference of opinion on how much the seller's IP is really worth to the buyer, the i-bankers, and their corporate clients tend to avoid including IP in the deal price calculus because of fear of creating a price gap that can't be closed.

Another IP-related risk factor responsible for the avoidance of IP value analysis in determining corporate value may be the fear that one or more disgruntled shareholders or investors of a party to the transaction will come forward after the deal is completed, claiming (in the form of a lawsuit) either that the buyer overpaid for the IP, or that the seller received too little—or both! IP-related shareholder derivative suits and Sarbanes-Oxley litigation are relatively rare, but as the IP portion of overall corporate value continues to grow, we can expect to see more litigation based on the mismanagement of IP, including the failure to properly estimate, or to consider at all, the value of the target's IP in an M&A transaction.

Still another environmental factor may be that those who know the most about IP are typically lawyers, and because lawyers often see their primary role as identifying and mitigating risk, (i.e., protecting their clients by developing every possible worst-case scenario no matter how unlikely), there is a reluctance to let the lawyers "into the room" during the initial business discussions about price and value. In this regard, a rough analogy may be drawn to presenting a draft pre-nuptial agreement for discussion on a first date.

An additional argument sometimes heard, particularly in the case of public companies, is that IP doesn't need to be separately valued because the market has already done so, and it is reflected in the share price/market cap. As discussed above, this may be partially true for IP that can be directly linked to past earnings, but has little applicability to IP that is used strategically or defensively, or to IP covering disruptive new technologies.

Yet another justification for ignoring IP in deal pricing is that much of the target's IP may be in the form of sensitive technical information, trade secrets, and know-how, which will not be disclosed, even under NDA, until the target knows that there is a reasonable chance that a deal is possible. (This is particularly applicable where the parties are direct competitors.) While this may be true, there is often substantial IP in the form of issued patents and published patent applications, which can be reviewed early in the negotiations, and even before the target is approached. The ultimate extension of this strategy is to use IP analysis to help drive the target identification and selection processes.

Finally, there is an organizational reason why IP analysis is typically restricted to risk identification (via due diligence), and allocation (via reps & warranties, indemnity, escrow, etc). In the early stages, because of secrecy concerns, the corporate deal team is restricted to a few senior "C-level" executives including the CEO, VP of Corporate Development, CTO, CFO and CLO (aka General Counsel or VP-Law). Because in most companies, including technology companies, the head of IP reports to the head of legal (the CLO), and is thus not himself or herself a C-level executive, he or she is often viewed as not senior enough to be made aware of the prospective transaction, at least until the due diligence process begins. This will be discussed further later in the chapter.

Second Generation M&A Mindset: Seeing IP as a Deal-Driver

While the general tendency in traditional M&A activity was to avoid any consideration of IP in pricing an acquisition, there are some notable exceptions. The first is in connection with pharmaceutical and biotech companies where patents play a critical role. One possible reason is the fundamental difference in the effect, and thus the value, of patents in the bio/pharma world, as contrasted to high technology. To oversimplify a bit, in high-tech, patents are sought that broadly protect markets, while in bio/pharma, patents generally protect products. Thus, if a semiconductor company, or electronics company or software company develops a solution to a particular problem that had not previously been solved, the company tries to protect all solutions to the same problem, regardless of the implementation details. On the other hand, if a pharmaceutical company develops and patents a blockbuster drug for the treatment of a particular disease, and a competitor introduces a drug with a substantially different formulation that is also an effective treatment for the same disease, the former company's patent position provides no market protection (in the form of exclusionary rights) against the latter company. Because the patents are so closely tied to products, they often become an important element of company valuation. Another difference is that the patent invalidity risk due to unknown prior art, and thus the valuation uncertainty, is much lower for a new molecule than for a software architecture for network control that is claimed by its developers to be novel and nonobvious.

The second exception to the general rule of not considering IP value in M&A deal pricing is where there isn't anything else to value. A dramatic example in this category, in which the author was involved, was the sale of a company named InterTrust in November 2002. Since 1990, InterTrust had been pioneering the development of DRM (digital rights management) software for securely distributing high-value digital content (such as software, music, and movies) in a way that integrated a payment mechanism into the distribution system. The initial distribution mechanism was via encrypted CD-ROMs, but that changed with the arrival of the Internet (more precisely the World Wide Web) around 1993. (IBM and Xerox had also been developing products in this area for some time.)

InterTrust had gone public in 1999, and at the height of its product development efforts, the company employed nearly four hundred people. By the time of the sale of the company, there were only a handful left. This decline was due partly to the collapse of the Internet bubble, partly to the fact that the DRM market did not develop as quickly as expected, and partly to Microsoft's anticipated dominance in this area. InterTrust had yet to introduce a product, and thus there was no earnings history (EBITDA) on which to base company valuation. In fact, at the time of the sale, the only assets were: a patent portfolio covering a wide range of different DRM implementations comprising 26 issued U.S. patents and 85 pending patent applications around the world, and a patent infringement lawsuit against Microsoft based on 11 of those patents.

InterTrust's board of directors and senior management decided to reposition the company from a product company to an IP licensing company and sell the company to a major corporate player that was, or wanted to be, in the DRM space. Several large investment banks initially contacted by InterTrust passed on sell-side representation of the company because of the lack of earnings history and absence of any "real" assets, and because of their inability to value the patents and the law suit against Microsoft. Ultimately, one of the smaller investment banks, Stephens Bank, accepted the representation and InterTrust was ultimately sold to a joint venture formed by Sony, Philips, and Stephens for $453 million! This was a highly strategic acquisition for Sony, which was planning to turn its PlayStation 3 game console into a full-fledged digital content delivery—and transaction payment—device, in direct competition with Microsoft's XBox 360.

In July of 2003, eight months after the sale of InterTrust was announced, the judge in the patent suit against Microsoft, in a so-called Markman ruling, adopted InterTrust's patent claim construction, and nine months later, the suit was settled on the basis of Microsoft's payment of a one-time license fee of $440 million (just a shade under the acquisition price of InterTrust).

After InterTrust, there could be no doubt that patents having significant strategic value, in terms of providing competitive market position, could be used to source a substantial M&A deal. This transaction signaled that the role of IP in the M&A world had indeed transitioned from a potential deal-breaker to a deal-driver.

Remaining Impediments to Fully Integrating IP Value Analysis into M&A Transactions—And Possible Solutions

As discussed above, the primary reason that IP value is typically not considered in pricing M&A deals is the lack of reliable methodologies to translate a company's IP position into quantitative economic terms. While the income approach—which seeks to estimate the risk-adjusted net present value of incremental future income attributable to the IP—may provide some useful data, by far the best indications of value are recent transaction prices for the sale of comparable (or at least, similar) patent portfolios. However, there are two problems with using "comp" data to value IP: first, the almost total absence of publicly available purchase price data; and second, even if the data were available, the analytic challenge of determining what is, and what is not, a comparable patent portfolio and/or transaction. The good news is that there are solutions to both problems on the horizon.

The primary reason that patent sale transaction data is hard to find is that one or both of the parties to the transaction, most often the buyer, wants it that way. If it were widely known, a company's patent purchasing activity would provide a window of competitive intelligence into the purchaser's market and product strategies. Thus, unless the buyer is a public company and the amount paid is "material" given the size of its business, price information generally will not be available from any public source. In fact, not only is price information difficult to come by, but even the fact that a given company has purchased patents at all may be concealed through the use of a shell company. It is quite common for a buyer to take title in the name of an LLC formed for that purpose and then record the patent assignments in the applicable patent offices around the world under the name of the shell company. (Of course, if and when the patents are litigated, the true owner will likely be disclosed in discovery and may be forced to join the suit on the basis that it is an "indispensable party.")

Notwithstanding this veil of secrecy around patent sale transactions, there is one good source of anecdotal data, and it resides in the minds of the patent brokers and other intermediaries involved in the majority of these transactions. Of course, the intermediaries are almost always contractually precluded from disclosing the details of a particular transaction, but the information can be used by them to give future clients at least a rough estimate of the market value of a given patent or portfolio. And obviously, the more transactions in which a particular brokerage firm is involved, the better the estimate.

As corporate IP strategy becomes increasingly visionary and proactive (as described in the book, *Edison in the Boardroom*[6]), demand will rise sharply for better IP transaction information that compliments existing data services subscribed to by traditional corporate development teams involved in the M&A process. Beyond the patent intermediaries as a source of anecdotal comp data, there is currently a new effort underway to create a trusted, standardized database of patent sale information that can be used by prospective patent buyers and sellers to make better decisions. The organization leading this initiative is Gathering2.0, based in Menlo Park, California,[7] and its initial members include some of the largest corporate patent buyers, and buyer/sellers, in the world, including both major technology companies and financial buyers.

Just as other markets have evolved with increasing liquidity and transparency fueled by the sharing of standardized information among participants through a trusted, neutral "informediary,"[8] Gathering2.0 is providing such an approach at a time when demand for patent transaction information is rising. By collecting standardized patent transaction data from patent buyers and sellers, and taking certain measures to ensure that their identities remain confidential and their data submission is valid, this service will be a valuable resource for prospective buyers and sellers for comparative data and trend analysis on patent sales, and eventually all other types of IP transactions.

Gathering2.0's standardized data set includes pricing, as well as other extremely relevant information such as the applicable technology, products or markets, the number and geographical distribution of the patents, etc. However, this data must be properly "anonymized" or it will not be made available. The obvious challenge here is balancing the need for confidentiality as to past transactions with the desire for useful information in pricing future transactions.

Addressing information-sharing in the form of "comp data" among IP market participants is a critical step in a process to more fully integrate IP value analysis into C-level corporate decision making, including M&A transactions. Certainly, other steps are needed to help improve transparency and efficiency in the transaction process. Gathering2.0 is working with several global leaders to develop other standardized "next" practices to address key IP diligence process issues including, for example, standard formats for offering documents (i.e. selling packages), dealing with encumbrances, standardizing on the right set of valuation methodologies for certain IP transaction types, appropriate time limits for due diligence, recommended reps and warranties for purchase agreements, and the like.

Collectively, the IP diligence process issues outlined in this chapter are key factors influencing the lack of liquidity; they are also creating an unacceptable level of uncertainty for valuations and the inability to predict if, and when, a deal will happen. Such inefficiencies in the diligence process are costly, as evidenced by high broker commissions (20–40%), and lead to far more deals cratering rather than closing. However, as more corporate M&A efforts get infused with proactive, visionary IP strategies supported by reliable data, analytics, and other standardized diligence tools, the market will benefit from increased liquidity.

The Role of the CIPO in Early-Stage M&A Activity

As mentioned above, one of the environmental impediments to integrating IP value analysis into early-stage M&A activity, (i.e., formulation of corporate growth strategy, target selection, and deal pricing), results from the organizational status of the IP function within most large companies. Typically, the IP function is embedded within the corporate legal department, with the head of IP (variously described as Director of IP, Chief IP Counsel, or Patent Counsel) reporting to the Chief Legal Officer (who may be titled General Counsel or VP-Law). This organizational locus is suboptimal for several reasons.[9]

First, the primary mission of the legal department is risk management, not value enhancement. The latter role is the function of the finance, R&D, marketing, and corporate development groups within the enterprise. However, while risk mitigation is a critical element of IP management, that mission can be executed through legal department oversight, without placing the IP function within (or at least, entirely within) the corporate legal organization. There are many examples of corporate functions that involve legal risk, but are not embedded within the legal organization. For example, the human relations department deals with legal risk on a daily basis, but the head of HR does not report to the General Counsel.

Second, unless the head of IP is seen as a member of the senior management team—generally defined as "C-level" executives (CEO, CFO, CTO, etc.)—he or she will not be viewed as worthy of a seat at the table in early stage discussions of potential M&A opportunities. For example, in the author's experience, the IP specialists in the outside law firms representing the acquirer and target frequently know about the prospective transaction before, and sometimes long before, the parties' internal IP counsel. In M&A-speak, the corporate IP group, including the head of IP, is viewed as not senior enough to be within the small group of key executives who are brought "over the wall" in the early stages of an acquisition, divestiture, or so-called merger of equals.

This environmental impediment will gradually disappear as more and more companies move the IP function, or at least the business-oriented parts of it, out of the legal department, and elevate the status of the head of IP to a C-level position in the form of a Chief Intellectual Property Officer (CIPO). The CIPO will become an essential member of the corporate M&A deal team and will be intimately involved in planning the company's growth (or downsizing) strategy, in selecting and ranking potential M&A opportunities, and, once a target is selected, in pricing the deal. Even in those companies, where the head of IP continues to report to the head of legal, companies are developing informal "dotted-line" relationships between the de-facto CIPO and the nonlegal C-level executives tasked with enhancing corporate value. Another organizational variant is to keep IP litigation within the legal department but "spin-out" the value extraction aspects of IP into a separate organization or even a seperate company. Early adopters of this model include Hewlett-Packard (Joe Beyers), IBM (John Kelley), AT&T (Scott Frank), and Philips (Rudd Peters).

The Role of the IP Investment Banker in Extracting Maximum Value from IP in M&A Transactions

The recent recognition of IP as a new commercial asset class means that monetization models that have developed in connection with other asset classes will be adopted, with appropriate modification, to exploit this new asset class. This has already occurred with regard to patent brokerage (which bears some striking similarities to real estate brokerage); IP collateralization (a new form of asset-backed lending); and securitization of IP royalty streams (although to date, this model has been generally limited to bio/pharma patents, music copyrights, and trademarks). The next step will be to adapt the existing M&A models employed in connection with the acquisition, divestiture, and merger of companies, and parts of companies, to encompass IP value analysis.[10] Enter the IP investment banker.

Two examples will now be described illustrating how an IP investment banker can either increase the acquisition price for a seller in the context of existing M&A discussions, or actually source an M&A transaction in the first instance in the form of a corporate spin-out of "stranded" technology and associated IP, a model that can be truly characterized as "IP-driven M&A."

When a larger company approaches a small or mid-sized technology company with a view towards potential acquisition, the conversation quickly turns to corporate valuation. For all the reasons described above, this process tends to ignore, or at least undervalue, the target's IP position, and in particular its patents and trademarks. In this context, an IP investment banker representing the target can play an important role in refocusing the acquirer's attention on intangible assets as an important element of the acquisition price.

One technique for achieving this shift in value perception on the part of the buyer, which this author has successfully used, is to transfer the target's patents and trademarks to an IP development company, which may be structured as a parent or independently controlled sibling of the target. The IP holding company then licenses the patents and trademarks to the target on a nonexclusive, and possibly royalty-bearing, basis. This means that acquisition of the target does not automatically transfer ownership of the IP to the buyer, but rather only the nonexclusive right to use it, in exchange for reasonable compensation. The IP holding company is free to license the same IP to others, including the buyer's competitors. The transfer of the target's IP to a holding company forces the acquirer to decide whether it wants to acquire the IP as well as the complementary business assets owned by the target—in which case the IP must be separately valued and priced.

Another technique to force buyers to focus on IP value involves the use of exclusive field-of-use licenses. Suppose the target has a patent portfolio covering several distinct and nonoverlapping technologies, commercial applications, or vertical markets. Suppose further that only one of these is applicable to the prospective buyer's current business. The buyer will certainly undervalue the patents that do not relate to its business. In this variant, the target can transfer ownership of its IP assets to a holding company, and take back an exclusive field-of-use license limited to its current business or to the business of the prospective acquirer. This will give the buyer an exclusive position in the IP for its core business, including the rights to license and to assert the patents against competitive uses, but not the right to license or sue others in different fields. This focuses the buyer on the question of whether it wishes to acquire the IP rights in fields outside of its current business. If it does, it must estimate the incremental value of doing so, and negotiate an appropriate price for those noncore rights.

An example of IP-driven M&A involves the monetization of "stranded" technologies and related IP that exist in virtually all large technology companies. In this context, stranded technology comes in two principal forms. One of these is "noncore" technology that doesn't fit with the owner's current business and future road map. This type of stranded technology and IP can result from many different scenarios. It may have once been core but has become stranded as a result of a change in the owner's business plan, technology focus, or target markets. It may have been acquired along with core assets in a corporate M&A transaction. It may have lost a powerful internal advocate that has left the company.

Regardless of why it is noncore, one thing is certain. Because it is nonstrategic, it can't compete for R&D dollars with core technologies. Thus, if it stays where it is, its value will surely diminish over time. Once the key inventors realize that they are no longer on the main track, they will move elsewhere within the company or find another employer. This will usually have the effect of rendering the recorded know-how unusable because the people who created it are no longer around to explain it. Finally, the associated patent position will wither and possibly disappear altogether because there will be no money for follow-on applications and issued patents will lapse due to nonpayment of maintenance fees.

The other type of stranded technology and IP can be characterized as multiuse, or "multistranded." In this case, the technology is in fact core to the owner's business but that business represents only a fraction of the total available market in which it potentially can be commercialized. The best source of this type of stranded technology is defense contractors, where the commercial (e.g., nonmilitary/aerospace) applications of the technology may represent 90% or more of the total available market.

Under a new IP-driven spin-out model,[11] the stranded technology and associated IP is assigned by its corporate owner to a Newco called a TACL (Technology Acquisition, Cultivation, and Licensing company) in exchange for some combination of a minority equity ownership interest in the TACL, an up-front payment, a continuing royalty stream, a convertible note, etc. The originator will typically also get an exclusive field-of-use grant-back license limited to its primary business. This is essential in the multiapplication type of stranded technology, but is also applicable to the noncore variant. The exclusive field-of-use grant-back may also extend to improvements on the transferred technology developed by the TACL or its licensees. The attractiveness of the exclusive field-of-use grant-back is that for all practical purposes, the IP position of the original technology owner remains essentially the same after the transfer of the IP to the TACL. For example, the originator can still sue and/or license competitors within the field of its primary business. The TACL value proposition to the corporate owner is simple—a partial interest in something of value is better than 100% ownership of nothing.

The TACL typically holds the technology and IP for a period of one to three years during which time the technology is brought to "commercializable" form, and the IP is enhanced through prosecution of pending patent applications, filing of follow-on applications, and possibly acquisition of complementary patents and applications from third parties via patent brokers, auctions, or direct negotiations.

On the financial side, the funding for this technology and IP development comes from capital markets, (e.g., high-net-worth individuals, private equity, hedge funds, etc). In contrast to traditional VC-backed spin-outs, the TACL model is very capital efficient because no investor money is spent on building out operating infrastructure, such as marketing, sales, and human resources departments. The reason is that the return on scaling infrastructure is typically low, zero, or even negative. Instead, all operating capital is focused on the improvement of the technology and IP which, if successful, produces a much higher IRR (internal rate of return) for the investors.

At the end of the holding period, the investor exit takes one of several forms including: M&A (i.e., sale to an operating company for whom the improved technology and IP are core); creation of a stand-alone business by wrapping operating infrastructure around the technology and IP; or in the worst-case scenario where the technology doesn't live up to expectations, sale of the IP to an operating company or a financial buyer. The most interesting exit, however, is the creation of a new kind of licensing entity, in the form of a strategic marketing company that develops and promotes multiple nonoverlapping applications or markets for the technology and IP, and then finds a commercialization partner within each "vertical" that is granted an exclusive field-of-use license.

Regardless of the particular exit chosen, one of the attributes of the TACL model that differentiates it from more traditional spin-outs is that the choice of the monetization model, (i.e., M&A sale, operating company, licensing company, or IP sale) can be deferred until both the value of the technology and the IP are significantly enhanced.

Conclusion

So far, the various models for extraction of value from intellectual property assets have developed independently of mainstream M&A activity. This adoption lag has resulted principally from traditional investment bankers' perceived inability to accurately value IP assets, and patents in particular, employing the accounting-based metrics used for tangible assets and companies. IP integration efforts are also impeded by a lack of engagement of IP business diligence early in the M&A process, and the absence of trusted comparable IP transaction data to aid decision-making. As better IP valuation models are developed, and as the IP function within a corporation moves up the org chart and is overseen by a CIPO IP value will become an essential consideration in early stage M&A activity. In parallel with the integration of IP into traditional M&A activity, new forms of IP-driven M&A will emerge and the IP investment banker will play a key role in extracting value from assets in the context of corporate transactions.

ABOUT THE AUTHOR

Ron Laurie has worked in Silicon Valley for over forty-five years, initially as a computer programmer and systems engineer, and then as an Intellectual Property lawyer. In 2004, he cofounded Inflexion Point Strategy, LLC, an Intellectual Property investment bank that advises technology companies and institutional investors in M&A and licensing transactions. Prior to launching Inflexion Point, Mr. Laurie was a founding partner of Skadden Arps' Palo Alto office where he chaired the firm's IP Strategy and Transactions Group for six years. He was also a founding partner of the Silicon Valley offices of Weil, Gotshal, and Irell & Manella.

As a lawyer, Mr. Laurie advised clients in the semiconductor, computer, software, communications, and media and financial services industries on intellectual property strategy—a subject he taught at

(*Continued*)

Stanford and Boalt (UC Berkeley) law schools—with a primary focus on the strategic use of IP assets in complex business transactions including mergers and acquisitions, technology divestitures and spin-outs, joint ventures, and strategic alliances. At Skadden, he led IP teams in some of the largest technology deals ever done, worth over $50 billion. Mr. Laurie is a registered patent attorney and a substantial part of his prior law practice involved strategic planning, competitive analysis, and commercial exploitation of patents. He wrote the Priceline "reverse auction" patent that was the first Internet business method patent to gain national attention when it issued in 1998.

Notes

1. The author wishes to acknowledge the valuable insights provided by Patrick H. Sullivan, Sr. of ICMG, and Michael Pierantozzi of Gathering2.0.
2. Raymond Millien and Ron Laurie, "Meet the Middlemen," *Intellectual Asset Management Magazine* 28 (2008); and Ron Laurie. "Business Opportunity Alternatives to Assertion-Based Patent Monetization." Patent Strategy & Management 8, nos. 4 and 5, *ALM Law Journal* (2007).
3. Nathan Vardi, "Patent Pirates," Forbes.com, May 7, 2007.
4. John Brindgardner, "Hedge Fund Spies in Courtroom," *IP Law & Business*, May 2007.
5. Patrick H. Sullivan, Sr. and Rob Mclean, "The Confusing Task of Measuring Intangible Value," *Intellectual Asset Management Magazine* 23 (2007); and Suzanne S. Harrison and Patrick H. Sullivan, Sr. "Extracting Value From Intangibles by Leading Companies in IC Management," *The Journal of Intellectual Capital* 1, Volume 1 (2000).
6. Julie L. Davis and Suzanne S. Harrison, *Edison in the Boardroom: How Leading Companies Realize Value* (Hoboken, NJ: John Wiley & Sons, 2001).
7. www.gathering2.com.
8. John Hagel III and Marc Singer, *Net Worth: Shaping Markets When Customers Make the Rules* (Massachusetts: HBS Press, 1999).
9. Robert Sterne and Ron Laurie, "The CIPO Manifesto," *Intellectual Asset Management Magazine* 25 (2007); and "The Recipe for CIPO Success," *Intellectual Asset Management Magazine* 26 (2007).
10. Ron Laurie and Robert Greene Sterne, "Integrating IP Value Assessment into Early-Stage M&A Activity," *IP Value* (2007).
11. "The TACL: A New Model of Corporate Spin-Out for "Stranded" Technology and IP" (paper presented at the tenth annual corporate venturing and strategic investing conference of the International Business Forum, February 5, 2008, www.ibfconferences.com/ibf/presentationdetails.asp

CHAPTER 13

Patents-As-Hedge: Wall Street's Emerging Monetization Model

BY JOHN A. SQUIRES[1]

PERSPECTIVE Since *State Street Bank* rendered business methods patentable a decade ago, financial institutions have sought to identify and capture the abundant innovation their employees generate. But filing patents on esoteric products like derivative securities and other financial instruments is not a simple matter. It requires an abundance of time and patience. Financial institutions hope to use patents not only to get a leg up on the direct competition, but also to prevent independent inventors, and NPEs backed by private equity capital, from asserting against them.

Business method patents are largely untested and their market value in most cases is insignificant However, their enterprise value to some owners can be very significant. Business method patents that cover financial and other products typically require five or more years to be issued by the USPTO, which is highly selective about granting them. It also remains to be seen how well methods' intellectual property rights will hold up to the scrutiny of litigation. Still, financial institutions as diverse as Citicorp, Merrill Lynch, Bank of America, and Goldman Sachs have been filing patents in increasing numbers and searching for the right ways to extract a return on them, preferably without asserting against each other.

"Wall Street believes in market solutions," says John Squires, Goldman Sachs' Chief IP counsel and director of their IP-related activities. "As

(continued)

a result, financial service firms are beginning to deploy their emerging patent base in a manner that is notably different from how other industries deploy, transact in, and even enforce their patents." Squires believes that outside of the financial industry, the value of a patent is in effect realized by the market exclusivity it provides. These traditional measures of value creation, however, have not yet become meaningful to financial institutions concerning their own intellectual property.

"An emerging model for financial institutions on Wall Street has started to focus on specific valuations for industry-generated and patentable intellectual property. The financial services industry is just now beginning to determine how to leverage its own intellectual property rights more fully and, consequently, is beginning to ascertain more precisely their enterprise value to its owners. In a nutshell, the view that is emerging is 'patents-as-hedge.'"

The upshot of this approach, notes Squires, is that financial companies see patents, for now at least, as an inherently defensive play. But that does not mean they can not have an important role in profitability. The use of patents, and patent applications, is growing in commercial consortia and joint-venture formation. This emerging use of IP can be found where several banks or financial firms come together to form a centralized marketplace for trading. Examples of operating ventures are beginning to paint a picture of a somewhat unique but still vital role for patents on Wall Street.

Valuing Risk Management

Some Wall Street firms have begun to participate in the slow march to procure, and even monetize, their own homegrown IP assets, which increasingly involve patents. So far, however, the emerging model for deploying financial patent assets appears to be based on risk-management notions rather than the traditional measures typically involved in commercializing innovative ideas. What kind of risk are financial service firms increasingly attempting to manage with patents? Operational risk.

In January 2006, major financial services industry associations provided a rare glimpse into their mindset concerning operational risk issues presented by patents. The financial services sector gave voice to their views via their first-ever Supreme Court amicus brief[2] on the patent-specific "automatic-injunction" rule at issue in *eBay vs. MercExchange.* Motivating the industry was the eyeful that they, as well as many other industries, had received as an injunction grant was imminent in the RIM/Blackberry patent dispute, and was avoided only by an 11th hour settlement for $612.5 million.

The *eBay* case ultimately carried the same legal issue forward—the "automatic injunction" rule (albeit too late for RIM)—and thereby provided a timely vehicle for the major financial services industry associations to forcefully, and, as it turned out, successfully, argue for modernization of patent enforcement doctrine. In their view, it was high time that patent issues begin to take into account the increasing role that critical technologies and interoperability considerations play in global banking and trading operations.

The brief argued that patent law had not been updated in over a century and was being applied in today's complex and interconnected economy in a manner that presented unacceptable operational risk to the U.S. financial systems, markets, and exchanges. Indeed, in looking at eBay's operational model—a classic exchange after all is said and done—the financial services industry saw much of itself. The industry immediately recognized the automatic injunction rule's propensity to disrupt and/or dislocate financial exchanges and markets to the far-wider detriment of the public at large.

Blame for the shutdown risk faced by eBay in its patent dispute, according to the financial services industry, lay squarely at the feet of an arcane, patent-only legal rule that eschewed any avenue for factoring the public's overriding interest in liquid and efficient financial markets. To the industry, this dynamic was a recipe for severe operational and systemic risk—arising from a private party dispute no less—which precluded the broader industry of any countervailing opportunities to mitigate. Worse, in the industry's view, was the rule's foreclosure of a reviewing Court's ability to do equity—even as between the private parties.

As such, the major industry associations implored the Supreme Court to fix the doctrinal problem before a major disruption occurred. The *eBay* amicus brief argued that the existing "automatic injunction" rule concentrated too much power in the hands of singular patent-holders, and this predicament, if permitted to continue, could easily compromise aspects of the nation's financial infrastructure—an infrastructure that increasingly requires both transparency and stability to thrive. In short, the ability to literally terminate and force the unwinding of ongoing, complex financial transactions through an "automatic" patent injunction created the industry's nightmare scenario.

While the industry's joint-amicus brief strikingly advanced their legal position, it also provided an extraordinary window into the still-developing mindset on financial service directed patents in general and on intra-industry patent matters specifically. In the end, the financial services industry received the legal result they sought with the Supreme Court's unanimous decision providing an avenue for equitable balancing of factors. And as a result permanent injunctions have become substantially less "automatic" and operational risk considerations correspondingly reduced in potential severity. But, the *eBay* decision did not necessarily "weaken" patents in many financial service firms' eyes. Rather, it clarified their role.

Much has been written about how traditional industry participants procure patent assets and how they are being monetized and rendered an asset class. Indeed, *Rembrandts in the Attic* is still widely viewed, as it should be, as the seminal work for the patent-as-corporate-asset model. As a result, the patent-as-asset intellectual construct has become more or less accepted as generally valid. The patent-as-asset approach recognizes the value of committing resources to innovation and research to develop a new technology with a competitive edge through the exclusion of others from using the technology. The patent is considered part of an asset class that creates economic value through competitive products and/or services offerings. The value of a patent is derived from the breadth of its limited, exclusionary rights and, at times, coupled with any additional value as realized via the exercise of patent rights through market share captured.

Generally, Wall Street prefers market-based solutions. As a result, financial service firms are beginning to deploy their emerging patent portfolios in a manner that is notably different from how other industries have transacted in and enforced their patents.

For example, industries outside the financial services sector, such as the semiconductor or pharmaceutical industries, generally realize their intellectual property values indirectly. In other words, the value of the patent is in effect realized by market exclusivity—such as is done traditionally with name-brand pharmaceuticals. This model, however, relies on the litigation club of an injunction to enforce exclusivity—a model that presents an unacceptable level of risk to financial institutions. In short, a new paradigm was needed.

An emerging model for financial institutions on Wall Street has started to focus on specific valuations within market-structure consortia or joint ventures for industry-generated and patentable intellectual property. The financial services industry is just now beginning to determine how to leverage its own intellectual property rights more fully and, consequently, is beginning to ascertain more precisely their worth to an enterprise and its owners.

In the case of Wall Street's *own* inventions and developments, for a variety of reasons (many of which are either self-inflicted by the industry or stem from patent office oscillations—and now perhaps Federal Circuit second-guessing on the issue), a general consensus view of patents is still taking shape—almost ten years after the landmark *State Street Bank* decision recognizing technology deployed in a mutual fund structure as patentable.[3] Even so, the Federal Circuit again visited the statutory subject matter issue en Banc in *In re Bilski*.

Another reason a financial services sector consensus view on patents is lacking is that the commercial and competitive relationships between banks and their operations involving merchant banking, investment banking, commercial banking, asset management and brokerage, to name a few, are quite complex. In some instances, banks, which are competitors in certain franchises, may also be partners/lenders to each other. For example, competitive institutions often must work together in a variety of roles, particularly in taking a company public, for the success of their client. The same is true in certain developing markets for trading. This dynamic has been aptly described as creating "virtual partners" while existing as "brick-and-mortar" competitors.

Yet another reason a consensus view of patents remains an open question on Wall Street is the excruciatingly long pendency times in the U.S. Patent and Trademark Office for what the Patent Office itself classifies as "business method" technology. Rightly or wrongly, patents filed by Wall Street have been reactively classified as "business methods" by the patent office.

At present, patent applications filed back in 2002 and 2001, and classified by the Patent Office as covering "business method" technology are just now beginning to be either reviewed or allowed as patents in any appreciable numbers—but by no means in any significant quantum for meaningful statistical analysis. Additionally, active and visible patent licensing programs within the financial services industry are relatively rare and intra-industry enforcement of patent rights is rarer still. The last major reportable decision occurred in 1981 in Paine Webber vs. Merrill Lynch, concerning Merrill's cash management account patent.

As a result, the role of patents as they slowly work their way into the infrastructure of the financial services industry is still emerging. That view is being fashioned by two industry realities. First, a growing recognition has taken hold that cross-firm and cross-technology interoperability considerations as to how financial services and products are developed, delivered, processed, tracked, and reported is commercially crucial. Second, an emerging industry acknowledgement is taking shape that new developments and the intellectual property rights that arise around them, can aid interoperability and, importantly, be deployed to help *mitigate* risk to operations. In a nutshell, the view that is emerging is that of "patents-as-hedge."

The upshot of the patent-as-hedge approach is that patents are seen as inherently a defensive play. While to a large extent this is generally true, there is a burgeoning use of patents, and patent applications to be more precise, in commercial consortia and joint venture formation concerning market structure entities and technologies. This emerging use of patents and patent applications can be found, for example, where several banks or financial firms come together to form a centralized marketplace for trading. While anecdotal, several examples of operating ventures are beginning to paint a picture of a somewhat unique role for patents on Wall Street and their concomitant valuation, and use in a particular niche in the financial services sector.

By exploring how Wall Street is deploying patents of its own origin, we can gain a glimpse into how these patents are valued and in effect monetized in the marketplace.

Attributes of Patents Wall Street Seeks to Procure

With the advent of the *State Street Bank* decision, financial service firms now faced a choice with respect to their own homegrown systems and developments. Before *State Street*, the only dynamic that existed was to hope for a first mover advantage and/or hope to, where possible, maintain secrecy. The rediscovered availability of patents deployed in financial services operations offered for the first time the possibility of both maintaining proprietary rights as well as affording transparency. This choice, of course, also created many downstream scenarios potentially affecting other industry participants. These scenarios may involve considering the potential enforceability directly against a competitor, which has generally been uncharted territory for financial service firms.

Given the lengthy pendency times in the U.S. Patent Office, the financial services industry is still struggling to conceptualize and determine what lasting role, if any, patented innovations arising from their own institutions have. To be sure, there are differing philosophies and camps of thought. The "patent-as-asset" camp recognizes the value of a patent in and of itself—that is, as an asset, the price of which could be affected by market and other conditions at any point in time. However, the "patent-as-hedge" camp views patents as market-positioning tools available for deployment to ward off certain identified risks—most notably operational risks. Both schools of thought are alive, well, and sometimes even simultaneously held.

Specifically, the differing and often complex competitive philosophies existing on Wall Street as to the role of financial services patents give rise to some firms embracing patents as an asset class, while others accept the patent-as-hedge view on patents as a defensive tool. Others still prefer a purely "open-source" world and generally wish the entire patent dynamic away. But in the modern economy, generally, and in the delivery of financial services in particular, both banking and technology are inextricably intertwined. Complicating matters is the near-universal, technology-based desire for system and service interoperability. This desire appears to run counter to adoption of a propriety-rights regime, particularly concerning the back-office. As a result the patent issue—and deployment choices—may be a permanent part of the competitive landscape.

As for the front-office, a common concern expressed, predominantly by financial service firms that compete best on scale, is that a patent adversely affects liquidity in the market. While this concern is occasionally voiced, what often goes unstated is that notions of frictionless adoption of new ideas by-and-between rival firms is premised on the expectation that financial innovation is freely available to all, and is somewhat enshrined in the thinking that "that's the way it's always been done." Wrapping proprietary rights around an otherwise disclosed or easily discernable innovation is counterintuitive—and still remains an anathema to many. This is somewhat quixotic as the notion of maintaining trade secrecy around various underlying financial models and practices is also "the way it's always been done."

Firms that generally see themselves competing more effectively with their intellectual capital, have more openly embraced a model of procuring patents in specific instances where they may aid in extending their first mover advantages. Patents may thus help support a firm's overall market positioning as it launches new products and services into the marketplace.

No doubt this divergence of competitive strategy on IP colors the extent to which any one particular franchise in one particular financial service firm may decide to deploy its intellectual property in supporting either its existing operational business or even more elusively, help further new market opportunities—or both. This dynamic alone makes it exceedingly difficult to collect sufficient data on how, where, and why patents are deployed as assets, and, therefore, tends to preclude any meaningful trend analysis and valuation modeling.

If that problem is not daunting enough, a number of other intertwined factors put valuation methodologies seemingly beyond the reach of the industry. Such difficulties in valuation call into question the patent-as-asset assumption for the financial services sector. One factor that is particularly disruptive to any patent-as-asset modeling is the snail's pace at which patents as assets are "manufactured" in the financial services industry. As compared to applications in other industries, financial services patent applications have exceedingly long pendency times—3–5-fold—prior to allowance as a patent.

Immediately following the *State Street Bank* decision, patent application filings for so-called and characterized "business methods" increased dramatically[4] and created a significant backlog of applications requiring review by the U.S. Patent and Trademark Office.[5] Between the years 2000 and 2006, patent application filings for business method technology averaged greater that 7,000 applications per year. Similarly, in the year 2000, the average pendency of an application to a first action, which typically included an analysis regarding patentability of an invention claimed in the application, was about 23 months, in comparison to the average pendency to first action in about 14 months for the entire U.S. Patent and Trademark Office.

Although the U.S. Patent and Trademark Office reports that it has worked through its backlog of business method application filings incident to the State Street Bank decision, the pendency of an application to a first action now appears to have gotten worse. At mid-year in 2007, the U.S. Patent and Trademark Office reported that the pendency to first action was about 44 months with the pendency to allowance for patent at about 54 months. In addition to the significant delay to review "business method" applications, there has been a gradual decline in the allowance of patents from 2001 to mid-year 2007. Initially, and in 2001, business method patents were allowed in about 45% of applications filed. Since then, the allowance rate of business method patents declined to about 14% for 2003 through 2006, and has rebounded slightly to about 20% for mid-year 2007.[6] These troublesome trends must clearly be factored into any decision to seek patents for financial services innovations.

Long delays and pendency times lead to another problem. Once the patent is granted—years later—the relevant market almost immediately adopts the view that the patent is merely someone trying to corner an old idea. The state of the art at the time of the patent is granted—many years later—may be much more advanced than at the time the patent application was originally filed. Thus, the correlation of the patent at the point in time it actually issues to the commercial shelf-life and market place for the product or service that patent covers diminishes into irrelevance. It becomes as if the patent rights are in a time-warp. This fuels a quality-perception problem for financial services patents and as a result works to undermine market-acceptance and industry adoption.

The average four-year pendency of financial services applications has specifically prevented firms in the industry from establishing any type of rights-based rhythm as to their innovations and from building any meaningful portfolio of patent assets to deploy in the traditional way—either in support of product or service exclusivity or to license. Additionally, and in the four-plus-year time frame of patent pendency, the market may have self-selected different technologies and thus rendered patent coverage obsolete.

In other words, firms must make decisions to protect financial services innovations, knowing that the process to obtain a patent will take at least four years if not longer. As an alternative to seeking patent protection, some firms opt to forego the process by instead protecting new innovation as proprietary, trade-secret information. Often, that is not possible, because banking, security, and exchange regulatory rules require explicit disclosure and transparency.[7] Protecting innovation as a trade secret presents wholly different risks. For one, many trade secrets lack the capacity to be self-standing, deployable assets in the traditional manner that patents provide. This inherent nature of some valuable trade secrets makes them therefore very difficult to license-out to others. Some trade secrets as a result may be incapable of generate a licensing revenue stream.

Another factor affecting patent valuation on Wall Street is the ever-moving target of what is legally considered "patentable subject matter." In the patent application process for "business methods"—a category in which most financial service industry innovation finds itself dismissively lumped—the requirements constituting what is allowable to be examined for patent protection has undergone several evolutions. As a result, predictability and clarity are lacking.

Far from laying these "ill-conceived notions"[8] to rest after the *State Street Bank* decision, the U.S. Patent and Trademark Office adopted a policy that required a patent application for business methods to meet a "technological arts" test to be eligible for patentability.[9] The technological arts test required claims to have a computer or other apparatus to perform the invention. Then, surprisingly in 2005, the Board of Patent Appeals and Interferences of the U.S. Patent and Trademark Office diverged from the technical art test and determined that as long as a claimed invention produced a "useful, concrete and tangible result" it fell within the scope of patentable subject matter as long as it did not cover an abstract idea, law of nature, or physical phenomenon.[10] With a push for patent quality improvement for 'business method' patents, the U.S. Patent and Trademark Office developed a second-pair-of-eyes review process. The implementation of an additional, critical review of a patent application by a supervising patent examiner after an initial review by the first reviewing patent examiner means in practical terms that applications categorized as claiming "business method" inventions are more scrutinized than any other field in the patent office.[11] Now, and more recently in 2007, the Court of Appeals for the Federal Circuit (the specialty patent appellate court) developed law that precludes a finding of patentability of a business system if it relies solely on operation of human intelligence alone.[12] In other words, the Federal Circuit has now has declared that patentable subject matter excludes mental processes standing alone.

The claims in *Comiskey* were directed at a particular type of arbitration that depended on the use of mental steps. While the holding itself is not particularly problematic, the Federal Circuit went on to state that the routine addition of modern electronics to an otherwise unpatentable invention typically creates a *prima facie* case of obviousness. This concept is completely unsupported in other areas of patent law where the claims are judged as a whole and appears to be another rearguard effort by the courts to treat patents in financial services under a different legal standard. Unfortunately, these efforts have only hampered the industry's ability to adjust to what should be a settled question.

With these critical shifts in what is considered patentable subject matter, financial industry firms have been left with a lack of predictability and clarity with respect to the patent process for protecting its innovation. This has hampered the industries' ability to patent innovation even when they decide to pursue it.

Patent valuation is also affected by the absence of any ongoing or robust intra-industry licensing or cross-licensing. This absence causes a lack of transparency for the economics of patent valuation. Conventional licensing of patented technology provides a clear, tangible, and ready means to evaluate and calculate the economic value of a patent based, in part, on licensing and royalty fees generated from the license. In cases where patented technology is not licensed, the process to value patented technology is a little more muddled and requires a greater evaluation of the economics of the technology in the marketplace, the value realized by the firm owning the unlicensed technology, and other market factors.

Patent valuation is also hampered by a lack of significant intra-industry enforcement of its patented technology. Firms are competitors in certain areas of the financial services industry, and partners and/or lenders in others. The complex business relationships on Wall Street create a less-litigious "competitor on competitor" environment in comparison to other industries such as the pharmaceutical industry. In financial industry circles, such a competitor-on-competitor patent infringement suit may be seen as the ultimate failure of diplomacy. This environment has therefore seen only a passive approach to enforcing patent rights against other firms. This approach effectively diminishes a patent's value because it is not being enforced against those with no right to use the patented technology.[13]

Innovation for Consortia and Joint Ventures in Market Structures

The absence of a ready market, or consistent data, combined with uncertain law or policy concerning patentable financial services innovation, impedes any patent valuation process. Stated differently, the traditional inputs and resources for building and operating patent-valuation models familiar to other industries are rendered functionally frozen in the financial services industry. The valuation landscape, however, is not completely barren. A slim reed of patent utilization in a specific niche may hold promise for understanding valuation in relative terms. Patent applications have recently begun to play an increasing role in the financial services industry in the area of market-structure joint ventures.

The construct for market-structure types of ventures typically involves founding firms contributing (licensing) patent applications (or patents if issued) to support the operations of the market-structure joint venture. In turn, the joint ventures deploy the technology in their market operations goals and objectives. Joint ventures use the patent-rights around their technology as a defensive tool should an allegation of IP rights infringement arise from a third party. The founding firm or firms contributing the patent application may receive slightly better ownership economics in the joint venture. Firms contributing patent rights as between nonpatent contributing members may receive perhaps an additional membership equity stake of 3–5%. Occasionally, patent contributing members may receive additional board representation in the joint venture.

Financial firms create and utilize these joint ventures to deploy useful innovations to create centralized platforms. Members and subscribers using such platforms may readily compete in trading, yet come together on a common technology to enable the market to grow. Such platforms therefore offer benefits for traditional participants and new entrants alike. This in turn maximizes the value of the underlying technology.

The role for patents in forming and operating these ventures is of a different stripe than the traditional patent-as-asset model. Patent applications are licensed or conveyed to these entities not necessarily to create "hard" assets for the new venture, but rather to be available for the venture to defend its operations from third-party patent infringement claims in the future, if needed. In other words, the patents are generally designed for, and deployed primarily by, the founders of the venture as a functional hedge for the operational risk that the venture may incur in the future.

An example of the typical licensing structure is shown in Exhibit 13.1.

In this manner and in connection with the formation by the founding dealers of the market structure joint venture (FD Corp.), a transaction is occurring to transfer the IP operational necessary for the JV, from the Founding Member possessing it to FD Corp.

Patents (as well as patent applications due to the long pendency times), often function as a "know-how" package of technology. The patents (applications) are far more valuable than just a pure contractual license grant to know-how. This is due to the better boundaries that are discernable around the contributed technology since the technology is defined within the four-corners of the patent document that is delivered to the joint venture. In addition, the publication of a patent application or issuance of a patent can provide helpful transparency as to specific modes of operation of the innovation. Ultimately, upon grant of the patent right,

EXHIBIT 13.1 **LICENSING STRUCTURE**

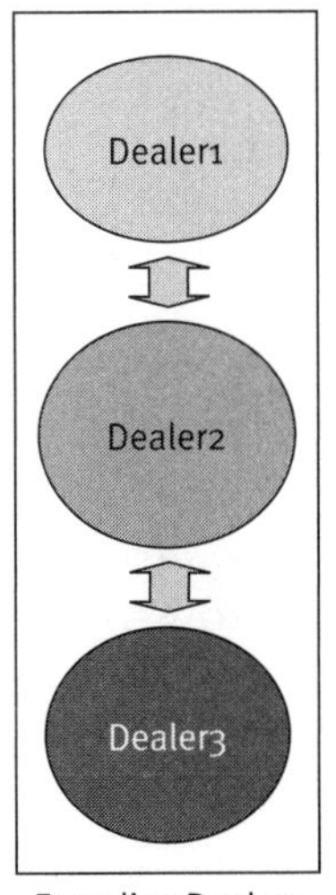

Founding Dealers

Founding Dealers –
Leverage 1: Patent contributor gets favorable economics in FD Corp for patent

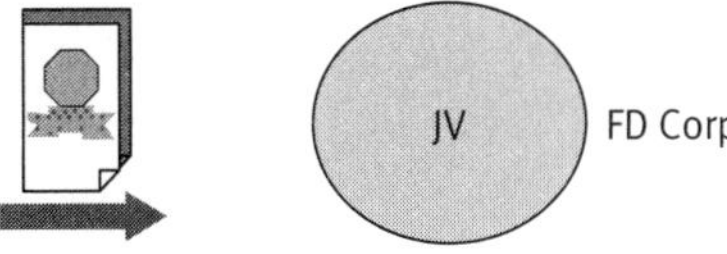

JV: Patent (application) licensed covering operational services

JV to Dealers:
Leverage 2: Services provide to Founding Dealers/Others

the patented "know-how" now has far greater defensive value for the joint venture.

In return for the transfer of the patent (application), the conveying or licensing founding dealer, will generally receive slightly more favorable economics in the venture in return for the transfer of the patent (application). (And these improved terms as discussed may result in a slightly increased ownership percentage over general members and perhaps increased representation on the JV's Board).

Upon commencing operations, the JV typically may provide patent (application) covered services back to the Founding Dealers as well as others who may subscribe. So in one sense, the patent asset is deployed to the JV in support of its operations, but the JV maintains the asset to be deployed to avoid third-party assertions against its operations.

The patent valuation, therefore, can occur up front in such circumstances. That is, "valuation" can now occur at or near the time of the formation of the entity. To be sure, this "valuation" is of a different hue than a patent valuation in support of a directly marketed product or service or a royalty-bearing license. Instead, this "up front" valuation is based on a model of the patent as an operational-hedge for the JV, not as a self-standing asset to be monetized.

A flagship example in the financial services of this model is Regulatory DataCorp. International LLC (RDC). RDC was formed by twenty-one of the world's leading financial institutions to aid its members and subscribers in combating terrorist financing and money laundering operations. Following the attacks of September 11th and as a means of helping to effectuate individual firms' USA Patriot Act compliance obligations, RDC was formed as result of Wall Street's recognition that in terms of combating illicit financing, individual firms could do far better deploying technologies collectively rather than individually.

But what role, if any, for patents in RDC? A surprising answer could be found concerning the role of patents as incentivizing the technologies that helped the allies win World War II. Gordon Crovitz, Editor, the *Wall Street Journal,* said it best in his review of the book *Tuxedo Park,* a biography of Alfred Loomis:

> Private enterprise, in Loomis's view, Ms. Conant writes, could move mountains in the time it took the government to pass a single bill.

★ ★ ★

> The idea of a private citizen funding military research off the government books was unusual in Loomis's time but would surely be a scandal today. Loomis filed valuable radar patents on the results—and, by the way, his first cousin was War Secretary Henry Stimson, whose strong support for Loomis would today raise red flags of conflict of interest. But without Loomis, the technology advances that helped win the war might never have happened.
>
> An equivalent feat today would be a dot-com billionaire locking himself and dozens of bright programmers in a garage on Woodside Road in Silicon Valley to write a code that would profile and identify would-be terrorists. Outside the bounds of cautious politicians or turf-minded agencies, he would access private and public databases to track terror suspects—and then patent the technique.
>
> In theory, if not in practice, a grateful country would forgo the otherwise obligatory hand-wringing over such a mix of public and private interests. Come to think of it, we could use some modern-day Loomises right about now.
>
> — L. Gordon Crovitz,
> "Doing Battle in the Lab—and Off the Books", *Wall St. Journal*,
> July 25, 2002,
> at D10 (book review) (emphasis added).

Mr. Crovitz penned these words in July 2002, the same month RDC was formed, and ironically, 18 months after the filing of the first patent application covering the innovation to be ultimately builtout and provided by RDC. Presently, 24 patents are licensed to RDC, many petitioned for expedited review by the U.S. Patent and Trademark Office under its process to speed-up examination of inventions used to combat terrorism.

The core technology of RDC is its "Global Regulatory Information Database" (GRID) system. The GRID system is a technological innovation that aggregates current, in-depth, risk-relevant data from public resources. The proprietary GRID system is implemented by RDC to answer inquiries from financial service customers for regulatory compliance. GRID is also to provide audit information on compliance requirements, such as those imposed by the USA Patriot Act.

Another uniquely suited role of the GRID system is its use in providing support for national security concerns and helping detect and potentially disrupt the flow of illicit funds through the global financial system.

The GRID technology can be used by subscribing financial service institutions to identify links between terrorist organizations and money laundering schemes. A critical value of the GRID system technology is that it contains continually updated information. GRID has at least 70% more up-to-date data than any competitive service provider. The GRID system is widely recognized as the most comprehensive, accurate, and reliable source of worldwide relevant regulatory, reputational, and law enforcement information for use in the financial services industry.

The GRID system does not involve credit risk, scoring, or analysis. Credit risk is the risk financial institutions face in extending services and not being paid back. So the GRID system is unconcerned with credit risk in its own right and does not contain personal information. The more relevant and predominant inquiry made by the GRID system is this—where did the money come from and where is it going?

The transparency afforded by patents (applications) is also very useful in terms of the GRID systems' operations. The publication of applications and issuance of patents demonstrate that the operations are not black-box, but instead are transparent. This transparency, coupled with the benefit of maintaining RDC's proprietary rights in its system, would be otherwise lost if only trade secret protection was available.

RDC itself offered a compelling and concise explanation in filing a brief with the Federal Circuit on the issue of patentable subject matter in *In re Bilski*:

> But why patents for RDC? The GRID database and RDC's related processes are predicated on *publicly available* information. RDC's modeling and detection processes are designed to help prevent suspect transactions from otherwise hiding in plain sight.[ ] Specifically, the risks RDC guards against are not credit risks—i.e., whether an institution will be repaid for extending services—but instead regulatory, legal, and reputational risks. [ ] In other words, institutions must protect their operations from being used to further suspicious, illicit, and perhaps illegal activity—particularly when such information may already be publicly available and, in theory, "knowable" at the time.
>
> AMICUS BRIEF OF REGULATORY DATACORP INC. TO THE UNITED STATES COURT OF APPEALS FOR THE FEDERAL CIRCUIT, SERIAL NO. 2007–1130(SERIAL NO.08/833,891), APRIL 7, 2008 PAGE 3.

Role of Patents in Market Structure Joint Ventures

Many in the global financial services community would like to see more joint ventures like RDC. The very conceptualization and formation of RDC was the result of financial firms seeing a critical need. The industry rallied around a new technological infrastructure to meet this critical need with a comprehensive approach to innovation, contribution, and development.

Other existing ventures have already taken shape and are successfully operating in various specialties. Several firms in the brokerage industry developed a technology based platform for transacting in overnight securities lending. In that instance, several broker-dealers contributed specific, complementary, intellectual property assets to the joint venture. The joint venture was then tasked with building the trading platform based on the contributed technology.

In this securities-lending venture, the operating business, now existing, resulted from the integration of two already existing at the time. The previously existing JVs were premised on a differing technical focus and each was supported by divergent patent applications and based on the differing operational ideas. The separate JVs were eventually merged, and the ownership of the JV ultimately expanded. The distinct patent applications are now housed under the single roof of the combined JV.

The resulting securities-lending platform is designed for use by brokers to compete in trading of overnight borrowed securities, also called "repos." As a benefit for contributing the trading technology, and ultimately combining the disparately focused JVs, the contributing financial firms each received an ownership stake in the joint venture.

Another technology based platform emerged in the burgeoning credit default swap market. Based upon a tested-concept by a founding firm, a joint venture provided with the patent-pending "know-how" to build out a database using an authentication and mapping methodology to ensure that reference entities and reference obligations concerning these complex securities were correctly allocated and tracked. Before the scrubbing methodology was developed—termed Project RED for Reference Entity Database[14]—real-world confusion and market losses resulted concerning similarly named operational and holding entities. One of those entities declared Chapter 11 bankruptcy. The bondholders of the entity declaring bankruptcy had different obligations than those of the nonbankrupt holding entity. The entire matter was made worse by misreporting in the press, leading to significant trade breaks between counterparties and unnecessary market disruption, losses and litigation.

As with the other joint venture examples, patent applications covering the new methodology were filed by a founding member concerning the scrubbing methodology. Both the rights and the technology were ultimately licensed to a multidealer owned joint venture. The joint venture currently administers the database for market participants and subscribers and enjoys the benefit of the defensive-availability of the patent (application).

These examples of market structure joint ventures show technological contribution and use of financial services innovation by different and often competing financial firms.

Patent Valuation and Implications for Use of Patents Moving Forward

Valuation of patents in the financial services industry is a difficult analysis. Numerous commercial and noncommercial factors that are not commonplace considerations in other industries affect how patents are viewed, procured, and ultimately deployed. In the limited instances where financial innovation is licensed, the valuation of a patent may be determined from the licensing terms and strategy. In other instances where there is a tension between direct competitors that are also partners and/or lenders, patent valuation may be more tenuous. One competitor/partner may adopt a stance whereby it will not pursue enforcement of patent rights against its competitor/partner. If so, the value of the patent is diminished because its exclusionary rights lie dormant—perhaps for the life of the patent.

Another critical component of patent valuation is the extremely long pendency of patent applications covering financial innovation. Some innovators have adopted a file and wait strategy while others forego the patent process and preserve rights in their innovation as trade secret or other proprietary information. All of these new patent valuation factors are a necessary consideration for patent valuation of financial services innovation.

In the future, financial firms may evolve their use of IP from a more traditional patent-as-asset to a patent-as-hedge strategy. Such use of patented-or patent-pending innovation can further the creation of the overall market size. This would be a natural outgrowth from how financial services innovation is adopted, used, and valued by Wall Street. The factors for valuation of innovation would further lend themselves toward the newly emerging patents-as-hedge view in the financial services industry. More market structure joint-ventures may then arise because these ventures can provide the infrastructure for developing technologies and enable the overall industry to capitalize on financial services innovation. Since the *State Street Bank* decision and with the *Bilksi* decision, patent valuation of financial services innovation may very well remain murky, but in the long haul, valuation methodologies and approaches will adapt to industry use and, over time will provide clearer indicators and a more accurate reflection of the use of patents in financial service company products and profitability.

ABOUT THE AUTHOR

John A. Squires is Chief Intellectual Property Counsel for Goldman, Sachs & Co. Mr. Squires is responsible for initiation, direction, and management of global intellectual property value capture and monetization efforts for all firm operations and franchises. Among the areas he oversees regarding IP are technology, e-commerce, and client-facing portals, producing business areas such as broker-dealer, specialist, asset management, and proprietary trading activities and investment and merchant banking, new ventures, and risk management. He managed the formation and launch of Regulatory DataCorp Int'l LLC (RDC), a for-profit, database and interdiction software venture, now owned by twenty of the world's leading financial institutions. Mr. Squires is Chairman of the Securities Industry Association IP Subcommittee and testified before the Senate Judiciary Committee on the Patent Reform Act of 2007. He also appeared on a cross-industry *eBay v. MercExchange* amicus brief to the United States Supreme Court.

Prior to joining Goldman Sachs, he held successive in-house counsel positions at AlliedSignal and was ultimately named General Counsel and Chief Intellectual Property Counsel for its Advanced Technologies division. Prior to AlliedSignal, Mr. Squires was in private practice with Rogers & Wells, specializing in IP litigation, and prior to Rogers & Wells, began his legal career with Morgan & Finnegan. He received his J.D. degree magna cum laude from the University of Pittsburgh School of Law where he was a member of the Law Review and Order of the Coif.

Notes

1. The depiction, views, and opinions expressed herein are personal to the author and may not necessarily reflect those of his employer, his employer's commercial interests, and/or those of his industry affiliations.
2. Brief of Amici Curae Securities Industry Association et al, No. 05-130 (January 26, 2006).
3. The patent at issue in *State Street* claimed a "system," thus eligible subject matter under 35 U.S.C. 101 as a "machine." The *State Street* court concluded there was not a separate "business method exception" to otherwise patentable subject matter.
4. For example, in 1998, the year *State Street* was decided, there were approximately 1,500 applications filed in class 705. By 2000, that number had risen to over 8,000. *See* USPTO.gov.
5. At the House Subcommittee Hearing in February 2007, PTO Director Dudas explained that more than 760,000 applications were waiting to be reviewed.
6. *See* USPTO.gov.
7. *See* Squires & Biemer, *Patent Law 101: Does a Grudging Lungren Panel Decision Mean that that USPTO is Finally Getting the Statutory Subject Matter Question Right?*, 46 IDEA 561 at 565 (2006).
8. "We take this opportunity to lay this ill-conceived exception to rest." *State Street Bank & Trust Co. v. Signature Fin. Group*, 149 F.3d 1368,1376 (Fed. Cir. 1998).
9. This is similar to the approach taken under the European Patent Convention.
10. *Ex parte Lundgren* (Bd. Pat. App. & Int., No. 2003–2088).
11. Patent Quality Improvement: Expansion of the Second-Pair-of-Eyes Review, www1.uspto.gov/go/com/strat21/action/q3p17a.htm.
12. *In re Comiskey*, 499 F.3d 1365 (Fed. Cir. 2007).

13. While there are some notable examples of patent litigation resulting in licensing in the financial services industry—see Electronic Trading Systems litigation and settlement with the Chicago Mercantile Exchange, the Chicago Board of Trade, and the New York Mercantile Exchange—these examples do not generally involve the traditional players on the street.
14. See "Mark-it Signs 16 To Reference Entity Database Service," http://www.finextra.com/fullstory.asp?id=10053

CHAPTER 14

Financing IP Assets—What Lenders are Missing

BY KEITH BERGELT

PERSPECTIVE The subprime credit crisis has cast a strangely positive light on intellectual assets.

Despite recent failures in the subprime mortgage and other debt markets, an ample supply of capital remains in search of attractive returns. In such an environment, intellectual property rights' position as a credible form of financing among alternative asset classes is generating increased lender attention. Collateralized IP assets, highly scrutinized and conservatively valued, have in effect become a safer alternative to the many broad bundles of risks like mortgage-backed securities that traditionally are not held but "flipped" to other investors. Imbedded in their portfolios, often, are dubious loans that are difficult to discern.

Until recently, financial institutions and private equity funds had not regarded IP rights as something that can be engineered for financial leverage. IP rights today, in fact, are emerging as an important source of capital formation and an alternative or complement to property plant and equipment (PP&E), accounts receivable (A/R), and inventory in support of private equity firm acquisitions. Throughout the history of banking and asset-based lending, observes Keith Bergelt, an investment banker who has helped to establish that IP is a cost-effective source of growth capital, specialty capital providers have emerged to put their stamp of approval on IP as an asset class.

"[Traditional investors'] strength was being able to access and manage risk associated with tangible assets, such as accounts receivable and

(continued)

inventory, when others found these risks unfathomable," says Bergelt. He believes that "creative sources of capital like IP-backed lending will become increasingly prevalent and the cost of growth capital will better align with the quality of the tangible and intangible assets that serve as collateral for loans and the underlying credit quality of borrowers."

"Current [narrowly focused] credit policies at the traditional asset-based lenders, such as banks and other large financial institutions, have yielded a seam in the market that is being filled by firms that are offering financing solutions that include IP-backed senior secured loans, IP-based venture debt, securitization structures, IP acquisition/aggregation, and litigation finance. IP finance is no longer merely a vision. It is a reality. As a result, IP is increasingly becoming the currency of the new economy and an asset around which capital is mobilizing."

The subprime mortgage crisis that had a negative effect on the world economy has triggered a shift (for now, at least) to more conservative lending and financial underwriting. Alternative assets, including IP, which are typically subject to more thorough diligence than traditional collateral, are benefiting from unease in the debt markets. The good news for IP is that for most investors still believe that proper financing structures and sound underwriting criteria make a difference about where and how they place their bets.

Financial Capital Availability to IP Holders

Intellectual property is increasingly central to how we live. As the advanced economies of the Group of 8 (G8) countries have developed and moved from an agrarian to an industrial to a service base, IP has come to form the core element of the enterprise upon which almost all business is built and value is created. This trend is also prevalent in South Korea, Taiwan, and other countries that up until quite recently were considered low-cost manufacturing centers. With the emergence of China, India, and a handful of others as low-cost manufacturing centers, these developing economies are now rapidly seeking to develop the capacity to author IP-based incremental and discontinuous innovations in much the same way as is occurring in the G8 countries.

It is on the trends surrounding financial capital and its availability to IP owners that the balance of this Chapter will focus. IP securitization,

IP senior secured debt, IP-based equity investments, IP-based venture debt, and IP-based royalty stream factoring are all methods that will be explored with examples of each provided. In addition, because of the increasing profile of IP in mergers and acquisitions, the role of IP for private equity firms seeking to value and finance their acquisitions will be considered against the backdrop of the subprime mortgage crisis.

Putting the Subprime Credit Crisis into an IP Perspective

Trends in Private Equity (PE)

- Migration of VCs to increasing "control" positions in mature companies

  The dramatic reduction in IPOs post-2000 has resulted in the migration of many traditional venture capital firms to hybrid approaches where they are now making control/majority stake investments in middle-market companies as a complement to their traditional minority equity investments in start-ups and early growth companies. All equity investors need to be assured of exits in reasonable time frames to ensure they meet their investors' expectations regarding return and a portfolio of purely venture based deals will often not provide sufficient exit opportunities, especially for some of the more sizable venture firms.
- Less leverage employed and less money taken off the table

  PE firms are generally looking to layer in a bit less leverage (i.e., a half or full "turn" less of EBITDA) and use more equity to support acquisitions so that they can more effectively control their newly acquired businesses and grow them without running a grave risk of defaults and debt rescheduling or worse. As a result, the number of high leverage deals where PE firms are immediately "taking money off the table" is reducing and debt capital is being used in most cases to pay out the seller/founders and support the growth capital needs of the acquired business.

Effect of Competition

- Control and noncontrol positions are often necessary to secure access to value

Due to the competitiveness among PE firms and with strategic acquirers, PE firms are increasingly willing to take minority (i.e., noncontrol) positions in companies in which they invest. This is only done in cases where the PE firm is comfortable with the preexisting shareholder(s) and is able to build-in protections and preferred positions that provide many if not all of the rights that it would have in a majority stock acquisition. Often, sellers are overly focused on majority share ownership and do not appreciate that a minority owner can secure rights to make or comake many of the most important decisions for a company (i.e., acquisitions, divestitures, compensation, management team hires, capital structure, etc.)

Impact of Hedge Funds

- PE firms and hedge fund lines are blurring

  Hedge funds are redefining PE to a great extent as they are investing equity, sub-debt, and senior debt in order to enable maximum returns. Their access to "flexible capital" and ability to participate across the capital structure offer a competitive advantage over some PE firms and senior and mezzanine lenders who would normally be active in different parts of the structure. As a result, asset-based lenders such as CIT have developed alternative risk or hedge funds to expand their capabilities and ensure competitiveness and traditional PE firms are developing business development companies (BDCs) (i.e. TPG-Axon, BlackRock-Kelso) to enable activity in the middle market and larger end of the market and ensure no loss of competitive advantage vis-à-vis the emerging hedge funds (i.e. Cerberus, Fortress, SilverPoint, etc.)
- Growth funds being raised to enable large PE firms to participate in the middle market and invest smaller amounts in deals

  Large PE firms are increasingly looking to explore the middle market and develop "growth funds" to enable investment in mid-cap companies. In this way, these PE firms are diversifying their risk, putting more aggregate capital to work and running parallel deal flow sourcing paths to ensure access to higher quality deals in an increasingly competitive market. Whereas large sponsors like Texas Pacific Group typically partnered with smaller funds like Golden Gate Capital by bringing them opportunities to invest in their sizable transactions, and spun opportunities for smaller capital investments out to them, an in-house or related fund now allows more value to be captured within the TPG family of funds.

- Hedge fund senior and sub-debt less welcomed by traditional PE firms

  PE firms, to some extent, are recognizing that their interests are not necessarily aligned with some of the hedge funds that have historically supported the PE Firms' acquisitions. The "loan to own" mentality in the hedge fund world that was popularized by Cerberus and Fortress is working against the funds and encouraging PE firms to look to lenders who have more congruent interests and a "relationship-based" approach that is commonplace in the corporate finance and asset-based lending world. In addition, the fact that hedge funds are starting to venture into corporate acquisitions puts them in competition with the PE firms to whom they provide debt capital (i.e., leverage for acquisitions or recapitalizations.)

IP's Emergence as an Asset Class and Source of Leverage in Acquisitions

IP is emerging as an important source of leverage and a fourth vertical next to property plant and equipment (PP&E), accounts receivable (A/R), and inventory in support of PE firm acquisitions. Throughout the history of banking and asset-based lending, credit based on asset classes such as accounts receivable, inventory, and PP&E have evolved over time, so in some respects, IP's emergence as an asset class is following a well established pattern. Those in the vanguard of the lending business who were capable of assessing and managing risk associated with tangible assets such as accounts receivable and inventory when others found these risks unfathomable drove the expansion of traditional lending beyond real property lending. Similarly, a group of innovative players came forward beginning in 1997 to enable IP to serve as an acceptable form of collateral in asset-backed transactions. As IP now constitutes the majority of the value of the "new economy" companies that predominate in the G8 countries, the untapped leverage in these businesses represent a significant source of well priced risk-appropriate leverage that PE firms that focus on brand/TM, copyright, and patent intensive companies covet.

Impact of the Subprime Crisis on PE, Credit Markets, and IP

- Higher cost of capital as lenders have somewhat arbitrarily elevated price by 100–150 basis points
- Lost opportunities as several large private equity deals were killed or put on indefinite hold due to the withdrawal of commitments by funding sources that retrenched from the market in Q307
- More limited universe of debt providers as many of the firms that were actively competing for PE firm debt capital opportunities are still not back into the market and several funds disappeared completely
- Tighter covenant requirements—the era of "covenant light" lending that was so prevalent in the period 2004–2007 is now over as lenders now have standing to assert their rights and to install protections in their loan agreements under which PE firms and their portfolio companies must operate
- Shift of advantage to strategic buyers vice PE, but this shift is temporary as capital will return to the market during 2008
- Fundless PE firms that were proliferating in 2005–mid-2007 are being rationalized as capital becomes more difficult to access. This effect should be temporary, especially in the middle market.
- In chaos, there is opportunity, and lenders with a unique niche and a well defined understanding of risk and its effective management are advancing their position in a market; a market that is temporarily crippled by indecision and deficient "sense making" of individuals and groups that lack the intuition borne of experience that allows decisions to be made under uncertainty
- IP of increasing importance as a source of asset-based debt in acquisition financing as leverage ratios tighten and a full and complete picture of a company's borrowing base of tangible *and* intangible assets is required to access sufficient debt capital to encourage PE firm acquisitions.

IP Finance

While there is still a large hangover of industrial era perceptions regarding the real sources of value in today's businesses, nowhere are these perceptions more entrenched and antagonistic to corporate growth than in the credit policies of traditional commercial lenders. Traditional lender credit policies have historically viewed IP (including patents, know-how, and trademarks) as "boot collateral"—entirely unsuitable as a form of collateral to support a loan but nonetheless susceptible to encumbrance as part of the blanket lien requirements that persist to this day.

The historical resistance to lending against IP has been attributable to:

- Perceived challenges associated with valuation
- Perceived challenges associated with monetization of IP collateral in the event of a default and foreclosure
- Limited motivation on the part of the lending community due to the fact that the IP assets would otherwise be encumbered and there was little or no incentive to take risk through lending money against the IP or unencumbering it so that a third-party lender could lend against it.

Throughout the history of banking and asset-based lending, credit based on asset classes such as accounts receivable, inventory, and PP& have evolved over time, so in some respects, IP's emergence as an asset class is following a well established pattern. Those in the vanguard of the lending business who were capable of assessing and managing risk associated with tangible assets such as accounts receivable and inventory when others found these risks unknowable drove the expansion of traditional lending beyond real property lending.

Similarly, a group of innovative players came forward beginning in 1997 to enable IP to serve as an acceptable form of collateral in asset-backed transactions. Initially, it was the so-called "Bowie-bond issue" conceived and led by David Pullman that raised awareness among the lending community as to the latent value of intangibles such as copyrights. Charles A. Koppelman's finance firm, CAK Universal Credit Corporation, then proceeded to serve as arranger of several transactions that enabled similarly cash flowing IP assets to serve as a source of cost-effective debt capital.

In addition, the lead specialty lenders involved in "factoring" pharmaceutical royalty streams such as Paul Capital, Royalty Pharma, and Drug

Royalty all entered the market with issues whereby their portfolios of cash flowing IP were securitized. Leading investment bank securitization businesses that had cut their teeth on mortgage-backed securitizations and then migrated to credit card and student loan facilities discovered IP during the late 1990s as well, as reflected in the sample listing of early-stage IP transactions summarized in Exhibit 14.1.

From mid-2003 to early 2004, IP lending was extended to noncash flowing IP for the first time. Firms like the Principal Financial Group-sponsored IP finance firm, IPI Financial Services, entered the market during this period and extended debt capital against naked IP irrespective of cash flows from licensing. Prior to this time, the cash flows that derived from IP as an underlying asset were utilized to support securitizations and bond issues. The sustainability of the cash flows and the ability to model them enabled rating agencies like Standard & Poor's and Moody's to rate these transactions, and facilitated the extension of partial guarantees or "wraps" by firms like MBIA, FGIC, and AMBAC. In a very real sense, these deals borrowed from structures used with great success for other asset classes (mortgages, credit cards, and auto loans) and were completed and sold down into the market with an almost agnosticism toward the IP that served as the underlying asset. In such transactions, the IP can be viewed as a means to an end, but it is not necessarily IP risk that is being taken by investors but instead investors looked to historical cash flows to give them comfort with future flows that would be used to pay down their notes. Obviously, this kind of approach does not require an in-depth understanding of IP and the risk associated with it.

Instead of using a sophisticated and costly sale-license back structure and the bankruptcy-remote special purpose entities that were commonplace in securitizations but unnecessary in more straightforward asset-based loans, IPI, of which the author was a principal, established itself as the first pure play IP lender and the first to simplify the lending process by requiring only a senior secured position in borrower IP. In this way, IPI's approach to IP lending was greatly simplified and, by design, made fully complementary to loans offered against a company's hard assets offered by traditional hard asset lenders.

Exhibit 14.2 is a graphic representation of the structure of a senior secured IP-based loan as conceptualized and implemented by IPI and, more recently, by Paradox Capital, an IP-based lender.

EXHIBIT 14.1 **EARLY IP-BASED SECURITIZATIONS**

Closing	Borrower	Type	Industry	Placement Agents	Amount
Feb-97	David Bowie	Royalty Income	music	The Pullman Group	$55
Nov-97	Dreamworks I	Royalty Income	film	Bear Stearns	$325
Jun-98	Motown Bonds	Royalty Income	music	The Pullman Group	$30
Nov-98	Ashford & Simpson Bonds	Royalty Income	music	The Pullman Group	$25
Jan-99	Corinthian Group	Master Recording & Publishing Income	music	CAK Universal Credit Corp. (aka UCC Capital)	$4
Feb-99	TVT Records	Master Recording & Publishing Income	music	CAK Universal Credit Corp. (aka UCC Capital)	$24
Apr-99	Sesac Inc.	Licensing Revenues	music	CAK Universal Credit Corp. (aka UCC Capital)	$29
Apr-99	L.A. Arena Funding	Naming Rights	sports	Bear stearns	$315
May-99	Curtis Mayfield	Royalty Income	music	CAK Universal Credit Corp. (aka UCC Capital)	$6
Jun-99	Barret Strong	Royalty Income	music	CAK Universal Credit Corp. (aka UCC Capital)	$4
Jun-99	James Brown	Royalty Income	music	The Pullman Group	$30
Jun-99	Iron Maiden	Royalty Income	music	Global Entertainment Finance	$30
Aug-99	A.B. Quintantilla III	Royalty Income	music	CAK Universal Credit Corp. (aka UCC Capital)	$2
Oct-99	Bill Blass	Licensing Revenues	apparel	CAK Universal Credit Corp. (aka UCC Capital)	$24
Jan-00	Dreamworks II	Royalty Income	film	Bear Stearns, Chase Securities	$540
Jun-00	Isley Brothers	Royalty Income	music	The Pullman Group	$20
Aug-00	Biopharma	Patent Rights	pharmaceutical	West LB	$100
Sep-00	Marvin Gaye	Royalty Income	music	The Pullman Group	$100

(*Continued*)

EXHIBIT 14.1 (CONTINUED)

Closing	Borrower	Type	Industry	Placement Agents	Amount
Nov-00	Arby's	Franchise/Licensing Revenues	restaurant	Morgan Stanley, Swiss Re New Markets	$290
Mar-01	Chrysalis Inc.	Royalty Income	music	Royal Bank of Scotland	$87
Dec-01	Gloria Vanderbilt	Licensing Revenues	apparel	UCC Capital	$30
Aug-02	Candie's, Inc.	Licensing Revenues	apparel	UCC Capital	$20
Apr-03	Guess Inc.	Licensing Revenues	apparel	JP Morgan Securities	$75
Jul-03	Royalty Pharma AG	Patent Rights	pharmaceutical	Credit Suisse First Boston	$225
Aug-03	Athlete's Foot	Licensing Revenues	apparel	UCC Capital	$33
Jan-04	Royalty Pharma AG (Neupogen)	Patent Rights	pharmaceutical	Credit Suisse First Boston	$263
Aug-04	Melrose Investors LLC	Royalty Income	film	Merrill Lynch	$210
Dec-04	BCBG Max Azria, Inc.	Licensing Revenues	apparel	UCC Capital	$53
Dec-04	Royalty Securitization Trust	Patent Rights	pharmaceutical	Bear Stearns, UBS Securities	$210

EXHIBIT 14.2 **IP LOAN TRANSACTION STRUCTURE**

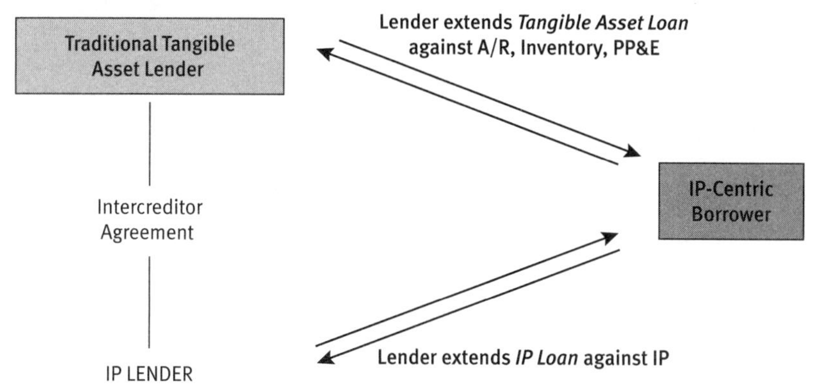

IPI did the pioneering work in establishing senior secured IP lending and drew on the $40 million fund that it raised from Principal Financial Group to essentially refine this lending model. During its existence, IPI extended debt capital against the IP of Wise Foods (maker of Wise branded potato chips, Cheez Doodles, and Quinlan pretzels), Cambridge Display Technology (owner of fundamental patent portfolio in next generation flat panel display technology—OLED), and BCBG Max Azria (leading contemporary women's fashion designer), among others.

Subsequently, the core operational team from IPI formed Paradox Capital and raised a dedicated $280 million IP fund through its relationships with the global investment bank, Babcock & Brown, and the structured products team at West LB. Since closing on the fund in Q406, Paradox has extended IP loans against the IP of Rachel Ashwell (home products/interiors designer and author of the Shabby Chic style), Cranium (leading board game), California Tan (premium indoor/outdoor tanning products), Robbins Brothers (retail jewelry chain), and Betsey Johnson (leading fashion designer in the vanguard of women's contemporary apparel), among others. Summary case studies of a sampling of these and other IP-backed finance transactions are sprinkled throughout the remainder of this chapter. These transactions range from traditional asset-based loans where IP supporting captive products was pledged as collateral to transactions where IP supporting both captive products and royalty streams served as collateral to securitization structures where a borrower's IP is synthetically converted to royalty generating and "securitized" (see the following section) to enable broad scale investment by funds and institutional investors alike.

CASE STUDY — BETSEY JOHNSON

- Status: Transaction closed August 2007.
- Company: Leading TM and brand-based fashion apparel and accessories business with extensive network of retail stores, a growing licensing platform, and a well established wholesale business with leading department and specialty stores.
- Sponsor: Castanea.
- $50 million IP-based term loan.

IP Finance Landscape

While the market entry of pure play IP asset-based lenders like IPI and Paradox Capital clearly signaled maturation in the IP finance market, it is important to understand the larger context of IP finance into which IP ABL fits. Toward that end, Exhibit 14.3 provides an overlay of the IP finance landscape and provides a jumping off point for discussion of brief consideration of some of the other businesses active in the space.

EXHIBIT 14.3 **IP FINANCE LANDSCAPE**

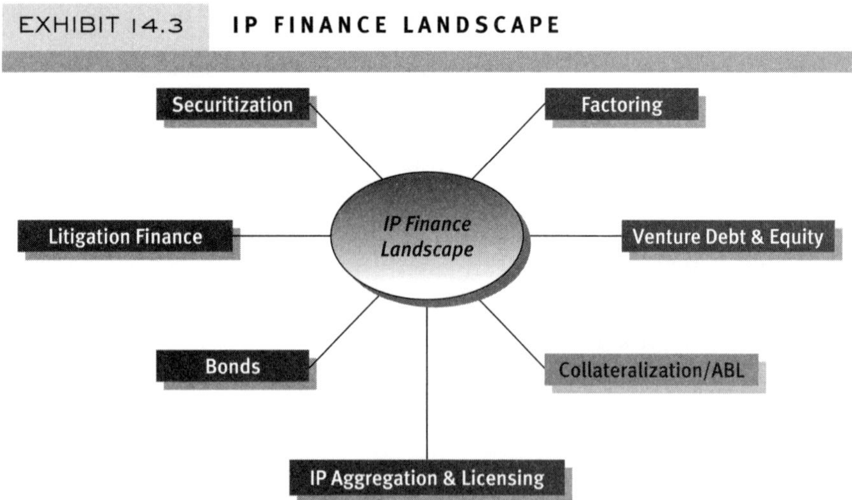

To round out the discussion of the evolving IP finance landscape, it bears mentioning that significant pools of capital are being raised and/or allocated to support new factoring businesses, litigation finance, and IP aggregation and licensing.

CASE STUDY **LENOX**

- Status: Transaction closed April 2007.
- Company: Leading TM and brand aggregator in the flatware and table top china and fine china space with such mature brands as Lenox, Gorham, and Dansk.
- Sponsor: None.
- $100 million Tranche B secured exclusively by IP and real estate.

For example, it has been reported that Altitude Capital has raised in excess of $200 million in capital to finance IP-based litigation and other high-yield IP finance activities (i.e., mezzanine and equity investment in IP-centric companies). IP aggregators such as Rembrandt, Intellectual Ventures, and Acacia have apparently raised capital to support the acquisition of largely orphan technologies. Venture debt providers like NewLight Capital and the more traditional banks active in this arena (e.g., Silicon Valley Bank) continue to deploy debt capital secured in large measure by the IP assets of venture-backed businesses; though a good number of these transactions are based as much on the credibility and pedigree of the lead venture capital investors in the deal as on the quality and value of the IP, it nonetheless evidences another means by which IP is enabling debt capital investment.

IP collateralization/asset-based lending is perhaps the most impactful of all those IP finance businesses in that it permits IP-centric companies to gain access to risk appropriate debt capital. The growing population of middle-market new economy companies that are brand/trademark and channel managers often have limited borrowing bases of accounts receivable, inventory and property, plant and equipment. Alternatively, they may be copyright owners with no complementary assets or patent rich companies with significant R&D budgets that support their technology advantage as a licensor to third-party manufacturers. As such, these companies are reliant on highly dilutive equity and/or expensive mezzanine capital to support growth.

CASE STUDY **WISE FOODS, INC.**

- Status: Transaction closed May 2006.
- Company: Premier regional salty snack company in the eastern United States. Founded in 1921, Wise is the largest regional manufacturer of salty snacks, holding a number two branded position in its target markets. TM-supported loan.
- Sponsor: Palladium Equity
- $9.75 million IP-based term loan.

Through the emergence of IP (cash flowing or noncash flowing) as an asset class and a fourth vertical alongside recognized hard assets, middle-market IP-centric companies that might hover in the "B"-rated credit range can access cost effective growth capital due to the introduction of IP collateralization/ABL (see Exhibit 14.4).

EXHIBIT 14.4 **IP LENDING IN CONTEXT**

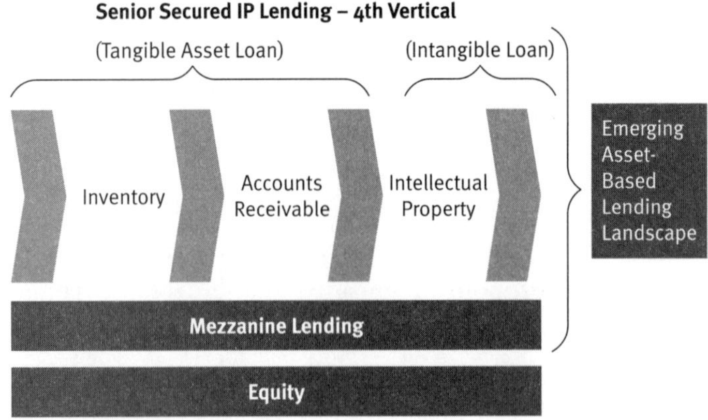

In essence, the lion's share of what second lien lenders loaned against in the late 1990s and into the early part of this decade was IP—not directly, of course, but indirectly and incidentally. Leading hedge funds minted during that period such as Back Bay Capital and, to a lesser extent, Fortress and Cerberus, started out by recognizing that traditional hard asset lenders could not sufficiently lend up to the debt servicing capacity of borrowers in the middle-market. The euphemism for what these hedge funds took second lien positions against in these transactions was surplus "enterprise value." In a very real sense, enterprise value is what the hedge funds were lending against but if one is more granular and analytic it was really the unrecognized and unarticulated value of the IP that makes up much of enterprise value in new economy companies that supported these high-yield second lien loans. IP-based collateralization/ABL loans, therefore, represent a natural and logical evolution of second lien lending to an asset-based transaction. The same systemic issue regarding traditional lender credit policies and attitude toward IP are addressed by IP collateralization/ABL as second lien loans, but the risk is made cognizable and the pricing of the capital deployed is brought more in line with that risk.

CASE STUDY — BCBG MAX AZRIA

- Status: Transaction closed December 2004.
- Company: Mid-market apparel company engaged primarily in the design, production, marketing, and international distribution of contemporary women's fashion apparel and accessories under the BCBG Max Azria, BCBG Girls, Max Azria Atelier, Parallel, To the Max, and Herve Leger trademarks. **Securitization News Deal of the Year.**
- Sponsor: None.
- $53 million IP-based securitization.

Comparative Cost of IP-Based Capital

For middle-market companies seeking to fully exploit their IP holdings, it is important to understand how IP can not only create much-needed growth capital availability but do so in a far more cost-effective manner than the alternatives. For example, a venture-backed company can outgrow venture capital and evidence a maturity in its business and its capital structure by taking in IP-based debt that is not dilutive and far less expensive than equity. In addition, any firm whose IP can serve as a sole source of collateral will create a rebuttable presumption that it has valuable IP.

CASE STUDY: CAMBRIDGE DISPLAY TECHNOLOGY

- Status: Transaction closed July 2004.
- Company: Market leader in the development and exploitation of LEP (light emitting polymer) intellectual property and technology – flexible/formable advanced display technology that is susceptible to roll process manufacture. Patent-based loan.
- Sponsor: Kelso
- $15 million IP-based credit revolving line of credit.

Similarly, a company with annual turnover of $200 million and positive EBITDA that does not have an abundance of hard assets but has a strong IP position can leverage that IP position to gain access to growth capital that is more attractively priced than second lien or mezzanine debt. The fact that traditional lenders do not often understand IP assets should not be an impediment for the creative manager cognizant of the real source of value in his or her company—IP—and looking to grow that business using external capital.

As a general guideline to the pricing that is typically applicable to the three core forms of investment (debt and equity) in IP-based companies, Exhibit 14.5 outlines the corporate characteristics and pricing attendant with qualifying IP-based risk.

EXHIBIT 14.5 **UNDERSTANDING THE IP-BASED FINANCING LANDSCAPE**

Libor + 10–15%	Libor + 20–25%	Libor + >30%
IP Collateralization	IP-Based Venture Debt	Equity
• Positive EBITDA	• Negative EBITDA	• Negative EBITDA
• Revenue or Non-Revenue Bearing IP	• Revenue or Non-Revenue Bearing IP	• Revenue or Non-Revenue Bearing IP
• Surplus Debt Servicing Capability i.e. <5X leverage	• No Surplus Debt Servicing Capability i.e. >5X leverage or otherwise in capable of qualifying for debt capital	• No Surplus Debt Servicing Capability i.e. >5X leverage or otherwise in capable of qualifying for debt capital
• Minimum Credit Rating of CCC+		
• Loan to IP Value (NOL) Ratio of <40%	• Credit Rating of <CCC+	• Credit Rating of <CCC+
• Asset Based Risk	• Mezzanine Risk	• Equity Risk

Conclusion

New economy companies that proliferate in developed nations are increasingly IP-intensive. As such, creative sources of capital like IP-backed lending will become increasingly prevalent and the cost of growth capital will better align with the quality of the tangible and intangible assets that serve as collateral for loans and the underlying credit quality of borrowers.

Current credit policies at the traditional asset-based lenders, such as banks and other large financial institutions, have yielded a seam in the market that is being filled by firms that are offering financing solutions that include IP-backed senior secured loans, IP-based venture debt, securitization structures, IP acquisition/aggregation, and litigation finance. Despite recent corrections in the sub-prime mortgage market, an ample supply of capital remains in search of attractive returns. In such an environment, IP's positioning as a credible form of collateral in the overall category of esoteric assets will garner it an increasing level of attention from investors.

CASE STUDY — LEVI'S

- Status: Transaction closed June 2004.
- Company: Leading global jeans and casual wear brand in market where over 30 countries maintain manufacturing capacity
- **Bifurcating Collateral**
  The financing package consisted of two different facilities:
  - *A $650 million asset-based revolving credit facility:* This four-year facility is secured by a first lien on Levi's receivables and inventory
  - *A $500 million senior secured term loan:* The six-year term loan is secured by a first lien on Levi's trademarks, and a second lien on its current assets.

Since the inception of a more active era of IP finance in the late 1990s, IP finance has evolved to far more than securitization and bond issues backed by royalty cash flows from music publishing or drugs. The quality and value of IP are becoming knowable to specialty lenders who understand the centrality of IP to enterprise value and can access its risk. IP finance is no longer merely a vision. It is a reality. As a result, IP is increasingly becoming the currency of the new economy and an asset around which capital is mobilizing.

The subprime mortgage crisis that surfaced in mid-2007 triggering a downturn in the U.S. economy will only serve to place more positive emphasis on IP-based assets, which because they are not fully captured by GAAP accounting typically are more highly vetted and conservatively valued than other classes of secured assets. Pools of capital are poised to redeploy out of the mortgage markets and into other assets where through the utilization of proper financing structures and underwriting criteria sound loans can be made. For those leaders in organizations responsible for stewarding and extracting value from IP, there is a real opportunity to take advantage of this trend and utilize selected IP rights as a safe and cost-effective source of growth capital.

ABOUT THE AUTHOR

Keith Bergelt is CEO of Open Invention Network (OIN), of which IBM, NEC, Novell, Philips, RedHat, and Sony are members. Previously, he was president and CEO of Paradox Capital, a subsidiary of the global investment bank Babcock & Brown. In this role, he led a team of asset-based lenders and structured finance experts in developing the intellectual property–based lending market. Prior to Paradox Capital, Mr. Bergelt served as president & CEO of IPI Financial Services, which was among the first financial services firms to offer specialty lending products supported exclusively by intellectual property and thereby enabled the emergence of patents, trademarks, and copyrights as a viable source of collateral in asset-based loans.

Mr. Bergelt previously served as an advisor to the technology investment group at Texas Pacific Group and headed business development, intellectual property, and licensing for the Kelso & Company portfolio company, Cambridge Display Technology, in the UK. In addition, he established and served as General Manager of the Strategic Intellectual Asset Management business at Motorola and cofounded the intellectual property advisory practice within the Electronics and Telecommunications Industry group at SRI Consulting in Menlo Park, California. Mr. Bergelt also served for twelve years as a diplomat with postings at the United Nations in New York and the American Embassy in Tokyo, Japan.

He holds an A.B. from Duke University, a J.D. from Southern Methodist University School of Law, and an M.B.A. from Theseus Institute in France.

CHAPTER 15

Assets, Property, and Capital in a Globalized Intellectual Value Chain

BY ULF PETRUSSON AND BOWMAN J. HEIDEN

PERSPECTIVE The emergence of knowledge-based economies has been accompanied by a fundamental shift from manufacturing to information resources. Transforming ideas into currency is fostering a more global perspective of innovation. How IP rights are viewed is very much a center of the transition. It remains unclear to what extent this epic shift will impact areas like the quality of innovation, shareholder value, and the economies of less industrialized nations.

Swedish researchers and teachers, Ulf Petrusson and Bo Heiden, of the Center for Intellectual Property in Gothenburg, contend that institutions have not caught up with the economic facts of life in the knowledge economy, and is leaving good opportunities behind. "To build an economy based on knowledge," they believe, "it is important to define, or redefine, what the meaning and role of assets, property, and capital is in contrast to the existing framework."

Petrusson and Heiden position their thinking about IP and knowledge management on the need to delineate between rights, assets, property, and capital—different aspects of the same universe.

"Just as water can exist in three states (solid, liquid, gas) so can financial objects (asset, property, capital), where each state is bound by

(continued)

different characteristics and consequences that are based on the belief and trust of economic and judicial actors as opposed to temperature in the case of water. For an asset, such as a house, to be considered as property, it must be trusted as an object of a commercial transaction."

The authors say that the creation, control, and management of intellectual resources and values are the primary contributors to the wealth of corporations and nations today. They contend that without fresh thinking, the knowledge economy, relying heavily on IP rights, will not have much room to spread or reason to be inclusive.

"The prospect of a knowledge economy is still outside of the consideration or comfort zone of society as a whole. With the majority of the world's population still living in a poverty-laden, agrarian economy, and the remaining minority blissfully captured in a physical property–based industrialized economy, it is not hard to understand why the notion of a paradigmatic shift in the economy is irrelevant, uninteresting, unwelcome, or just plain off the radar."

(Re)Defining Intellectual Assets, Property, and Capital

In a knowledge economy, all business is becoming global, unbound by physical boundaries. This creates a competitive pressure for entrepreneurs and managers to adopt an intellectual property rights (IPR) focus in order to control the development of their innovations and to profit financially. This ongoing global development can be described as an evolutionary path that is leading us into an intellectualized economy where the core of business is focused on intellectual assets, property, and capital.[1] However, in order to build an economy based on knowledge, it is important to define, or redefine, what the meaning and role of assets, property, and capital is in contrast to the existing industrial economic paradigm.

In a capitalistic economic system, the formation of "capital" is fundamental for the creation of wealth. While this may seem evident, the mechanisms of capital (i.e., wealth) formation are not obvious and require explanation. To better understand wealth creation, let's start by analyzing the relationship between three key terms conventionally used to describe valuable business objects: assets, property, and capital (see Exhibit 15.1).

EXHIBIT 15.1 **CONCEPTUAL FRAMEWORK FOR ASSETS, PROPERTY, AND CAPITAL**

Assets as Valuable Objects

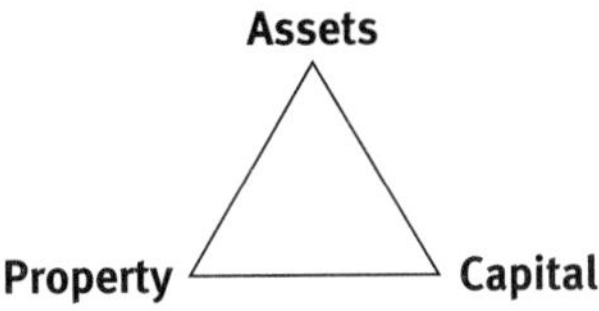

Property as objects for commercial transactions

Capital as objects in an machinery for creation of wealth

In this context *assets* could be defined simply as valuable objects, *property* as objects for commercial transactions, and *capital* as objects accepted by the financial establishment.

Just as water can exist in three states (solid, liquid, gas) so can financial objects (asset, property, capital), where each state is bound by different characteristics and consequences that are based on the belief and trust of economic and judicial actors as opposed to temperature in the case of water. For an asset, such as a house, to be considered as property, it must be trusted as an object of a commercial transaction. Fundamental to this belief is a system of well-established ownership rights, which can be validated by the judicial system, which in turn are used and accepted by market actors in particular and society in general. When well-defined ownership rights are not established, commercial transactions can still occur, but they will lack the necessary trust required by financial markets to consider the property to be capital.[2] In order for capitalization to occur, assets must be trusted as potentially secure objects in commercial transactions before they can be considered as capital by financial markets, for example as security for debt financing such as bonds and loans. For wealth formation to occur, assets must be *propertized* and *capitalized*, both of which processes are based on trust provided by well-functioning economic and legal institutions.

Thus, one important approach to deal with the challenges we are facing is to creatively experiment with the interplay between what can be labeled as "intellectual asset management" (IAM), "intellectual property management" (IPM), and "intellectual capital management" (ICM). In a knowledge and network economy it is unavoidably the intellectual assets that must be the center of attraction. Technical functions, design, content, brands, systems, and databases, etc., are the companies' most important assets. To develop and manage intellectual assets is however not enough. The assets must be convertible into value propositions and property in commercial transactions (IPM). Inventions, designs, brands, patents, copyrights, licenses, etc., are all intellectual building blocks that must be exploited in the construction of innovations, companies, and network-based markets and platforms. To enable successful intellectual property management, it is at the same time important that the intellectual assets constitute capital in the financial machinery. The assets must be included in financial accounting, be part of the basis for taxation, and most importantly be managed as capital in financial transactions (ICM). If intellectual assets don't constitute collateral security, cannot be subject to seizure or be included in bankruptcy estate, it is very difficult to build successful companies based on intellectual property.

The meaning of concepts such as intellectual assets, property, and capital, is further clarified in the development observed in three different areas. Perhaps most obvious and famous is the transformation driven by advances in information and communication technology. This development has led to a number of hybrid business solutions combining aspects of the industrially manufactured product and the service—solutions that are variously termed virtual products, IT-services, "features," and "content." The technological advances surrounding software, databases, and Internet solutions have created a platform with an enormous potential for value creation, partly in terms of technological functions and innovations, but also in terms of design, cultural expression, and even moral value systems. The lack of tools for developing IP, however, is forcing software developers to still burn instances of their software to hard media in physical packaging, and deliver it to customers through traditional channels of distribution. The lack of an adequate approach to intellectual capital means that accountants given the task of quantifying the value of company resources face an insurmountable challenge, and the banks naturally refuse to grant loans. IT-based features, content, conceptualized IT-services, and virtual products are not accepted as financial securities.

Another important example is the transformation taking place within the different biotech-based markets. Innovations within the field of biotechnology often arise at a great remove from the market, and the majority of ideas within this area will therefore first be implemented in commercially complete products within a span of five to ten years in the future. At the same time, however, in many cases it takes millions of dollars to bring a biotech product to the market, which means that the entire existence of the industry depends directly on the ability of companies to trade amongst each other with licenses tied to various intellectual properties. If this weren't possible, the considerable entry barriers would mean that only a small number of multinational giants could survive on the market. This would in turn mean an incalculable loss of valuable knowledge from research groups around the world, which would never be developed to the point of benefiting humanity. The unwillingness to accept research results regarding genomes, proteins, and stem cells as financial security and comparable capital is of course obvious.

The third and final development that clearly demonstrates a growing focus on IP is the branding culture. For some of the most sophisticated actors, the brand has become their most valuable resource, and it has grown far beyond simply being a distinct signifier of the product. Today, the entire value proposition of the company can very well be said to be comprised by the brand. This value proposition, in turn, does not merely contain a description of the functional utility and quality of the proposition, but also the experience the buyer can expect, as well as the identity that the buyer will project to other people. The importance of this is demonstrated, for example, in the fact that Coca-Cola was recently valued in excess of $70 billion, and other world-leading brands such as Intel, Microsoft, and IBM, are not far behind. Increasingly, companies are realizing the inherent potential in building the business around the brand as an intellectual resource. The brand is realized as property in commercial transactions such as franchising, merchandizing, image transfer, and cobranding. Nevertheless, it is only recently that a small number of American actors have created at least limited opportunities for borrowing against these often central resources.

Thus, it is becoming increasingly recognized that management today has little choice but to adopt a more active intellectual property management and licensing stance. However, the risk is that this spiral focus on IP will lead to the blocking of innovation and wealth creation as more and more actors assert their IPR, such as patents, trademark rights, copyrights, and trade secrets. While IPR will continue to play a critical role in determining wealth and welfare in the 21st century, whether this role is positive or negative will depend greatly on our ability to use IPR to build instead of block innovation.

The Transformation of Industry to Knowledge-Based Business

Thus, recent use of IPR in management and entrepreneurship can be regarded as one path to the increased intellectualization of business, as well as the economy at large. The usage of IPR on new technologies, primarily the fields of information and communication technology (ICT) and life-science oriented technologies, is reshaping business drastically. As discussed, the transformation progressively leads us to a new entrepreneurial era, where the creation of value and wealth has to be reconsidered.

A good example of the emergence of the knowledge economy can be seen through the transformation of farming. It wasn't that long ago that over 90% of the population of the world was engaged in farming, where productivity was constrained by the limits of physical labor, and value creation was based exclusively on the sale of crops. With the advent of industrialization, overall productivity increased substantially through the introduction of chemicals and machinery into the value chain, whereby a major portion of the value added was appropriated by the industrialist in relation to the farmers (see Exhibit 15.2). Today we see the creation and extraction of value even further upstream in the value chain, where companies such as Monsanto own the differentiating genes of valuable crops and thereby control their development and distribution. The important

EXHIBIT 15.2 **THE TRANSFORMATION OF FARMING FROM AN AGRICULTURAL TO AN INDUSTRIAL TO A KNOWLEDGE-BASED PARADIGM**

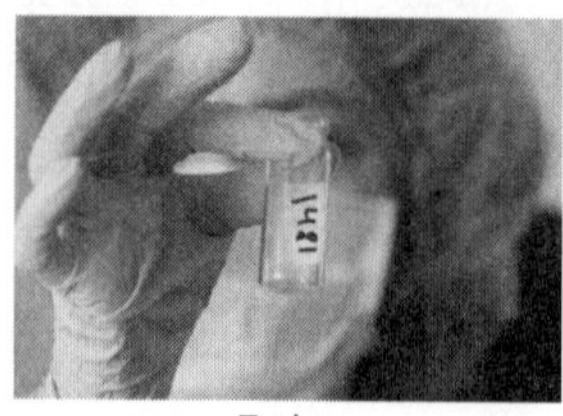

Before → Today

message in this example is that the development of a knowledge economy doesn't mean the elimination of agriculture and industrial production, but instead it shows how the value chain is transformed to include different actors and business models resulting in the redistribution of wealth. In the knowledge economy, farming will still be important though the creation and extraction of value will be organized vastly different than it once was.

The Intellectual vs. Material Value Chain

The industrial economy is typified by a relatively few, well-known commercial means from which to create and extract value through the production, distribution, and sales of physical goods. This material value chain (MVC), shown in Exhibit 15.3, can be characterized as follows:

- The product and factors of production are the main focal points
- Wealth is created in the transaction of physical goods and the number of business models is limited
- Competitive advantage is determined by the closest actors operating in a similar context of differentiation and cost strategies

While much of the developing world is still captured in the agricultural economy described above, the developed world is captured in the material value chain where capital is only created through the creation of physical assets and property. Possibly the greatest challenge in the

EXHIBIT 15.3 THE MATERIAL VALUE CHAIN

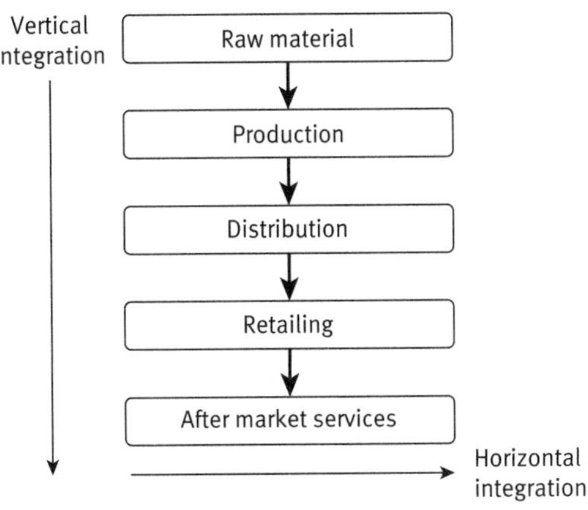

transformation from an industrial to knowledge economy is our long, deep-rooted, historical belief that intellectual assets and property are not (and should not be) part of the financial system on both Wall Street and Main Street.

It is precisely this focus on the material value chain and the production of physical products that has shaped the view of IP as a "static" right with the primary purpose of blocking others from copying manufactured products. Given this prevalent static, no-trespassing view of IP propagated in the industrial paradigm, it is of course understandable that society is concerned with the future extrapolation of static-oriented IP strategies on innovation for both developed and developing countries.

In knowledge-based business, value is created and extracted through the management of intellectual assets, property, and capital. This means that the industrial material value chain must be complemented by what we call an intellectual value chain (IVC) as shown in Exhibit 15.4. The IVC helps us to realize that all value creation stems from human intellect and the intellectual assets that are generated in the form of know-how, relationships, inventions, etc. Taking our starting point in the intellectual assets allows for the full complexity to be revealed, analogous to the chess game below. While the production of physical products is still a viable

EXHIBIT 15.4 **A FRAMEWORK FOR AN INTELLECTUAL VALUE CHAIN ADJUSTED TO KNOWLEDGE-BASED BUSINESS**

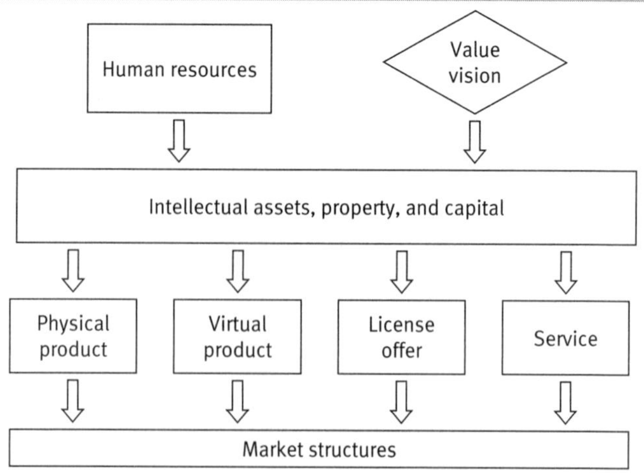

option, it is not the only option. Firms can also leverage their intellectual assets through virtual products, license offers, and services which in turn will affect the market and the distribution of value. For example, in the music industry, starting from an intellectual assets perspective, one can see multiple options, such as the creation of CDs (physical products), downloading MP3s (virtual products), acquiring and brokering copyrights (license option), or performing music to live audiences (service). In a knowledge economy, all of these options, even the production of physical products, are based on the management of intellectual assets and property as prerequisite for successful commercialization. Modern information and communication technology has opened up the whole playing field to new business models and new actors on a global scale. Competitive advantage will be determined by which actors are best able to recognize the potential strategic options and manage the opportunities and threats presented by the intellectual value chain.

It is important, especially for entrepreneurs and managers in knowledge-intensive firms, to acknowledge and accept this transformation. A fundamental entrepreneurial challenge is not to only understand the transformation, but to be able to grasp the opportunities generated. By analyzing the transformation process, its character and origin, it is possible to develop an operational approach concerning which tools and skills are needed in order to become a successful entrepreneur and business actor. At the same time, it is important to recognize the risks and the potentially destructive consequences. The usage of IPR is an important course of action in order to create value, but it can also be destructive and prevent creation of wealth. The increased use of knowledge-based business models in industry is, from this perspective, a good starting-point in the quest for understanding wealth creation in an intellectualized economy (see Exhibit 15.5).

Knowledge-Based Business Models

One good way to see the differences stemming from the increased use of the intellectual value chain is to examine how intellectual assets are being leveraged in new ways as both a substitute for and complement to the traditional economic processes of R&D, production, hourly services, and marketing. Below we will provide a brief set of emerging business models

EXHIBIT 15.5 **AN IVC APPROACH CHANGES THE PLAYING FIELD AND THE RULES**

Knowledge-based business models not only provide more options but the ability to change the rules of the game.

where intellectual assets are the most important drivers of value creation and extraction.

The Physical Product in a Supporting Role

To say that the factors of production are not the most important determinant of success is not to say production is unimportant. Neither does it mean that physical products will cease to exist. As mentioned before, agriculture did not cease to exist because of industrialization, it merely evolved such that the difference is that now 3% of the population can produce more food and lower prices than 50% of the population could 100 years ago. Physical products will continue to be produced though it will be the intellectual dimension of these products that will generate more and more value. The following three illustrations will exemplify this evolution:

1. The brand as a carrier of the product

   While the product once carried the brand, increasingly, the brand carries the product. The value proposition of the physical product is often supplanted by other values that are captured by the brand, such as moral values, artistic values, and identity. For example, a car as a technical product designed to get you from point A to point B is replaced with other values such as environment friendliness, safety, and driver's joy captured in the brand. Certainly, nobody thinks of Volvo without thinking of safety, which is a moral value that they have capitalized.[3] Adding an alligator to my sweater neither makes it warmer nor necessarily last longer, but it does raise the price. Does anybody believe anymore that people buy a Rolex because they need to know what time it is or a Burberry scarf just to keep their neck warm? Even when we know, for example, that Nike shoes are produced for a small fraction of the sales price, it is difficult to tell your child that he or she will have to wear the generic shoe when the rest of the team is wearing Ronaldhinhos. While it may seem that these are just marketing ploys, we would submit that brands represent real values for many consumers and increasingly represent the greatest fraction of the profit of many products.
2. The concept beyond the product

   Building on the use of the brand as a core asset, many firms have begun to focus their value propositions around a broader concept where the physical product is just one part. For example, companies such as Starbucks and IKEA tout that they provide a concept that generates customer loyalty well beyond the utility of the products they sell. The opening of a new IKEA is often characterized in some countries by a massive stampede of humanity, for what? The right to go home and spend the afternoon swearing while you put together a piece of furniture with a strange Swedish name you can't pronounce? Obviously, they sell more than put-it-together-yourself furniture. Another good example is Nespresso, which on the surface appears to be just a coffee machine. But with a wide range of gourmet flavors, aesthetically designed machines, an online coffee club, and George Clooney, it becomes rather obvious that the luxury experience is just as important as the coffee itself. At the center of this transformation is the recognition by most industries for the need to "de-commodify" their products from value propositions once sold by the kilo to more sophisticated concepts that return greater value for the consumer and company alike.

3. Building and controlling markets, not only products

   In the industrial economy, the interaction of the product and market was treated as black box controlled by the invisible hand of the price mechanism. In this model, actors controlled technological innovation, supply and demand determined market structures, and actors could only indirectly influence market structures through marketing and price strategies. However, in the knowledge economy, it is often impossible to separate the creation of the innovation (i.e., product) and the market. This is extremely evident in the information and communication industries where competitive advantage is determined by conscious strategic effort to build and control the market, or at least part of it. In telecommunication, for example, actor networks create the structures for market control through standards and IP management. Thus the market is often shaped to accommodate technological innovation where strategic network activities become as significant as research and development. Companies such as Qualcomm, Microsoft, and Apple among others have all recently been under scrutiny of the competition authorities in relation to the dominant position afforded to companies that don't only sell products on an existing market, but have pioneered the creation of these markets. When a firm such as Apple created the market for efficient downloading of music through iTunes linked to the product IPod, they, by definition, became dominant on that market, since they created it. The blurring of the line between competition and collaboration and innovation and market creation will no doubt transform the way antitrust behaviour is typified in the knowledge economy.

R&D as Both a Product and a Business Development Platform

Traditional post-war industrial R&D activities, especially research, took place far upstream of commercialization and primarily in-house. Below is a discussion on why this has changed and how business models must adapt.

1. Research as commercial tools

   In no industry has the time between research and commercialization been reduced so significantly as in biotech. Today, discoveries, and we use the term loosely as often as they are being patented, at the lab bench can be commercialized rapidly as research tools by actors further down the value chain as diagnostic tools, or in pharma R&D. Much as companies have traditionally paid for microscopes and test tubes, they are now being asked to pay for tools in the form of knowledge, such as biomarkers in the form of genes, etc. This has opened up for license-based business models targeted at R&D institutions and hospitals, which has raised flags from many actors regarding patentability of research tools and the ethics of their commercial use. Myriad Genetics, a firm that controls important genes related to breast cancer diagnosis, is a classic case fueling debate over the ever-blurring line between discovery and invention and the proprietary use of research tools by a single actor. Even pharmaceutical companies, always the bastions of pro-patent sentiment, are expressing their concern over the patenting of research tools. As this debate continues, it is important to realize that for many entrepreneurial biotech start-ups, research tools are products backed by significant investment in R&D and deserve their place in the value chain—the question is where and under what terms.
2. R&D as an open innovation platform

   It was once possible to manage R&D under one roof, but for an increasing number of industries, this is no longer possible. Instead, firms must learn to manage their R&D as transactions of IP among various actors both in and outside of the hierarchy of their own firm. An important distinction regarding open innovation is to differentiate between the development interface and the distribution interface in the management of innovation, where openness in development is much more sophisticated than simply overcoming a "Not Invented Here Syndrome." There is no question that the innovation process is becoming more open across most industries.

Even firms that sell physical products as a distribution model are under pressure to manage their innovation development process, with actors both upstream and downstream in order to control the knowledge required to build competitive value propositions. Thus, all industrial firms are becoming more knowledge orientated in their approach to innovation. To move beyond the mere rhetoric of open innovation requires firms to acknowledge the management of intellectual assets and property as the key to successful implementation. However, many companies struggle with this transition as new capabilities are a prerequisite. Openness is a sophisticated process of control where IP is the enabler. Without advanced licensing capabilities to manage relationships as IP transactions, opening-up innovation will justifiably remain a risky endeavor for most executives to endorse.

Leveraging Content and Know-How as Property

1. The age of the virtual product.

   Information and communication technology has completely transformed the possibilities to package and leverage know-how. Today, almost any service that was once sold on an hourly basis or was previously fixed to physical media can be digitized and commercialized as a virtual product.

   Companies such as Google, Microsoft, and eBay are examples of huge success stories, but IT-based decision support systems, features, and tools are prolific. Combining graphic user interfaces with databases and software applications allows know-how and content, as will be discussed below, to be leveraged as never before. However, along with the possibilities of capitalizing on virtual products are the difficulties in defining ownership and building the belief among consumers that these products should be respected commercially in the same way as physical products. New business models based on IT solutions are destroying traditional industries where the physical production and distribution of goods formed the basis for value creation and extraction, such as in the music industry. In the context of virtual products, licensing takes on a new meaning compared to traditional business-to-business (B2B) patent licensing. This new business-to-consumer (B2C) license model has become ubiquitous and has allowed for the creation of copyright-base industries to flourish by regulating the distribution of proprietary content directly to consumers. One can barely surf the Web these days without entering into a content provider agreement or other B2C license contract. Other examples of B2C licensing include sales of features, shrink wrap, and Web wrap transactions, service subscriptions, and open source agreements. In fact the use of B2C licensing models is a perfect illustration of how IPR and contracts can be combined to create openness. For example, through the means of copyright licenses, we are able to create open source models. This is ironic for most open source is an IP-based business model, though this fact never seems to make the popular press.

One interesting challenge for the knowledge economy will be to treat virtual products as property and capital. Already eBay has been reluctant to support the sale of virtual products as title issues are difficult to regulate. While property issues related to software and digital music have made great strides, the capitalization of virtual content is still a great challenge. Just for fun, call your bank to see if they will take your Second Life simulated island as collateral for a car loan.

2. Capitalizing content through licensing

   Long before MTV, in the age before copyright, if you wanted to make money from music you needed to perform, likely to the amusement of some royal benefactor. While artists and authors successfully managed to leverage their works with the help of copyrights through physical books and records, these activities seem almost primitive in comparison to current evolving practice. Let's take J.K. Rowling as an example. When she thinks up a story, she has an almost boundless number of commercial options ranging from books, movies, video games, theme parks, cartoons, toys, clothing, and so on. In 2006, Pixar's library of eight stories (plus potential future endeavors) was bought by Disney for $7.6 billion. The ability to transform content into financial capital through licensing has exploded in recent years with companies such as Disney using merchandizing as a core business model to extract maximum value from their content. Given the number of merchandise following each of their film releases it's hard to know what is marketing and which the commercial products are. Is Disney channel a product or is it marketing for merchandise? Are the movies marketing for Disney World or vice versa? The relationship between Lego and Star Wars is another example of using both cobranding and merchandizing business models to leverage content. One interesting questions emerges—who is paying who when I order a Scooby Doo Happy Meal? Is it Warner Brothers or McDonald's? The intersection of branding, content, and creative licensing and distribution models is redefining the content industries and is spilling over to other industries as well.

The Road Ahead

It has been roughly ten years now since Thomas Stewart's groundbreaking work on intellectual capital, and Kevin Rivette and David Kline's treatise on the latent value of intellectual property in the corporate world.[4] Both these contributions, together with numerous others[5] over the last decade have helped to mainstream the realization that knowledge (or more broadly the creation, control, and management of intellectual resources and values) is the main contributor to the wealth of both corporations and nations.[6] While obvious to some and plausible to many, the revelation that wealth in society will increasingly be dependent on the control of knowledge is still either foreign and/or alarming to most. The prospect of a knowledge economy is still outside of the consideration or comfort zone of society as a whole. With the majority of the world's population still living in a poverty-laden, agrarian economy, and the remaining minority blissfully captured in a physical property based industrialized economy, it is not hard to understand why the notion of a paradigmatic shift in the economy could be irrelevant, uninteresting, unwelcome, or just plain off the radar. Nevertheless, the last ten years has seen an exponential increase in knowledge-based business models and financial activity focused on utilizing the economic potential of intellectual assets, property, and capital. However, we have just scratched the surface.

In the developed world, we are still very much captured in an industrial paradigm where IPR are a means to support the production of physical goods. Wealth and welfare tied to the material value chain remains the predominant paradigm in business schools, accounting practices, courts, financial markets, management practices, and so on. In most developing countries, capitalism has not even been able to take root. Thus the whole world is facing the challenge of how to create wealth and welfare in the knowledge economy.

Economic systems exist for the purpose of generating welfare—wealth is a means to this end.[7] Thus, the impact of all economic activities needs to be measured in relation to the advancement of the human condition through increased freedom, opportunities, and standard of living. The promise of the knowledge economy is that wealth can be generated through the capitalization of knowledge, art, values, identity, and other products of the mind and spirit as opposed to through physical labor. As industrialization increased productivity and capital formation freeing the now developed world from a life of subsistence farming, knowledge-based business promises, a concomitant increase in productivity, and greater pursuit of intellectual value adding activities beyond the production floor.

In this struggle to build greater global welfare, IPR are tools. People are responsible for their construction and their use. The future promise of the knowledge economy surely balances on the right blend of entrepreneurship and responsibility.

ABOUT THE AUTHORS

Ulf Petrusson is the cofounder and Director of the Center for Intellectual Property (CIP). He also is Professor of Law at Göteborg University, Sweden and cofounder and Senior Principle of CIP Professional Services AB. For the past twenty years, Professor Petrusson has worked in the field of IP as both a scholar and a practitioner where he has advanced the cause for creating wealth and welfare through IP management. He has been recognized by *Managing Intellectual Property* magazine as one of the fifty most influential IP persons worldwide. Professor Petrusson is directly responsible for the research program at CIP, which blends new operational theories with the creation of IP-based business and technology management tools. Prof. Petrusson holds master and doctoral degrees in law from Göteborg University and

(*Continued*)

is the author of numerous articles and three books, the latest of which is *The Role of University in the Knowledge Economy.*

Bowman J. Heiden's role as Deputy Director of Center for Intellectual Property Studies (CIP) at Göteborg University, Sweden, is focused on the building of collaborative innovation platforms to facilitate the creation of business. He teaches knowledge-based business and has developed CIP FORUM, which is one of the leading IP business events worldwide. Projects he is working on include the construction of an Intellectual Capital Incubator designed to package intellectual assets with partners worldwide, and the creation of social entrepreneurship platform focused on developing countries. Professor Heiden holds degrees in engineering and technology management, and his Ph.D. work is in the field of innovation and entrepreneurship, with a focus on IP finance. Professor Heiden worked for IBM early in his career and played professional basketball in several of European countries.

Notes

1. For a more rigorous discussion on the intellectualized economy and its impact on wealth and welfare creation, see Petrusson, *Intellectual Property and Entrepreneurship* (CIP Publishing, 2004).
2. This property state, or lack there of, is called "dead capital" by De Soto in his book, *The Mystery of Capital* (Basic Books, 2000).
3. Recently, Honda has also announced that their core values will be safety and environment, which highlights the difficulty in exclusively claiming intellectual assets, such as moral values. http://corporate.honda.com/america/public-policy/
4. Stewart, Thomas, *Intellectual Capital: The New Wealth of Organizations* (Doubleday Business, 1997); and Rivette, K. and Kline, D, *Rembrandts in the Attic* (Harvard Business School Press, 1999).
5. For example, see early works by Patrick Sullivan, Leif Edvinsson, and Karl-Erik Sveiby.
6. The late 1990s is obviously not the beginning of human thought on the issue of knowledge in relationship to economic development. However it could be said to mark the beginning of a mainstream recognition by leaders in the business, financial, and political spheres.
7. Aristotle: "The life of money-making is one undertaken under compulsion, and wealth is evidently not the good we are seeking; for it is merely useful and for the sake of something else," *Nicomachean Ethics,* Book I, Chapter V.

Index